In Memoriam

Gareth Jones

August 13th 1905 August 12th 1935

"Made Perfect in a short time, he
hath fulfilled a long time."

All rights reserved. No part of this publication may be reproduced or transmitted, in any form or by any means, without permission.

Copyright ©2001 by Margaret Siriol Colley.

Published by: Nigel Linsan Colley,
1 Crown Street, Newark,
Nottinghamshire, NG24 4UY.
Email: Nigel@colley.co.uk
Tel: +44 (0) 1636 605772

For supplementary background material, errata, sales enquiries and any matters relating to this book please visit:

Web: www.colley.co.uk/garethjones

Further information including copies of Gareth Jones' originally published articles relating to his 1930s travels in the Far East, Germany and the Soviet Union are also included on the website.

Printed by Alphagraphics, Nottingham, England.

ISBN 0 9537001 0 0

First Edition: July 2001
First Reprint: March 2002

Gareth Jones
A MANCHUKUO INCIDENT

By

Margaret Siriol Colley

**Additional material, editing and website design
By Nigel Linsan Colley**

IN MEMORY

I have endeavoured to write this story in the treasured memory of my grandparents, Taid and Nain, Major and Mrs Edgar Jones of Barry, Wales, who bore the grief of the death of their beloved son Gareth so bravely.

Heraclitus

They told me, Heraclitus, they told me you were dead,
They brought bitter news to hear and bitter tears to shed,
I wept as I remember how often you and I
Had tired the sun with talking and sent him down the sky,

And now that thou art lying, my dear old Carian guest,
A handful of grey ashes, long, long ago at rest,
Still are they pleasant voices, thy nightingales awake,
For death he taketh all away, but these he cannot take.

W. Cory

(Translated from a poem by Callimachus in the Greek Anthology.)

CONTENTS

Curriculum Vitae — i

Preface — ii

About the Author — iii

Acknowledgements — iv

Foreword — v

Method of Research — vii

Gareth's 1934-5 World Tour Itinerary — viii

Maps — x

Introduction – My Uncle Gareth — xv

Part 1 – Inner Mongolia

    Chapter 1. The Final Journey. — 1

Part 2 – Gareth's Travels

    Chapter 2. En Route to Japan. — 43
    Chapter 3. From Kobe to Manila. — 67
    Chapter 4. The Philippines. — 75
    Chapter 5. Java. — 80
    Chapter 6. Singapore. — 89
    Chapter 7. Siam (Thailand). — 96
    Chapter 8. French Indo-China
                     (Cambodia & Vietnam). — 107
    Chapter 9. Hong Kong. — 116
    Chapter 10. Canton (Guangzhou). — 124

Chapter 11.	Journey to Changsha.	132
Chapter 12.	Changsha to Shanghai (Via Hankow & Nanking).	142
Chapter 13.	Peking (Beijing).	151

Part 3 – Capturing the News

| Chapter 14. | Bandits. | 161 |
| Chapter 15. | The Tragic End. | 172 |

Part 4 – Gareth: A Man Who Knew Too Much?

Chapter 16.	Dr Müller's Parole.	179
Chapter 17.	The British Embassy in China.	188
Chapter 18.	Lloyd George Contacts The Foreign Office.	202
Chapter 19.	Baron von Plessen.	214
Chapter 20.	The German Doctor.	222
Chapter 21.	The Japanese Involvement.	228
Chapter 22.	A Manchukuo Incident.	237

Appendix I	Historical Background.	249
Appendix II	Tributes.	264
Appendix III	Eulogy.	267
Appendix IV	Death Certification.	273
Appendix V	Bibliography.	275
Appendix VI	List of Characters.	277

Index   286

CURRICULUM VITAE
GARETH RICHARD VAUGHAN JONES,

1916-1922	County School for Boys, Barry.
1922	County Scholarship.
1922-1923	University College of Wales, Aberystwyth.
1923-1925	University of Strasbourg: Diplôme Supérieur des Etudes Françaises.
1925-1926	University College of Wales, Aberystwyth. First Class Honours in French, University of Wales.
1926	Entrance Exhibition, Trinity College, Cambridge.
1927	Medieval and Modern Languages Tripos, Part I. First Class Honours in French and German, with distinction in the Oral Examination. College Prizeman.
1928	Senior Scholar & Prizeman, Trinity College, Cambridge.
1929	Medieval and Modern Languages Tripos, Part II. First Class Honours in German and Russian, with distinction in the Oral Examination. College Prizeman.
1929	Supervisor of Studies, Trinity College, Cambridge.
1930	Private Secretary for Foreign Affairs to Mr Lloyd George, O.M.
1931	Visited New York to study the economics of American business.
1932	Returned to his former post with Lloyd George.
1932	Visited Italy in official capacity to report the measures adopted for the relief of the unemployed in the draining of the Pontine Marshes.
1933	Studied conditions of living in the U.S.S.R.. Master of Arts, University of Cambridge. Joined the staff of *The Western Mail*.
1934	Left for a "Round-the-World" tour.
1935	Died, August 12th, 1935.

PREFACE

Gareth Jones, my uncle, was killed in Inner Mongolia on the eve of his 30th birthday in 1935. The last words he wrote, before he was captured by bandits were: "There are two roads to Kalgan to where we go back; over one 200 Japanese lorries have travelled; the other is infested by bad bandits." A ransom of £8,000 was demanded by the bandits.

The story commences in Japan where Gareth interviewed a number of Japanese politicians of worldwide influence. He was a journalist on a 'Fact Finding Tour of the World'. That he had been David Lloyd George's Foreign Affairs Adviser gave him entrée into the presence of these famous men. Leaving Tokyo he visited a number of Far Eastern countries and in each he made exhaustive enquiries into local political opinion for it was his ambition to write a book on the intentions of the Japanese in the Far East. He travelled through China and his eventual destination was to be Manchukuo, from where he never returned alive.

Gareth's death at such a young age, in my opinion, was not an act of local Chinese banditry, but should be seen in the light of the global events of the nineteen-thirties.

To quote Mr R. Barrett of *The Critic* of Hong Kong in a letter of condolence to Gareth's father:

> There is no doubt that Gareth was in deep waters, for the swirl of Far Eastern politics is more ruthless and treacherous than anything conceivable in the West, more a mixture of petty interests of money and 'face' with the enormous clash of national interests. They knew what he had discovered in Russia and they knew what he had found out in the East.

ABOUT THE AUTHOR

Though Siriol Colley's early years were in London, she is proud of her Welsh ancestors. Her mother, father and husband were born in Wales and she knows the principality well. In 1940 she was evacuated to Canada where she commenced her medical education. For 35 years she was a General Practitioner in Nottingham. She has four sons and eight grandchildren. After the death of her husband in 1973 she took up scuba diving and has dived with sharks in the South China Seas, with sea lions off the Galapagos Islands and with many colourful fishes in the world's oceans. She has explored the wrecks of the German battleships scuttled in 1919 in Scapa Flow and assisted in the underwater survey of the East Indiaman, the *Earl of Abergavenny* whose captain, John Wordsworth (William's brother) in 1805, went down with his ship.

The murder of Gareth Jones has intrigued her family and almost 15 years ago she commenced researching the story hoping to find a reason for his premature death.

ACKNOWLEDGEMENTS

I have many personal acknowledgements to make to the numerous friends and relatives who have helped me in preparing this book. Firstly, my late mother who could still recall the terrible ordeal of the death of her brother, Gareth. The Rev. John Heywood Thomas gave me initial advice as to how to set the story in its present form and improve my 'turn of phrase'.

I should like to particularly thank my son, Nigel, as he has not only given me constant support and enthusiasm, but also on-going computer advice, having introduced me several years ago to Mr Bill Gates' word-processing technology. Furthermore, he has helped me editorially to separate the political intrigue from the travelogue, spending in excess of several hundred hours over the past few years reading all the source material, re-structuring the investigative chapters, providing additional research and alternative opinion (resulting in much heated discussion and on-going e-mail correspondence). Finally he oversaw the extremely long process of sub-editing through to eventual publication and created the supporting website.

Jane Colley sketched the map of Gareth's final journey into Inner Mongolia. Miss Bronson Ward gave me infinite encouragement and reassurance. Dr Alun R. Jones (a distant relative of Gareth's) gave me my first constructive sub-edit and later checked the final proofs including the Welsh spelling. Dr Richard Sims and Tristram Hicks have advised me on the 'Historical Background'. Sarah Honeychurch in the main but also Richard Surrey, Christine Walters and Dr Alistair Strang, who have edited the transcript for improved readability. Dr Dennis Witcombe and the Welsh Book Council for their constructive editorial direction. Sheila Sellars who originally deciphered Gareth's handwriting and transcribed his original diaries.

My son Philip investigated the murder in China and Japan, and my sons Graham and Richard and their families have shown great interest. My Chinese friends have also given me encouragement.

Thank you!

FOREWORD

Eryl, Porth y Castell, Barry, was until burgled some 10 years ago, the Jones' family home. Miss Gwyneth Vaughan Jones, Gareth Jones' sister, then in her nineties had hoped to end her days there, but due to the burglary this was not to be the case. The house, which once echoed with the sounds of happy, lively conversation and was full of life and laughter had taken on a lonely, melancholic air. Clearing the house was of great sadness to her relations as its contents spanned a hundred years of family history. Old photos of relatives long since gone, many unnamed, kept as memories of the past by my grandparents along with many other items of our family heritage were uncovered in every room. At the bottom of the second flight of stairs leading to the attic with paper peeling off the walls with age and plaster crumbling, amidst old domestic equipment, I found a brown leather suitcase monogrammed with 'G.R.V.J.'. On opening it to my surprise I discovered that Gareth's diaries had been lovingly kept by my grandmother. Under the bed in what was my grandmother's room, thick with dust which nearly choked me, was a black tin box with many of Gareth's letters and other documents relevant to his death. Nothing had been thrown away.

Since then I have found many other items connected with his death and I am still doing so. Recently, I discovered Gareth's copy of Hitler's *Mein Kampf*. In addition within a book in German entitled *Krieg in China [War in China]*, a letter from Baron von Plessen (who will be referred to later in the story), fell out which has possibly never been read until now. He had returned the book that belonged to my uncle and referred to him as 'poor Gareth Jones'.

In the Introduction, the reader will discover a brief history of his short but eventful life. Then the story begins with a copy of his last letter home. As a result of my investigations into his death, I realised that Gareth's tale of political intrigue commenced in Japan so my story then covers his experiences from that country until his eventual capture by bandits in Manchukuo. I have incorporated this into a 'travelogue' from his diaries and letters to his parents. Though it may appear to be a separate story, it is none the less, a colourful description of the Far East in the mid-thirties and portrays the adventurous and inquisitive nature of a young journalist. His diaries were written as an aide-mémoire, intended for the book Gareth eventually planned to write on his return. This will become apparent on reading some of the chapters, particularly those on the Philippines. His letters home are affectionate, showing his great love for his family, and his diaries often contain rather serious interviews with some of the most outstanding politicians of the time. A scrapbook of worldwide newspaper reports on his capture, subsequent murder by bandits was given by a journalist to his family, and extracts from these reports as well as many others appear in chapters 14 and 15. In the final part of the book I have tried to piece together whatever evidence there was and from this to investigate the reason for his premature death. With this in mind I have researched many books, the applicable Public Record Office documents and letters sent to my grandparents by Mr A.J. Sylvester, Secretary to David Lloyd George. It must be added that Mr Sylvester gave my grandparents much support in their grief. Ultimately, this is a story constructed faithfully from Gareth's papers

Gareth appeared to have been very influenced by a best-selling travelogue by Peter Fleming entitled *One's Company*, published in 1934. From this book describing the author's adventures in the Far East, Gareth planned his own journey through China en route to Manchukuo.

Every photograph, card and newspaper cutting (except the maps) that I have used in the book have come from those kept and treasured by my grandmother showing the depth of loss that she felt from the death of her beloved son on the eve of his 30th birthday. The quality reproduced may not be excellent, but they are worthy of reproducing and this book is a dedication to my uncle's short life and a personal labour of love.

The names of people and places in China are written in the form used in 1935 and generally follow the Wade-Giles system of Romanisation. Occasionally, the more modern system of pinyin has been added in parentheses.

To understand Gareth's tale, a background history of the period so relevant to his death is to be found in Appendix I.

METHOD OF RESEARCH

On finding Gareth's diaries in my aunt Gwyneth's house in 1990, I was determined to investigate his death. I knew the story started in Japan and not in China as most people thought. First Mrs Sheila Sellars transcribed those diaries relating to the Far East in 1935. At least six years ago I transcribed his weekly letters to his family, which were written in the last six months of his 'Round the World Fact Finding Tour'. Following this I endeavoured to merge the two into a story. The section on his capture by bandits was taken mainly from newspaper articles that had been kept by my grandmother, Mrs Edgar Jones, and from those which were given to her in a book a fellow journalist had compiled in his memory.

I commenced his personal history 'My Uncle Gareth', compiled from oral family history and from perusing a 'scrap book' containing many of his articles dating from 1930. There had been much correspondence between Lloyd George's Secretary, Mr A.J. Sylvester and my grandfather, Major Edgar Jones, and this was collated with extracts from Public Record Office documents.

I was no nearer finding the solution to his death and subsequently I felt it necessary to study the period of history prior to the tragedy. Books and documents I read are recorded in the Bibliography. The final interpretation of his death is my own opinion. On commencement of the transcription of his diaries and letters I presumed that the story was to be a personal one, but have found that as it evolved it became one of political intrigue.

GARETH'S 1934-35 WORLD TOUR ITINERARY

Late October	1934	Gareth left Great Britain
November	1934	Arrived in New York on *SS Manhattan*
November	1934	Left Washington for Chicago
December 2nd	1934	Visited Frank Lloyd Wright at Taliesin
January 2nd	1935	Present at Randolph Hearst's ranch
January 20th	1935	Embarked from San Francisco on *SS President Monroe*
January 30th	1935	Sailed from Honolulu on *SS President Coolidge*
February 9th	1935	Arrived in Yokohama, Japan
March 15th	1935	Left Tokyo sailing on *SS President Grant*
March 16th	1935	Docked at Kobe
March 19th	1935	Shanghai
March 22nd	1935	Hong Kong
March 25th	1935	Arrived in Manila in the Philippines
April 4th	1935	Left the Philippines on-board the Dutch ship *Tgisadane*
April 7th	1935	Crossed the equator
April 12th	1935	Disembarked from the ship, the *Op de Nook* in Semarang in Java, visited Mr Fletcher's plantation and from thence to Batavia, (Jakarta) Dutch Indo-China
April 20th	1935	Left Batavia on the *Ophir*
April 22nd	1935	Arrived in Singapore
April 26th	1935	Left Singapore for Bangkok on *SS Kistna*
April 30th	1935	Arrived in Bangkok
May 11th	1935	Left Bangkok
May 13th	1935	Arrived in Phnom Penh, Cambodia
May 14th	1935	Arrived in Saigon, French Indo-China
May 18th	1935	Arrived in Hong Kong on May 17th on-board the *D'Artagnon* and left on June 1st to Canton
June 8th	1935	Left Canton for 'Yale in China' in Changsha
June 12th	1935	Arrived in Changsha
June 16th	1935	Left Changsha
June 20th	1935	Hankow
June 30th	1935	Shanghai
July 2nd	1935	Nanking

July 4th	1935	Arrived in Peking
July 11th	1935	Left Peking to go to Prince Teh Wang's Palace before proceeding on his fateful journey
July 15th	1935	Left Prince Teh Wang's palace
July 19th	1935	Arrived in Ujmutchin
July 23rd	1935	At Larsen's Camp where Dr Müller and Gareth saw Sir Charles Bell
July 25th	1935	Arrived in Dolonor
July 26th	1935	The final entry in the diary
July 28th	1935	The day that Gareth and Dr Müller were captured
August 12th	1935	The date of Gareth's murder

MAPS

Gareth's journey from Hawaii took him first to Tokyo in Japan, from Kobe to Shanghai, to Hong Kong, Manila in the Philippines, Bali and Batavia (Jakarta) in the Dutch East Indies (Indonesia), Singapore and then to Bangkok in Siam (Thailand). Following this he crossed into French Indo-China, returning to Hong Kong. From there he went to Canton (Guangzhou). He travelled north to Changsha en route to Hankow, Nanking and Shanghai. Returning to Nanking he went to Peking (Beijing) and finally to Kalgan (Zhangjiakou) before embarking on his final journey to Inner Mongolia. His eventual destination he intended to be Manchukuo, which was previously known as Manchuria before the Japanese invaded the area in 1931.

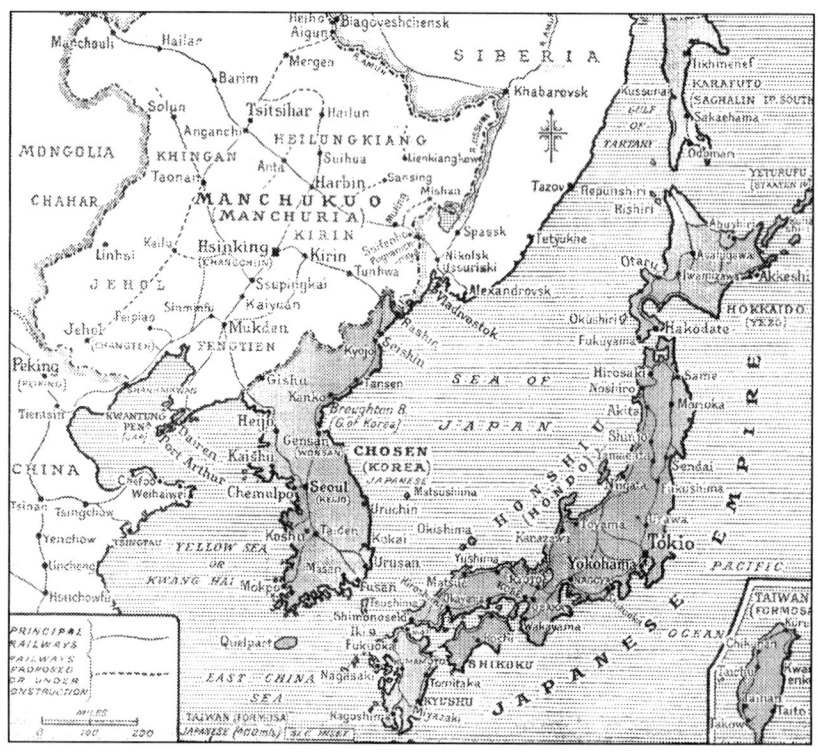

Taken from The Daily Telegraph Supplement on Japan and Manchukuo 1934.

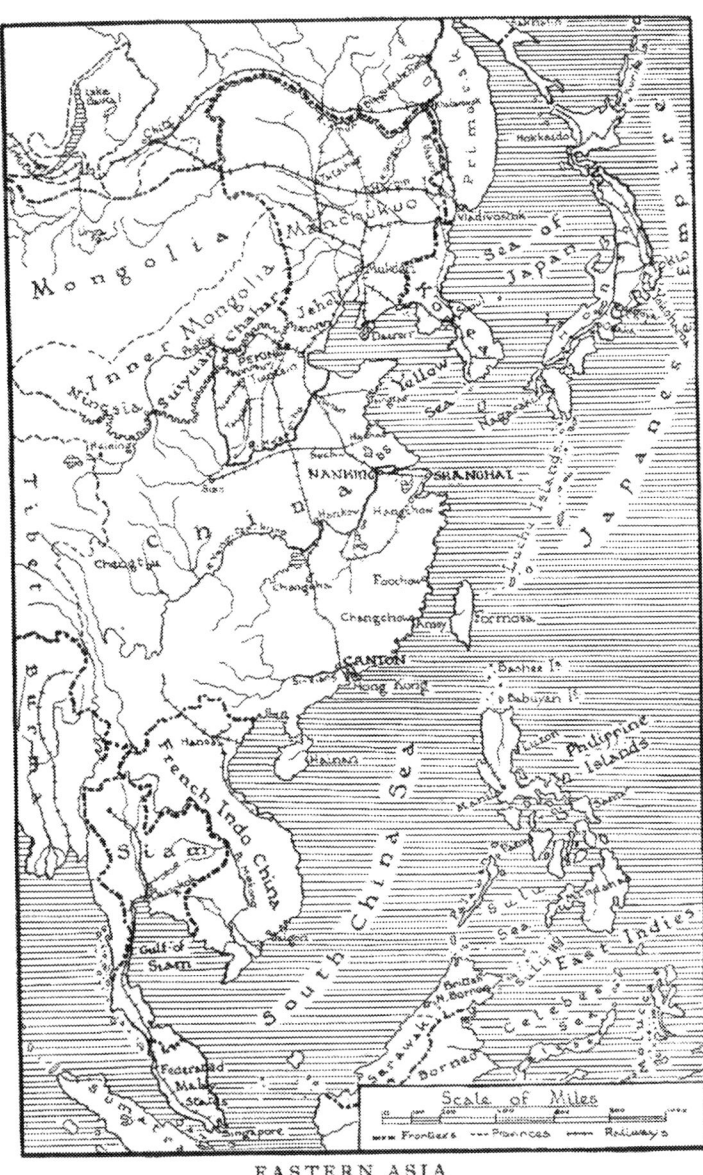

East Asia from the Institute of World Affairs Report on China and Japan 1937.

From the Institute of World Affairs Report on China and Japan 1937.

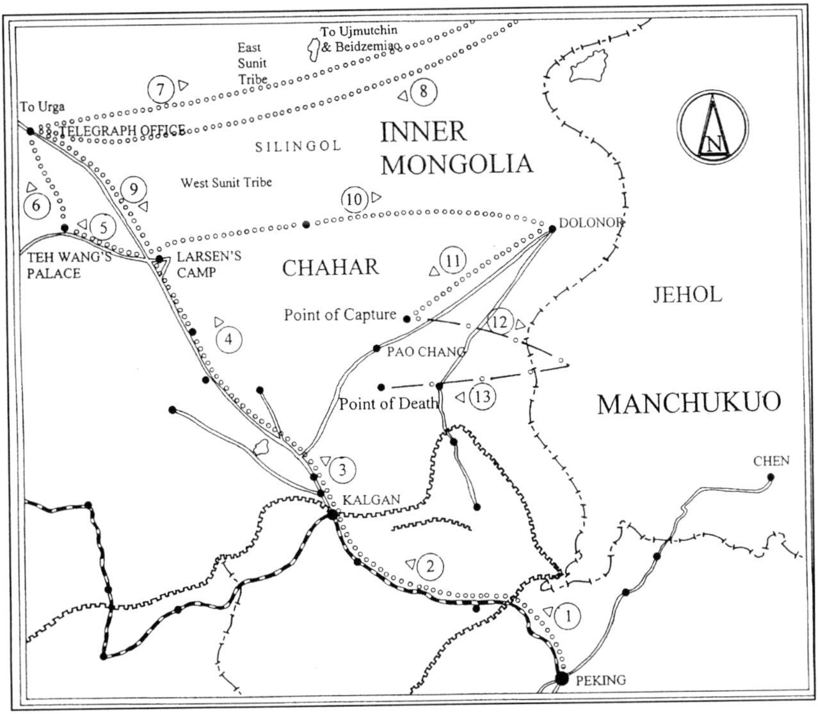

xiii

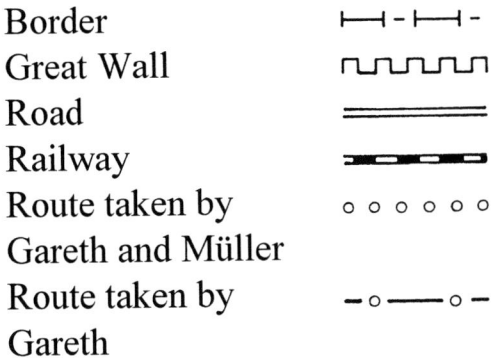

KEY

Border	⊢-⊢-
Great Wall	⊓⊔⊓⊔
Road	═══
Railway	▬▬▬
Route taken by Gareth and Müller	○ ○ ○ ○ ○ ○
Route taken by Gareth	–○——○–

Map of Chahar and Jehol (Gareth's Journey)

Introduction

Gareth with his mother – circa 1911-12.

My Uncle Gareth

Gareth's soul has never been laid to rest and his family speaks of him frequently as if his death only occurred yesterday. His mother considered that her beloved son had been the first victim of World War Two. After Gareth's death she always wore the black of mourning: it was a terrible tragedy for her to bear. She had lived her life through him and it was the stories of her youthful experiences in Russia that gave Gareth the interest in foreign travel. To his father it was the most traumatic event of his entire life.

I remember clearly being told by my father that bandits in China had killed Gareth. I was standing holding onto the banisters three steps from the bottom of the stairs in our London house. I remember the harrowing journey from Paddington to Cardiff by Great Western Railway with his ashes in a casket on the seat directly opposite me. They had been brought back on the *SS Rawalpindi* to be borne to their final resting-place in Barry. It was a cold December day in 1935. There was thick fog, which delayed the train and the journey seemed to take so many, many hours.

Gareth was born in Barry on August 13th 1905. His father was Major Edgar Jones, O.B.E., T.D., M.A., LL.D., for 35 years the headmaster of the Barry County School for boys, respected and loved by the thousands of pupils who passed through his school. He was considered by some to be the "Matthew Arnold" of Wales and that great English headmaster described the loss of a son in these words: "Be think thee for an only son what was that grief". Edgar Jones, known to all as 'The Major', was the noblest of characters. He understood tolerance and imparted to his students an understanding which enabled them to live in harmony with one another. He was modest in nature and a Christian gentleman in the true sense of the word. He had infinite interests and fostered these in the many boys that passed through his school. Many honours were bestowed on him not least that of being made a Freeman of the Borough of Barry. He was active in his support of the League of Nations and was a man of peace.

Introduction – My Uncle Gareth

Gareth's mother, Mrs Annie Gwen Jones was an equally interesting person. As a young girl who had never previously left Wales, she travelled to Russia in 1889 to be the tutor to Arthur Hughes's children, the grandchildren of John Hughes, the steel industrialist who founded the town of Hughesovska, later known as Stalino and now the City of Donetz. In old age she was a very fine, distinguished lady - a woman with high principles - and so it was difficult to visualise her in her youth riding with the hounds from the Court Estate of Merthyr Tydfil or skating on the lakes in the bitterly cold Russian winters. She was a woman with a strong personality. Early in the century she became a suffragist and the first meeting of the suffragettes in South Wales was held in the family home, Eryl. Crystabel Pankhurst, the daughter of Emily Pankhurst, attended this meeting. The town of Barry held her in high esteem and in her later years she accepted the honour of being made a Justice of the Peace.

The family home was first in the Colcot, Barry and then in 1932, Gareth persuaded his father to buy 'Eryl' in Porth y Castell, Barry. This imposing house commanded a magnificent panoramic view of the Bristol Channel in the distance and nearer Cold Knap and Pebbley Beach, Barry Island and the old Barry Harbour. I have cherished memories of the Sunday afternoon teas when many friends both great and humble gathered in the drawing room for the animated conversation and the warmth of hospitality for which the Jones' family was renowned. Auntie Winnie, Gareth's aunt on his mother's side and affectionately known as Ninnie, was well known for her lively nature and her delicious Welsh teas.

Gareth's early life seems to have been uneventful. His class reports from his father's school were unremarkable. One story remembered is of how he entered the drawing room to the amusement of a number of guests, wearing a top hat on his head and sporting a walking stick announcing he was the Governor of Taganrog. (His mother had acted as hostess to the Governor when Mrs Hughes was away from their home in Hughesovska.) It is strange that though there are very many documents that she saved about her son there is not one letter from her to him despite the fact that it is said she wrote nearly every day. His death affected her very deeply and perhaps that is why there are very few references to his early days.

Gareth with his father, Major Edgar Jones.

It is difficult to do justice to Gareth's brilliance in a short biography, which in itself is merely an introduction to his epic journey to the Far East. He was taught by his mother until the age of seven years. From his father's school he went to the University College of Wales, Aberystwyth, Strasbourg University and then on to Cambridge

Introduction – My Uncle Gareth

University where he obtained first class honours in German, French and Russian. Therefore including his native English and Welsh, he was able to write and speak fluently in five languages.

Gareth gained top marks in the Civil Service Examination for the Consular Service and was subsequently offered a posting in China, which he did not accept. In view of his exceptional knowledge of European languages, this offer would have been seen as derogatory and a great disappointment to his family. He was a Barry County Schoolboy from Wales in the era when the possession of public school education was considered of great importance. Gareth travelled widely throughout Europe and the United States. He worked his passage on a dirty French steamer, signed on as a stoker on a Norwegian boat and travelled steerage on small Swedish and German steamers. He was the 1920's version of the back-packer. In 1923, due to the fall in the German Mark he travelled through Germany for the sum of five shillings.

In 1930 he became research advisor in Foreign Affairs to Mr David Lloyd George, the former Liberal Prime Minister, and the following year he became Assistant to Mr Ivy Lee, public relations counsel to Rockefeller, Pennsylvania Railroad, Chrysler and other American business institutions. During this time Mr Lee, who knew Russia well, requested Gareth to accompany Jack Heinz II, grandson of the founder of the Heinz Organisation, on a tour of the USSR.[1] Gareth's sister, Mrs Eirian Lewis told of how she visited them aboard a dilapidated Russian ship, the *SS Rudzutak* in the Port of London before their journey. She vividly recounted that Jack's suitcase

---

[1] "With a knowledge of Russia and the Russian language, it was possible to get off the beaten path, to talk with grimy workers and rough peasants, as well as such leaders as Lenin's widow and Karl Radek [Secretary of the Communist International]. We visited vast engineering projects and factories, slept on the bug-infested floors of peasants' huts, shared black bread and cabbage soup - in short, got into direct touch with the Russian people in their struggle for existence and were thus able to test their reactions to the Soviet Government's dramatic moves. It was an experience of tremendous interest and value as a study of a land in the grip of a proletarian revolution." Extract from Gareth's Preface to Jack Heinz II's [anonymously written] book *Experiences in Russia – 1931. A Diary.*" [N.B. In 1931, the U.S.S.R. was still politically unrecognised as a sovereign state by the U.S.]

bulged with the '57' varieties of Heinz produce [which she presumed were for their future personal sustenance in Russia].[2]

Gareth only spent a year with Mr Ivy Lee, on account of the Depression in America, before returning to spend a further period in the office of David Lloyd George. The latter assigned him to make enquiries into Mussolini's relief measures in the Pontine Marshes, attempting to rid Italy of the scourge of malaria. In 1933, he was sent to Eire where he interviewed President De Valera of the Fianna Fail Party. He wrote of the I.R.A. and its hatred of the British. Prior to his 'Round the World Fact Finding Tour' Gareth worked for *The Western Mail* and the Managing Director, Sir Robert Webber, wrote to Gareth enclosing a copy of a letter from John Buchan, the famous author congratulating him on his articles written in 1933 exposing the current situation in Russia. Sir Robert thought very highly of him and in his tribute to Gareth considered him to be a brilliant writer, a most interesting lecturer and a linguist of extraordinary cleverness fitting him to be a most successful journalist. Sir Robert Webber considered that Gareth's ambition was to be a foreign correspondent:

He travelled extensively in Europe and America. It was to increase his practical knowledge of world affairs that he decided to travel in Asia. He had a most enquiring mind. He was only satisfied with the most thorough research. The relations between China and Japan profoundly interested him and it was in the pursuit of first-hand knowledge that he made the supreme sacrifice.

As a prolific writer, Gareth left a legacy of articles published in many British newspapers including *The Western Mail, The Times* and the *Manchester Guardian,* in Germany in the *Berliner Tageblatt* and in American newspapers through the International News Service. These articles are a graphic and historic portrayal of the critical events of the early thirties and are worthy of an in-depth study in

---

[2] "Mr Zuckerman (Chief of the Supply Department of the Narcomsnab (the People's Food Commissariat) was kind enough to send us [Gareth and Jack Heinz II] off in an auto with an interpreter, to see the President of the Torgsin stores concerning the purchase of the "57" (varieties) ... I [Jack Heinz II] wanted Mr Jdanoff, of Torgsin, to try some hot beans, and made an appointment to see him in an hour. Just as I arrived, with my hot tins, the rascal drove off in his car." From: *Experiences in Russia – 1931. A Diary.*

Introduction – My Uncle Gareth

themselves. In 1932 he wrote in *The Western Mail* of his reception by Lenin's widow, Nadezhda Krupskaya, in the Commissariat of Education in Moscow. As she was opposed to Stalin's policies they did not discuss politics. It was whispered in Moscow that she and the dictator had had an argument. Stalin had lost his temper with her and shouted: "Look here, old woman, if you do not behave yourself I'll appoint another widow to Lenin!" This woman of great character was enthusiastic about the educational aims of the Communists and the need to raise production. "She mentioned production in the same tone as a Welsh minister might mention God or religion."

The following year in his articles Gareth dared to expose the folly of Communist Russia's Five Year Plan of industrialisation and collectivisation. On his last visit to Russia in 1933, he disregarded an Embassy warning, packed his rucksack with bread, cheese, butter and chocolate and travelled hard-class to the Ukraine. There he wrote:

> I walked through the country visiting villages and investigating twelve collective farms. Everywhere I heard the cry: "There is no bread. We are dying!" This cry is rising from all parts of Russia; from the Volga district; from Siberia; from White Russia; from Central Asia and from the Ukraine – "Tell them in England we are starving and we are getting swollen."
>
> Most officials deny that any famine exists, but a few minutes after one such denial in a train I chanced to throw away a stale piece of my bread. Like a shot a peasant dived to the floor, grabbed the crust and devoured it. The same performance was repeated later with an orange peel. Even transport officials and O.G.P.U. [Russian police department] officers warned me against travelling over the countryside at night because of the number of starving desperate men. A foreign expert from Kazakhstan told me that 5,000,000 of the 11,000,000 inhabitants there had died of hunger. After the dictator Josef V. Stalin, the starving Russians most hate George Bernard Shaw for his account of their plentiful food, but there is insufficient food and most peasants are too weak to work on the land.

Dr Ivy Lee.[3]

---

[3] Dr Ivy Lee, America's greatest publicity expert, had a face which the Americans called "dumb pan". Ivy Lee never took a fee that did not run into five figures. Perhaps it was his recognition of his somewhat grandiose ideas that, according to him, Soviet commissars used to entertain him exclusively off gold plate. He was the first person to urge the United States to recognise the Soviets, and paid a visit to Russia twice a year. This did not prevent him, however, from accepting - with his son - $58,000 a year from the Nazi Government. His connection with the Rockefellers and other magnates is well known and he was proud of his title "family physician to big business". He was said to have kept even millionaires waiting for an appointment. [From a newspaper obituary (Date and source not known).]

The Right Honourable David Lloyd George.[4]

---

[4] David Lloyd George, Chancellor of the Exchequer 1908-1915 introduced in 1911 the National Insurance Act. The Insurance Certificates were known as 'a Lloyd George'. He was Prime Minister of Great Britain from 1916 to 1922 and one of the signatories of the Treaty of Versailles in 1919.

These reports confirmed the grim situation and followed shortly after Malcolm Muggeridge's accounts in the *Manchester Guardian* and, as Muggeridge's biographer mentions, Gareth's stories were incorporated in his book *Winter in Moscow*.

A rebuttal was promptly presented by Walter Durranty, U.S. correspondent - long in the Soviet 'good graces' to which Gareth replied in the *New York Times* reaffirming that starvation was widespread in Russia. Soviet propaganda, fed by the party activists who were imbued with a religious fervour, so impressed foreign visitors and delegates that the outside world was unaware of the catastrophe that had befallen 90% of the Russian people. In a letter to Gareth of April 17th 1933, Muggeridge describes Durranty as "a plain crook, though an amusing little man in his way" and offered to write a letter of protest to the *New York Times* if he had sight of Durranty's piece. Later that year Muggeridge wrote again having seen the Durranty contribution and commented: "He just writes what they tell him". [Letter of September 29th 1933.]

Gareth wrote that the success of Stalin's plan of collectivisation and industrialisation would strengthen the hands of the Communists throughout the world. As early as 1930 he was one of those who predicted that the 20th century would be a struggle between Capitalism and Communism. Now we have reached the new millennium and are able to look back over the history of the twentieth century we can see that his belief was remarkably accurate.

His fluent German greatly facilitated his reporting of German affairs and in 1933 he was the first foreign correspondent to fly with Hitler in his plane, the famous 'Richthofen', the fastest and most powerful aeroplane in Germany at that time. His article starts as follows: "If this aeroplane should crash the whole history of Europe would be changed. For a few feet away sits Adolf Hitler, Chancellor of Germany and leader of the most volcanic nationalist awakening which the world has seen".

He described Hitler as an ordinary-looking man and was mystified how fourteen million people could deify him as 'The Great Dictator'. The flight was from Berlin to Frankfurt-am-Main where

Introduction – *My Uncle Gareth*   xxv

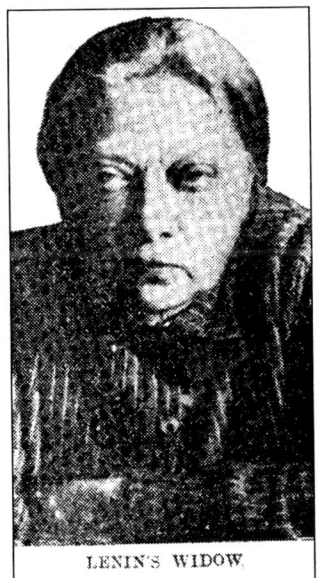 

Photo of Lenin's widow, Nadezhda Krupskaya taken from one of Gareth's articles written at the time and one of Joseph Stalin from a postcard sent to his mother in 1930.

A unique photo taken in 1933 by Gareth of the starving children in the Ukraine. One of the very few pictures that recorded this great tragedy of the Stalin era.

Russian posters found in Gareth's room in Eryl in 1990. Gareth brought them back in 1931 and presented one to David Lloyd George. The right hand one represents the Hoover plan in crisis.

'Tractor is in the field. It is the end of the Will of God' by the artist Cheremnykh.

Hitler was to speak at a rally of Nazi supporters. At the rally Gareth described the people as being "drunk with nationalism", and that the atmosphere was one of hysteria in the auditorium. 25,000 men rose to their feet, 25,000 arms were raised in salute and 25,000 voices shouted 'Heil Hitler'. The dictator's speech completely mesmerised the audience.

Later Gareth met Hitler's private secretary in a private suite overlooking the Chancellor's Palace. He confirmed that Germany must look east and unite with East Prussia across the Danzig Corridor. Gareth forecasted then that the dispute between Germany and Poland over the Corridor would bring about the Second World War.

Adolf Hitler, Chancellor of Germany.

Gareth's writings and his radio broadcasts were often illustrated with delightful and amusing anecdotes. "The microphone preserved every iota of his (Gareth's) personality, the enthusiasm and vivacity ... a peculiar impression of intimacy, as of addressing a single person across the fireside." One such tale was circulated among the anti-Nazi Lutherans in Germany of a staunch Nazi priest who, before commencing service, ordered that anyone who was a Jew should leave the church. There was a brief pause and then the figure of Jesus Christ stepped down from the crucifix over the altar and silently went out of the building.

Heading of one of Gareth's articles wrote after he attended the Frankfurt rally.

There was a joke whispered in Germany of a humorist who asked:

Do you know how Hitler is going to put 3,000,000 unemployed to work?" Then he, himself answered: "He will make the first million paint the Black Forest white. The second million will build a one-way road to Jerusalem, and the third million will cover the Polish Corridor with linoleum."

Yet another was that of an airman who was passing over a lonely lake and saw a man struggling in the water and rescued him. When he had done so he found it was Stalin and immediately considered the advisability of dropping him overboard again: "because of what all the other Russians would say for not letting him drown".

Another anecdote that he had heard in Kharkoff was that of a louse and a pig meeting on the frontier of the Soviet Union. The louse was going into Russia while the pig was leaving. "Why are you coming into Russia?" asked the pig. "I am coming" the louse replied, "because in Germany the people are so clean that I cannot find a single place to rest my head. So I am entering the Soviet Union. But why are you leaving Russia?" The pig answered: "In Russia today the people are eating what we pigs used to eat, so there is nothing left for me, and so I am saying goodbye". Gareth was to see proof of this in the market where a slice of doughy black bread was selling at the exorbitant price of one rouble [(2/-) or equivalent to about 24 loaves of bread in 1933].

The Frankfurt Rally that Gareth attended in 1933.

After Gareth's death, *The Western Mail* paid tribute to him by re-publishing a selection of his articles from their newspaper and the proceeds from the publication of this book, *In Search of News*,[5] went towards a travel scholarship which was founded in his memory. The title page bears a quotation from the eminent journalist, John Garvin, the editor of *The Observer*, describing Gareth as a journalist who had won every step of his way by personal force. That force is precisely what the book reveals; it is a newspaper's testimony to the achievements of one of its brightest stars and a recollection of the kind of brilliant informative writing he had contributed over the years. The little book - published over half a century ago, but still quoted as a record of Welsh life in the 30s and of Welsh awareness beyond Wales - is a wonderful example of Gareth's powers of description and evocation. His articles describing Wales excite the imagination, setting the scene with the sounds and sights of the countryside. He describes local characters whose trades have long since fallen into obscurity and recalls such characters of folklore and legend, telling the story of Bob, the Raven of Brechfa, or the legend of the Lady of the Lake, the Mystic Maid of Llyn y Fan Fach. One only needs to read that lovely recollection of an evening in a Welsh farmhouse to see his passionate love and appreciation of his Welsh heritage. Turning to the pieces in the Eisteddfod is to see him feeling that love for historical investigation and observation of the continuing influence of that tradition. Even the articles on his foreign topics - Lenin's widow and the Seven Japanese Virtues reveal a journalist who was essentially a Welshman abroad.

It was Gareth's ambition to *Search for News* that eventually led him to explore further afield. Although he had already travelled extensively in Europe and the United States, the Far East remained unknown territory to him, and, wishing to investigate its growing political problems, it was to this turbulent region that he was next to turn his attention. Over several months, his work took him throughout Asia, before bringing him, on July 4th, 1935, to Peking (Beijing). It was from here, a week later, that he was to embark on a journey into

---

[5] Please refer to the website: www.colley.co.uk/garethjones for a full transcription of these articles by Gareth.

Inner Mongolia, a journey which would prove, tragically, to be his last.

The following pages take up the story after his arrival in Peking. It consists of a letter that Gareth wrote to his parents in the form of a narrative, in which he also incorporates extracts from his diary. It was to be the last letter that Gareth ever wrote.

Gareth at the Wrexham Eisteddfod. With Richard and Eryl Hall Williams.

PART 1

INNER MONGOLIA

Chapter 1

The Final Journey

In a magnificent yurt, coloured red and gold inside, in the palace of Prince Teh Wang, Prince of the East Sunnit, direct descendant of Genghis Khan and leader of the Free Mongols.

(A yurt is the same shape as an Esquimau hut, but bigger and made of wool on wooden framework.)

Sunday, July 14th, 1935

My Dearest Everybody,

    I have written my Sunday letters from lots of strange places - from a rubber plantation in Java, from the ruins of Angkor, from a horrible Chinese inn - but this is the strangest of the lot. I am the guest of His Highness Prince Teh Wang, the greatest man among all Mongols, whose forefather, Genghis Khan, formed the huge Mongol Empire which reached Hungary, nearly overran Europe and whose other forefather, Kublai Khan, Dada used to read about in school (Coleridge). It has been the most colourful day I have ever had - a Mongol feast in honour of the spirit of the mountain, just near, and I also had a good interview with Prince Teh Wang, who wants to set up an independent Mongol Empire, including the Mongols under Soviet rule in Outer Mongolia and the Mongols under Manchukuo. The splash of colour, with bright silks and gorgeous head-dress, the fine horses, the Mongol tents, the spirit of worship and the wrestlers, riders, lamas and archers, has been magnificent.

    <u>Journey into Inner Mongolia.</u> On Thursday July 11th, I got up at 5.30 a.m., breakfasted and went by rickshaw from the Legation Quarter, Peking, to the station which is very close. There, Baron von Plessen, who is the double of Tom Ellis, was waiting for me. He had shorts and I also brought shorts. We had a first-class compartment and soon the train steamed off. At the next station Dr Herbert Müller, a friend, entered and we formed a trio. (Dr Müller and I are left. The Baron had to return to Peking on Monday.) Plessen and Müller were

extreme opposites. Plessen is tall, sensitive, and nervous about catching trains and buses, exact, correct, speaking public school English. Müller is small, pleasantly cynical, and philosophical. Does not worry about anything, jokes all the time, as do all my German friends. When we are almost bumped to pieces going over a mound he grins; if the lorry nearly tumbles on one side he roars; he never loses his good humour and is an excellent companion.

Thus the train left Peking with its 'Three Musketeers'. We travelled towards the fine, towering mountains about 20 - 30 miles to the north of Peking, and saw the Great Wall; or rather there are many walls, which defended China against the Mongols. The Mongols have been slowly driven back for over 150 miles to the north of the previous frontier and all the villages we passed through are Chinese. Poor old Mongols! They have a hopeless position and have been losing their land to the Chinese. We went under the Great Wall in a tunnel, came out and saw a magnificent view, a vast plain surrounded by blue mountains, which are full of iron ore and which the Japanese wish to develop.

<u>At 3.30 in the afternoon</u> (after 8 ½ hours), we came to a huge collection of mud houses, with some stone in the middle surrounded by hills. It was Kalgan, the outpost for trade between the Mongols and China. There, two magnificent cars were waiting for us. We were to be the guests of Mr Purpis, a Latvian, the "King of Kalgan" who is the chief trader in Inner Mongolia and sells about 30,000 horses each year to the Chinese Army. Our chauffeur was the former chauffeur of the Panchen Lama, who with the Dalai Lama is the chief lama of Tibet and Mongolia. He drove us through the dirty town to a kind of mud-wall fortress on the outskirts of the town. It was Wostwag, the company for trading with the Mongols, a German firm. We entered a courtyard, which was full of hides, tobacco, boxes of silks, wool. There were many lorries, which go from Kalgan across part of the Gobi Desert to Urga in (Soviet) Outer Mongolia. Mr Purpis, a very lively man, very strong and vigorous, in breeches and leather boots, came to welcome us. He gave us a wonderful dinner that night. We had a warning to beware of Mongol dogs that are said to leap at men's throats if the men are afraid. (But I do not have the slightest trouble with Mongol dogs. Either they take a liking to me or

Chapter 1 – The Final Journey

they are terrified of me and slink away. They can tell at once that I have no fear of dogs.)

Our caravan consisting of two cars and a lorry was to start off next morning at four o'clock, just about dawn. Plessen woke Müller and myself before four o'clock. (The Baron was just like an alarm clock). He shaved, whistling and put on his shorts. We dressed, drank tea without milk or sugar; the effect of the sunrise over the hills was fine; our caravan rattled out of the fortress. Two cars were leading and one had a trunk with all kinds of goods for the Mongolians.

The evening before a Chinese Foreign Office representative asked us to sign the following: -

We, the undersigned herewith certify that we are going to visit Inner Mongolia on our own risk for any eventualities, which may happen during our travelling.

We carefully considered all warnings of the local Chinese officials who will take no responsibilities should anything happen to the undersigned:
  Von Plessen
  Herbert Müller
  Gareth Jones.
Kalgan, 11th July 1935.

Next to me in my car was a tremendous Cossack, he had a head like a melon - only square, shaved bald; he was terrifically strong and fat; he had bandy legs from being so much in the saddle. He laughed and joked all the time. He was very much of a child. His name was Vishnevitch and after the Revolution he walked 800 miles in winter across Mongolia, from Urga to Kalgan! There were three Russians and myself in the car and the driver said: "don't be disappointed if we don't get further than twelve miles, for floods may have blocked the road". When we left the town boundary, the day gradually getting lighter, we had to show our special visas for Chahar and Suiyuan (as the Inner Mongolian Province is called) while blue uniformed soldiers, formerly of General Sung, stood there with fixed bayonets. And so we rattled on along <u>horrible</u> tracks into Inner

Chapter 1 – The Final Journey

Mongolia. We left the last Chinese town behind, gradually cultivated fields disappeared; we entered the Steppes and were in real Mongolia by afternoon.

At three o'clock - after we had seen our first yurts and herds of camels and of cattle, we left the main Kalgan-Urga road; (Urga is of course Bolshevik) and came to Larsen's Camp. The scenery was similar to that around Hughesovska; dark green hills and rolling plains. Larsen is the Duke of Mongolia, a Swede, formerly a missionary, who has become a great man in Mongolia. He lives in an old temple on the side of a hill, surrounded by yurts.

Kalgan. The headquarters of the Wostwag Company, a German firm that traded with the Mongols.

The railway terminal at Kalgan.

Chapter 1 – The Final Journey

The lorries of the Wostwag Company being loaded with hides, boxes of silk, wool and tobacco.

One of the Wostwag lorries being loaded.

The bread and butter there was wonderful, just like Breconshire or Cardiganshire, but before I had eaten two or three pieces the shout came: "Caravan! Forward!" And off we rattled towards the west, sometimes along a cart track, sometimes over the

Steppes. We did not see a single tree for 150 miles, from Kalgan to Larsen's Camp.

About four o'clock, we saw a great sight - over 1000 horses on the plain. They all stick together side by side affectionately. This is against the wolves that will kill them. In Outer Mongolia, they reckon five percent die from the wolves that even kill big horses. A few dark blue tents had been pitched. It was Mr Purpis' horse camp where he had 1250 horses. There we were to camp for the night.

It was like the Wild West! A number of Mongol horsemen were there and a great performance began. Mr Purpis was to choose some of the best horses to bring to Kalgan. Mr Larsen and he directed the Mongol horsemen to choose one out of the wild horses. The Mongol armed with a long whip, which was also a lasso, would descend on the chosen horse that would then fly away. A great race would follow, the Mongol catching the fugitive horse, throwing the whip-lasso round his neck and bringing him to a stop. Five or six Mongols on foot - very plucky - on this horse being brought back – would leap on the horse or hold him by the mane and tail. Then another Mongol would brand the wild horse with "P" for Purpis. Then supper - soup with big lumps of mutton - cooked by the Russians. We ate it in wooden Mongol bowls. We then slept in tents.

We woke up early the next morning (Saturday July 13th) after a good sleep. It was a cold morning and we could hear the sound of horses' hooves and those of camels. We had kippers for breakfast and then watched more horses caught by the Mongols. Then one car with Plessen, Müller and myself left towards the palace of Prince Teh Wang at Pai Ling-miao. "This is puzzling," said Plessen: "When one is invited for a weekend in England, one knows what to expect. But a weekend at the palace of a Mongolian prince! I just can't picture what it is going to be like". We drove bouncing up and down over the Steppes. There was no road and the sensation was that of an aeroplane. The ground was sandy with heaps of flowers. We saw one lone rider and sheep grazing. Müller said: "That's where the aeroplanes land. The Japanese planes come very often. The Japanese have wireless stations (sending and receiving at all places) and motorcars and aeroplanes connect all stations. In Teh Wang-fu there is a Japanese hospital and they are planning to develop roads there.

Chapter 1 – The Final Journey

Probably before long there will be an autonomous Mongolia with treaty of friendship and commerce with Japan".

Prince Teh Wang owns about 35,000 horses, 30,000 camels and the land all the way to the Outer Mongolian border. About 20,000 Sunnit form the tribe and the Prince is the judge. Everyone of the tribe must come, one time or another, to serve for one year. They are very independent characters and it is very hard for the 'Japs' to control here.

After 10-18 miles of rushing across the Steppe, we went over a hill and in the hollow, we saw two collections of strange buildings. The first was of grey stone with brightly coloured roofs in Chinese style. A number of yurts surrounded it. We saw a wall with pictures of big blue birds upon it. That was the palace of Prince Teh Wang. The other collection of buildings was a number of temples about 500 yards away, with their Chinese fantastic gables of dragon designs, rising above a series of mud houses. That was the residence of the Panchen Lama, who, they say, cannot go back to Tibet because he is anti-British and, of course, we control Tibet.

We drove towards the Prince's palace, when about five Mongol soldiers rushed out with rifles. They had very dark old uniforms, but with very fine silverwork on their daggers and belts.

They had very prominent teeth and pigtails (all Mongols, except lamas, wear pigtails). One barred the way with his rifle and grinned. He would not let us go to the palace, but pointed to a building on the hill with yurts round it. (We learned later that only the Prince and his family could come down the straight way to the palace and that ordinary mortals should come the side way, although we could leave by the princely way.) The soldier in a blue-grey ragged uniform jumped on to our sideboard and directed us to a low white washed building with a grey roof and the yurts on the hill. A yurt is round, made of sheepskins and wool and is warm and comfortable. Here a number of Mongols in brilliant, though dirty, red and blue silks bowed to us and led us to a yurt where we sat cross-legged on Mongol carpets (which were about a yard square). They brought us Mongol tea with mare's milk in it. It was <u>awful</u>! We sat in silence for some time, and then afterwards wandered about the yurts. After about one hour and a half, word came that the Prince was ready to receive us.

A group of guests outside a yurt.

Pai Ling-miao. A soldier on guard outside the Temple of the White Tomb.

Chapter 1 – The Final Journey 9

Gareth carrying his bag into the yurt.

The interior of the yurt that Baron von Plessen, Dr Müller and Gareth shared.

We went down the hill. We entered the courtyard, and saw this dazzlingly painted entrance with the two green statues of lions. They looked like Chinese lions, but with funny heads. Two soldiers stood with fixed gleaming bayonets. They saluted and presented rifles to us as we passed and we entered another courtyard. We waited, seated, in a room in the palace until a big man in a dark blue silk robe with a skullcap, on which there was a red button and having a very long pigtail, came in. He had a reddish face, rather cunning and looked about 45-50. He was the Prince. His counsellor, a dignified wrinkled man with a strange headdress, accompanied him. We bowed and grinned. Müller said we would like to sleep in a yurt. The Prince bade his servants take us and we went to a courtyard where there were three yurts. We were taken to the further one (a soldier with a fixed bayonet guarded the second, because it contained the Prince's seal).

We entered the tiny door and found ourselves in a brilliantly coloured interior. All round the circular wall there were bright red, shut boxes with golden designs of bats, which is a sign of good luck. There were two big chairs, opposite the door, against the wall, but we were requested not to sit in them, because they were for the high lamas. Just near the door there was a red and gold open box full of dry horse manure. In the middle under the opening there was a space with a fireplace. On the left of the two lamas chairs was a Tibetan Buddhist altar with three gold Buddhas. On each side were offerings of raisins, dates, sweets and dried prunes. A piece of yellow cloth hung down from it. Beside it was a blue tapestry and cylinders for prayer in a glass case with gilt dragons above and fishes below. As well as these, was a picture of the Panchen Lama with a fluffy, hairy dog and a painting of Buddha with four hands (two folded and two outstretched) arising out of a lotus flower. There was room for four of us to sleep on the floor.

When Mongols greet each other, they take out their beautiful snuff bottles of different colours and stones, hand them to one another, pretend to sniff and hand them back. I met Mr Pao, a Chinese man, who had been captured by the Communists and had been kept prisoner. He seized one of their hats, walked out, and escaped.

The temple has a Chinese influence. Before the entrance is a courtyard and on the north and south sides are prayer wheels. A man with a conical hat and a red cloak and prayer beads turns each cylinder. On the roof of the temple are dragons with heads looking down and a collection of bells with beautiful sounds hang down. The carvings of dragons are in gold and green. An old man sits at the door of the temple, mutters into his hand and the boys reply. They are dressed in purple and some in dirty yellow cloaks and have hats like Roman soldiers with a yellow mane. The chief priest is very fat, laughing and chuckling all the time, holds a coloured joss stick. The lama priest and children think it is a great joke. The boys look at each arrival and the priests come to see my hairy legs, look in wonder and point. It is 5.30 in the afternoon and the service begins. The festival is in honour of the spirits of the mountain. There are larks in the sky and the swallows swoop about and chirrup. The priests sit cross-legged. The chief on the floor makes a noise, loud like rub-a-dub-dub and seems to wink at us. A big gong bursts into a crescendo of noise. There is more laughter and then a roar from the man on the floor with a big moustache about five inches long.

Plessen said: "It is the most extraordinary divine service I have ever attended". Then the fat chief suddenly draws a heavy stick and right in the middle of the service strikes a boy on the back and on the head in punishment. "What's that for?" asks Plessen thinking it was part of the ceremony.

The Prince had 50 guests. There were Chinese officials, the British Military Attaché, Sir Charles Bell, the High Commissioner for Tibet and daughter, an American artist, some people from Peking Embassies, but mostly Mongol princes and lamas. Sunday was to be the greatest feast of the year, but there was not a single lavatory in the whole palace! Not even for the Prince. That night there was a great feast at the palace. There were Chinese dishes: lotus seeds, seaweed, shark's fin, date and 20 kinds of soup including mutton soup. Fermented mare's milk, which is horrible, is the number one drink, the champagne of Mongolia.

12 Chapter 1 – The Final Journey

Prince Teh Wang, leader of the Mongol Princes and head of the Sunnit Banner.

Prince Teh Wang arriving at the festival of the Mongol Princes on his white horse.

Chapter 1 – The Final Journey

Prince Teh Wang with his young son.

The young Prince.

14   *Chapter 1 – The Final Journey*

Ceremony at the Tibetan lama temple.

Gareth at the lama service.

The feast.

The obo.

On Sunday morning, I woke up to hear the Baron say: "Gentleman it is five o'clock." He woke us up much too early! We dressed, breakfasted from our own supplies and before 7 a.m. we dashed off to a hill about seven miles away, where the great feast was to be held. Dozens of blue tents had been put up. Hundreds of Mongols in silks of reds and blues, princes with peacock feathers in their hats and also some in purple and red robes - all the cream of this part of Inner Mongolia had come to pay their respect to the Spirit of the Mountain. On top of the hill was a cairn of stones with a pole. (They call the piles of stones in sacred places here "obos"). In front of the pile were about 25 lamas in yellow silk and broad-rimmed hats looking like Cardinals, chanting Tibetan music. Then the Prince, who was now in red, came riding up the hill with horsemen following. He came and sat down in front of the lamas. With him sat his little son aged about five years old. He had a little red hat on with a number of pearls, a jade brooch and a brown silk coat with a design of yellow squares on his back. He had a lama guard. The lamas sang, shouted and threw rice. Then they all marched round the obo three times and suddenly started throwing coarse flour at each other. They roared with laughter. They threw flour at the masses of stones, then bombarded each other. It was just like an old-fashioned slapstick comedy where people threw cakes at each other. Round the obo were numbers of offerings of meat, cheese, cakes and other delicacies! That religious ceremony over, we all descended the hill. Lambs (sheep) had been brought to be slaughtered and soon we were eating mutton with our fingers.

The Prince sat in his tent to watch festivities. He was clad in yellow with a conical hat with red threads. He was seated on a throne with a dragon design and before him is a huge mass of cakes. Next to him on his left sat his elder son adorned with pearls and jade jewellery playing with a smaller pile of cakes. The number depended on the importance. Looking out of the tent we could see the riders and retainers who are allowed to wear peacock feathers on their heads, which makes them very official. The button on top of the skullcap signifies rank and a direct descendant of Genghis Khan. Before the Prince's tent, there is a square cloth, about 20 yards in front, directly in line with the entrance. It is to prevent evil spirits from entering the tent. The Prince joined the revellers and with his bow and arrow shot the bull's-eye twice.

A boy jockey described by Gareth as having a yellow shirt and a red kerchief on his head.

  Then came the horse races with boy jockeys who were wearing yellow shirts on which were bright red Buddhist prayer wheels and they had brilliant red kerchief on their heads. After that there was archery for some hours. Next came the wrestling. Before a bout, mare's milk was served and the wrestler prays and also after the fight. He wears a leather coat studded with white metal studs with a Buddhist wheel on the back. He leaps and dances and the winner comes to the Prince's tent and is given a block of tea, money, presents and cake. He dances up and down, prays on his knees and bows with his head on the ground. He goes back into the field and throws a piece of cake on to the roof of the tent. The wrestlers are very sporting. There is no quarrelling as to the decision and the loser just grins. The winning person has a swastika branded on him. What would Hitler say? The wrestling of Mongols went on for many, many hours.

  A boy priest came and sat down by me while I ate my mutton at lunchtime and stared at me, as do many of the Mongols. One young boy with a pleasant face came up to me and pulled the hair on my hand, pulled the hair on my knee and drew the zip on my shirt to see the hair on my chest. The Mongols love being photographed and they lacked self-consciousness as I took photos of them. I was amused to see another old ruffian who had an embossed sixpenny piece of 'Queen Victoria' attached to his pigtail.

One of Teh Wang's guests was Dr Erskine and I asked what was the Prince's Mongolian name. He told that the Prince's name is sacred; that it is blasphemy to say it and that it must not be uttered. He is known as Vang Yi, the Prince. No son or daughter should say the name of a parent. The doctor had treated the Prince for a disease and all his children died until he cured him of the condition. Now his children live, and because of this he is very grateful to the doctor. I was surprised to hear from him that the Mongols do not bury their dead for they believe it is wrong to touch the surface of the earth. A dead man is tied on a rope on to a horse and is dragged by the horse with the rider, off into the Steppes, until the corpse falls off or is lost; the rider must not look back. There, the body is left on the Steppes and the birds and the wolves come and eat the body.

I heard a Japanese aeroplane arrive with officials flying low over the crowds. The future of Mongolia is in the balance and at the same time as the festivities a lot of political talks went on. Prince Teh Wang summoned me to his presence and gave me an interview, guarded by two pigtailed Mongol soldiers. He sat bow-legged in his tent wearing magnificent light blue heavy silk with beautiful dragon designs. It had a dark blue collar and he had a thick black silk skullcap with a red button on top. The throne was a dragon in blue and red. Servants came in and stared. He wants to have a great Mongol Empire, uniting the Mongols of Inner Mongolia with those currently under the control of the Soviet Union or the Japanese in Manchukuo. He would prefer to rely on the Chinese for help, but if they treated the Mongols badly by colonisation they would turn to the Japanese. Only as a last resort, if the Japanese squashed them, would they turn to the Russians. I asked him if the best method to attain a united Mongolia would be with Japanese help. To which he replied that they wished to obtain independence without any outside help. He said that the attitude to the Japanese giving help would be that anyone who sympathises with the Mongols was their friend. He had cunning eyes, gave skilful, sharp diplomatic replies. He appeared tired and yawned during my interview.

Chapter 1 – The Final Journey 19

The entrance to Prince Teh Wang's palace.

Gareth with a lama.

Mongolian Princes at the festival.

Prince Teh Wang's troops.

Chapter 1 – The Final Journey

I pressed on and asked if the Japanese had plans to build any roads, which their cars could use and whether they planned to build aerodromes, but this he denied. I asked him what the significance of the visit to Pai Ling-miao by the Japanese (the occupants of the plane) was and I was told that it was merely social.

After my interview the Embassy people especially our Military Attaché, descended upon me to hear the Prince's views. I then spoke with a Mongol officer who speaks Russian and was in the Artillery College in Moscow, he told me:

> People in Urga are discontented; there are still bread cards there. Two years ago there was a big rising. The Soviets fought against the lamas and the princes, and people don't like the economy plans. Perhaps there will be a revolt as there are many that want to join a big Mongolia. I am a nationalist, I believe in a big united Mongolia with Outer Mongolia, Manchukuo Mongolia and free Mongols. Prince Teh Wang is a great man, and I hope he will be the leader of a united Mongolia.
>
> If there is a war, we will be in a bad position. If the Russians win then we will lose all, the princes will be crushed and the lamas broken. If the Japanese win they will set up a 'Great Mongolia', but Japan will enslave it. We are in a difficult position. We don't like the Chinese, or the Japanese, or the Russians. The Russians will give in on all hands, they know they are too weak, and they will yield to the Japanese for at least two years.

<u>About seven o'clock in the evening</u>, we returned, tired, to our yurt. After we had eaten, a Chinese diplomat, knowing I had heard the Japanese point of view and the Mongol point of view came in to impress upon me the Chinese point of view!

<u>Monday, July 15th</u> was a day of all days. "Gentlemen, it is four o'clock!" shouted the Baron just before dawn. Plessen had decided to go back to Peking, because there was practically nobody at the German Embassy. Müller and his 'boy' servant Liang (aged 46), who was as superior with the Mongols as an English butler among the

Hottentots, Anatoli, the Russian chauffeur and I decided to cross a big part of Inner Mongolia, almost as far as the Soviet-Manchukuo frontier.

We said goodbye to Plessen and off we went at 5.30 in the morning, when the sun was shining over the palace and hundreds of swallows flying round it. Our destination was a lama's town and temple called Beidzemiao where the second most important Living Buddha in Outer Mongolia was staying. There was an early morning haze over Mongolia. The sentry at the gate was snoozing and another sang a Mongolian song reading it from Mongolian writing. A woman was squatting on the floor arranging a silver headdress. Priests squatted facing the sun. A boy with crooked legs strolled about.

We passed a Japanese hospital, which had increased in size over the last three months, and then by four long, low buildings and three gasoline tanks built on ground close by where the Japanese planes land. The Mongols dread the aeroplanes and have fantastic legends about them, because the Japanese once took a skeleton away for research. Even the camels are terrified by the shadows of the planes. The Mongols are frightened of the Japanese; they said there was no snow last winter, because of their presence.

We drove over uncharted land. No map contains the features of the roads or rivers. Perhaps the Japanese have military ones. The roads were terrible, just ruts here and there. We very nearly bumped the roof every other minute. The lorry-car nearly tumbled over. It was like being in a tank during the war. We went on for hours and hours. How we stuck it I don't know and how the car kept together I also do not know. We had to go the long way round the Sacred Mountain, as we crossed the southern fringe of the GOBI DESERT. (Did you think a year ago that I would be crossing part of the Gobi Desert?)

It was very sandy and the scent from the wild thyme was beautiful. Fine birds and eagles circled in the sky and antelopes crossed our path. Skeletons of cattle lay strewn on the wayside. There was a sudden descent in the track and we could see ridges and

Chapter 1 – The Final Journey 23

Mongolians examining the car before Gareth departed on the final journey from Pai Ling-miao.

The sign says: 'Welcome to the Daban lama temple meeting'. It is northeast of Dolonor.

plains stretching for miles. There were very few yurts to be seen and eventually we came to some temples where we grinned at a solitary Tibetan monk.

Midnight came and we seemed to have lost our way. All the maps are bad and the distances are wrong. Luckily it was the night of the full moon. "I am afraid", said Anatoli, the Russian chauffeur: "Are we anywhere near the Soviet frontier? If so, we'll be shot. I have no documents". "We had been earlier", said Müller. Earlier we had been within 30-40 miles from Soviet Outer Mongolia, but now we were about 100 miles away. "We'll have to camp out", said Müller. We then passed the skeleton of a camel in the moonlight. "Killed by desert foxes," said Müller. All day long we had passed skeletons of cows and horses killed by desert wolves. "Let's go", said Anatoli: "Soon we'll come to Beidzemiao". So we rattled on.

At 1.30 a.m., after travelling for 21 hours we gave a shout: "Hurray!" We could see a town of mud walls and with temples. We were all about dead-beat and we thought: 'time now for a good rest'. Suddenly we came to a river, which was about 150 yards from the town. It looked like a ford. Our car splashed through and then, just as the front wheels had gone on the other bank, the back wheels got stuck! The car could not get out. We tried until about 2.30 a.m., pushing, but it was no use! Anatoli and I went into the town and shouted, but no one came although a lot of dogs barked. We went to some Mongol yurts half a mile away, but the Mongols just grunted from inside. We went further on, but we could find no help anywhere. Finally at 3.45 a.m. we came back to the car where we decided to stay until dawn.

I slept for nearly two hours and when I woke up I was bewildered. There were two camels tugging in front and a host of Mongols. I got out of the car and we all pulled at ropes. Next we got some oxen, but they were no use at all. Then a lama in salmon coloured silk robes came down in a car from the temple. About eight o'clock we decided to go to the town and leave the car. We came to an inn that was occupied by Japanese who were most hospitable and charming. At nine o'clock, they gave us a room and after 29 hours I lay down on the floor and slept!

Chapter 1 – The Final Journey

<u>On Friday, July 19th</u>, we arrived at Ujmutchin. It is 25 miles from Soviet Outer Mongolia and 35-40 miles from the Manchukuo border, in the northeast wedge of Inner Mongolia. This is a lama town, where the head Prince of the Silingol League of Mongols has his residence.

Bogged down in the river.

This has been the most exciting week I have ever had in my life, packed with adventures and strange encounters. It has been so full that I have not had the chance of continuing my letters, when one rattles along for 20 hours a day in a lorry, over sand dunes and through rivers, when one interviews Living Buddhas and Japanese agents and Buriat and Mongol princes. It is hard to find a minute to write beyond the notes, so I will continue my story where I left off having had a very long sleep.

After arriving in Beidzemiao where 1000 ignorant lamas live, I slept all day and all night. The place was a collection of mud houses with magnificent temples. Next day (Wednesday) the Living Buddha, Diluwa said he wanted to see me and give me an interview. So Müller and I went past the temples where the lamas were busy praying in yellow robes and came to a small temple dwelling where the Diluwa was staying.

I entered the reception room of the Living Buddha. It had a throne and a place for about 14 people on bright coloured mats around the wall. The High Lama was in a salmon coloured silk robe with a purse of gold. I liked him very much. He had a frank smile with white teeth. He had a sense of humour. He did not sit on his throne, but beside it. He 'told' brown beads all the time. Priests came in with gifts of silk - in rolls of bright blue and red. We were given Mongolian tea. Then Diluwa took some Mongolian butter-like cream and stuck masses in my cup of tea. He started speaking in Mongolian to his secretary who was wearing a dark long brown robe. He translated into Chinese, which Müller translated into German and which I wrote down in English. It was an appeal for help for refugees from Soviet Outer Mongolia. Many, about 40,000 to 50,000, had had to flee, unable to rescue much of their property and arriving at most with only their riding animals, either camels or horses. The poverty among them is terrible. They have few household utensils and only a small pot. They started to come in 1931 when the Communists started to press their ideas. They did not bring their herds, because the Bolsheviks confiscated these. They had a difficult time to escape the guards. The Nanking Government has given £30,000 for rice, but this is not enough. While we talked lamas peeped through the windows like schoolboys. Then a Japanese man rode by in brilliant Mongol dress, on a fine Mongol saddle, with a little skullcap and a button on top. Müller says: "A lot of them do it. It is much more comfortable and they think it makes them more popular".

After my interview with Diluwa, we motored on and got stuck in a river for three hours and twenty minutes and eventually we arrived late at night at Ujmutchin, not far from the Soviet and Manchukuo frontier. The leader of the Buriat Banner, Prince Otcheroff gave us a room near his palace and we slept well. Next morning, we went to the Yamen and paid a visit to the Japanese representative of the Kwantung Army, as the Japanese occupied it. The leading Japanese in the yurt was a man of great charm with fine teeth, a tuft of beard and brilliantly humorous eyes. They had a wireless there. Into the room came a Mongol who had a purse with a swastika, black on white with a red border. The Japanese man said he had been there since March and had not yet had a bath. He was having great difficulty with the superstitions of the local people. He could not hunt, because the Mongols feared their guns as it disturbed the spirits of the mountains; he could not dig, because the Mongols believed it wrong to disturb the surface of the earth, and he had not yet had the chance to speak to the Prince. He considered that Mongolia is a hopeless job.

I also found that a lot of lamas were very superstitious. I had seen a part of a temple with pictures of laughing skulls and of devils and I returned to photograph it, but a lama rushed out terrified and barred the door. I tried to enter the temple, but a lot of lamas collected together and they looked very menacingly at me and shouted. Then I saw a sundial, but it was covered with a sheet of wood to keep the sun away! Obviously, it was a very great treasure. A soldier with a rifle came out to stop Dr Müller and me going into a house, which was being built, and again the lamas shouted threateningly at us. I have never seen such a suspicious place; the Japanese were quite right.

I strolled about in the Yamen in Ujmutchin and came to a school where four youngsters were writing in Chinese and Mongolian script. There was a picture of the Kangte Emperor [Pu Yi], most elegantly and 'fadedly' clad in morning dress and 'Come to Jesus' butterfly collar, striped trousers and two Manchukuo flags painted on it. There was a propaganda poster for a Mongol feast in Manchukuo probably under the auspices of the Japanese with wrestling, riding, singing, etc.. Mothers were invited to bring their children to very good Japanese doctors (however they would rather die than go to a Japanese doctor). Children loved the silver paper from cheese or camera film that I gave them. I did tricks with a coin in front of the lamas and they were amazed. I was entertained by an acrobatic goat, which marched on its front legs, with its back legs lofted into the air, much to my amusement.

I spoke to a Russian that I met called Kulagen, who told me that the Japanese are building barracks in Beidzemiao where we had stayed and that everyone expected that the Japanese would soon send troops there. He said that in 100 years that the Mongol race would be dead. The spread of venereal disease is terrific and the people have no idea why they have no children. Prince Otcheroff has a son and daughter, but no grandchildren. The chief cause is Lamaism for it leads to the lack of young men to work and there are no husbands for the young girls. These girls sleep with the lamas and spread the disease, but they will not go to the Japanese doctors for treatment.

Kulagen continued to tell me that the Mongols, who had recently visited Manchukuo, had returned, bringing back bad news and all of them loudly curse the 'Japs'. While in that area they heard how the Japanese have beaten and killed their fellow Mongols. In Manchukuo there is great discontent focused against the Japanese. No one in Inner Mongolia has any desire to join with Pu Yi and the Mongols say it is foolish to look up to him as a descendant of the former Emperor. The leaders realise that he is a puppet of the Japanese, that he is their prisoner and to swear allegiance to him would be the same as swearing allegiance to Japan. To say that the Mongols are loyal to Pu Yi is merely Japanese propaganda. The priests are especially afraid and say that the coming of the Japanese will bring evil to the land.

<u>Now on Friday evening July 19th</u>, I am in a Buriat (Mongol) camp on a hill, in a tent with a wonderful view of great herds of cattle, horses and sheep in the distance.

I did not have time to continue the letter this morning; because we decided to return westward and here we are back with the Buriats, who are very hospitable and clean. There is a wonderful view with blue hills in the distance for about 30 or so miles, over the border of Manchukuo. Soviet Mongolia is about 110 miles to the north. Our Russian chauffeur is now preparing soup with mutton. I have almost forgotten what a bed is like, and to sit around a table and not to eat meat with my fingers will be very funny. We went very slowly from Beidzemiao to the land of the Buriats, through lovely grass with flowers, irises and mauve marguerites, much better than the sand we went through on our way to Beidzemiao. More people including Russians have arrived at the camp of Prince Otcheroff, who speaks perfect Russian. I am told that the Prince came here after the Revolution, but the Mongols would not give him any land. But he told them of their history of Genghis Khan and what the Mongols did 500 to 1000 years ago. They were amazed and became friendly. He went to the Panchen Lama who said there was some free land and gave his permission for him to live there. Another reason given for him obtaining land was that he took the offensive against some Mongolian robbers who were stealing and killing cattle. Otcheroff stole back some of the cattle and captured some of these Mongols. He then cut them up and hid their bodies. When the Mongols could find no trace of their bodies, they became terrified, presumably, because they are afraid of their spirits.

When we arrived, the horsemen went to fetch some sheep to be killed for the feast tonight. We could see the flock far away in the distance, a perfect white mass. The Buriats are much cleaner than the previous Mongols we met and have beautiful milk and butter. On our arrival, I was given a fine bowl of milk before going into the yurt of the Prince. It was big, spotless and it even had a bed. It had an altar with silver cups and photographs of lamas. He studied law at Petrograd before the war and by an amazing coincidence had met Müller there in 1911.

Prince Otcheroff invited us to have brandy and vodka. Suddenly he started making a political speech to me:

You were the secretary of Lloyd George, he is a vigorous old lion and he must come to the help of the Mongols for we are the finest race in the world. Under Genghis Khan, we conquered half the globe, but what do we see now. We see parts of Russia like Latvia and Lithuania, which were mere Provinces, are now independent nations, while we are scattered and under submission; we, who received the tributes of Russian princes, we who conquered Moscow and had Russians as our slaves.

What do we want? We want to become an independent nation under the protection of the League of Nations; we want England to help us. You see we are a dying people, perhaps we cannot be saved, but we know we are doomed if the Japanese, Russians or the Chinese dominate us. We hate the Japanese, as they want to control us. The Chinese are too weak and they have been bribing some of the Mongols with money and gifts. The Japanese are doing the same. Teh Wang is too friendly with the Japanese.

Müller, who was tight, went out to play with the dogs and then came back into Otcheroff's yurt. The German was red in the face and drunk. "You have insulted me", the Prince cried: "You from England, Germany and Russia come, and then you and the English go, and only the Russians remain". He went on with his speech: "The Japanese, they lie, they want to get a grip on the country". The group including some Russians began to drink toasts. "To the glory of the Buriats!" "To an independent Mongolia!" Koster, a Russian, says for a joke: "Well here's to the 'Japs'" and drinks to them.

I did not grasp for several minutes what was happening, when suddenly the Prince shrieked to one of the company, Shuskin: "What! You drink the health of the 'Japs'. No!" Otcheroff was in a terrible temper and in great fury and with terrible cursing in Russian said: "You son of a ----- Mother!" To which Shuskin replied: "I did not say anything". A Mongol present shouted at Shuskin: "You are a traitor to your country, the Japanese beat you in 1905[1] and yet you drink their health. They are now trying to choke the Mongols and you drink their health". However, it was actually another person, Koster, who had made the insulting toast. Shuskin denied the remark vehemently, but nobody believed him. "You lie. You lie. You said it. You are a traitor", stated the Russians present. Poor Shuskin controlled himself: "I'm going now, thank you for your hospitality". "Come back. You're afraid. You know you drank to the health of the cursed 'Japs'." Shuskin came back, very dignified and sat next to Otcheroff. "Look I am a Russian Officer." Otcheroff breaks in: "Yes, yes a Russian officer and you drink the health of the enemies of the Mongols, the people who are trying to smash the Buriats. You son of a Red!" As Shuskin leaves, Otcheroff in a drunken state draws up his sleeves and attempts in vain to strike the departing officer.

As we leave, there are terrific flashes of lightning towards Manchukuo and others from the north. It lights up the sheep that are huddled together and the lambs that are sheltering in the deep furrows. Neureutz winds blow and the tents are very exposed on the hill and rattle. We are pleased to get into our beds.

---

[1] Russo-Japanese War 1904-1905 – Refer to General Nogi for further details.

<u>Saturday Morning.</u> It got too dark to write last night and it was bitterly cold, because Inner Mongolia is nearly 4000 feet high, somewhat higher than Snowdon. Prince Otcheroff, our host, has gone off to catch horses and we are waiting till he comes back before going to call back on Diluwa. He has a motorcar and we shall travel together to visit some Mongol princes. I am presently sitting on a box covered with a very bright, small Mongol carpet. The nine yurts of the Buriat settlement, our tent and the tents of some Russian traders (from Kalgan and Tientsin) are behind me. As we are breaking camp, we shall say good-bye to Prince Otcheroff and then off we go in search of the Living Buddha again.

<u>Sunday, July 21st, one o'clock.</u> "On the track of the Living Buddha" - we have been following his motorcar track across the Steppes, but cannot find him. We followed his tracks last night till dark and then pitched our tent near a spring about one mile from a Mongol camp. I am afraid we cannot find the High Lama, so we will have to make our way southwards.

<u>Six o'clock.</u> Hurray! We have tracked Diluwa like boy scouts from one prince's camp to another. We are going to spend the night in the camp (seven yurts, and about 20 camels) of the Prince of East Sunnit and we leave tomorrow morning for Larsen's Camp, the Living Buddha leading us in his car. There are black clouds and it has become very dark and overcast. If it rains, we may be stuck here for days. The Prince of this Banner has returned and offered us his yurt. I am very glad because the tent is cold. It is hot during the day and very cold at night – so Nos Da. [Good night.]

<u>Tuesday, July 23rd.</u> We came 150 miles yesterday, Monday, to Larsen's Camp. We have just left Larsen's Camp where we saw Sir Charles Bell and our Military Attaché. We are going through bandit country to Dolonor. I am told they are very pleasant bandits and do not attack foreigners. Dr Müller knows the bandit leader quite well and we may call to see him. I don't think there is any danger, because 35 bandits were seen on the road yesterday and they were driven off into the mountains. We were stuck in the mud for three hours; got stuck again later. I am afraid we will have to camp out tonight. Dolonor is on the map but the other places are not.

Wednesday, seven o'clock. We have drifted off on to the wrong road into the mountains, and we have lost our way again. We came down tracks, which were very deep and bumpy into the plain. We were just going to pitch camp near a well, when a Mongol rode up and invited us to stay in a yurt. The host offered me his wife and this also happened in other places. We expected to be in Dolonor by this time. We are going towards the east in the hope of finding the town. It is raining and we have run out of bread and biscuits, but we still have plenty of tinned stuff. I do hope we'll get to Dolonor today.

No bandits have come our way, and in any case, they are a pretty harmless lot here and would not dare to attack foreigners, because the Japanese would capture them at once. We have not met the bandit leader whom Dr Müller knows as he is in another part.

Dr Müller and Gareth's car being pulled out of the mud.

<u>Wednesday, July 24th 3.30 p.m.</u>. Again, we have been stuck in the mud for many hours and it has been pouring. I have no idea how we shall get out. Perhaps we shall have to wait until the land dries out which might be a long time. We had hoped to have a Chinese meal at Dolonor last night. Peking seems a very long way indeed. There is a Mongol village a few miles away and we have sent for some men to push.

<u>Five o'clock</u>. At last, we are out of the mud after five hours here. It took 20 villagers to tug us out. There was a huge cloudburst, which brought down torrents; there were masses of hailstones; the biggest I have ever seen, some almost as big as marbles. It is becoming increasingly more difficult to write my notes.

<u>Two hours later</u>. We are in the most outlying Chinese village bordering on the Mongol lands - in the most miserable mud hut I have ever seen – the only furniture is a mat. People are very poor here. The cloudburst, which has caused so much trouble, has wrecked their few crops. We have travelled 110 miles from Kalgan, but in the last eight hours, we have travelled four miles!! Just think of that speed when you speed on perfect roads in your Lanchester car. This village is quite different from the Mongol places. There are masses of children to be seen here compared with the Mongol places where we have been where there are almost none.

We are now 50 miles from Dolonor. We may have to wait until there is sun to dry the roads. When I get back to Peking I'm going to the Grand Hotel de Peking to have really good dinner - although we've had good tinned stuff. We have little food left, because we expected to get to Dolonor in about six or seven hours, but we've already been two days. So, we'll be hungry by the time we get to Dolonor. The people here have not much to eat.

Yesterday we passed some mounds just near the place where Kublai Khan had his summer house. Dr Müller believes that the mounds are Zanadu.

<u>Thursday, July 25th</u>. I have left home exactly nine months today and shall be home in something over three months. Then it will be fine to have the usual dinner cooked by Auntie Winnie and invite our great friend, Mr Davies.

Last night we slept four in a row (Dr M., self, Liang and a Mongol guide) on the floor in a very poor Chinese mud hovel - on a mat. During the first part of the night, the dogs howled everywhere and mad donkeys brayed. Dr Müller thinks there were bandits in the vicinity disturbing them, but I am told that the bandits here are just horse and cattle thieves and do not kill. Anatoli slept in the car and also had a bad time, because the entire village came to peep in at him. This area is exceedingly poor, but the villagers are having the time of their lives watching us. They came to see us get up. They believe that foreigners have webbed feet like ducks and came to verify it while we dressed this morning. The roads are very bad after the rains, but we are going to make an attempt to get through to Dolonor. I haven't slept in a bed for a fortnight. We got eggs from the villagers and we solved the problem of having no bread by mixing eggs with flour and milk and making a sort of hard pancake.

1.20 p.m. A very narrow escape! We thought we would be stuck for 4-5 days in the village, because the roads were slippery after the cloud burst. We had the help of 20-30 villagers and what a relief! We got out of the valley to drier hills.

First signs of Manchukuo! Hurray, because it shows we are getting near Dolonor, which is near the Manchukuo frontier. We have just met an ox cart with a Japanese flag flying on the front and a Manchukuo flag at the back - an indication that we are near the border. It is beautiful country with larks singing everywhere and the meadows covered with wonderful flowers - just like a field in June. There are deep blue larkspurs, butterflies, yellow and red flowers, and mountains around. What a contrast to the village we nearly stayed for many days in. We are exceedingly happy, because we are out of the region where the cloudburst was. I really thought we were going to be there for nearly a week. We are now in Mongol lands, which have been colonised by the Chinese; the Mongols have been driven north and westward. Dr Müller has just come into the car with a bouquet of flowers. When I hear the larks and see the June and early July flowers I can almost imagine that I am coming home to strawberries and cream! A few days ago, we saw a herd of over 1000 antelopes; the hill was coloured brown with them.

I shall write this letter while we stop for the engine to cool.

Thursday, July 25th at six o'clock. We were stuck in the mud again this afternoon, and now we are stuck again just near the river, which we must cross. Across the river, a boy is waving a Manchukuo flag, although this is really China. While we wait for the oxen and

Chapter 1 – The Final Journey

men, I shall continue to write. It is a lovely evening. Today I saw a little Chinese girl with half a dozen buttons on her dress of which she is very proud. On each button was printed: "for Gentlemen!" Dr Müller has gone off to talk with the villagers. On his return, I see Anatoli wading the river with wood to get under the wheels and now oxen are being tied up to the car. Finally, we are pulled out and we carry on.

<u>Ten o'clock at night.</u> Hurray! AT LAST DOLONOR! After a terrific journey traversing across high hills in the dark. Just outside the town, there was a poppy field and the West Gate, which we came through, was not guarded. On each corner, soldiers with fixed bayonets guarded the streets. Many of the houses are made of mud and lanterns lighted the streets. We waited in a rough inn for supper and eventually we had a good meal. In the same room, there is a man with no hair, just a bald shaven head. He is boiling opium in a deep frying pan on a wood stove and is fanning the wood stove with a Chinese fan. The room is papered with Chinese account books. Every now and then he drains the opium mixture through leaves or filters. There is a sickly smell of opium and in the next room; there is an opium pipe and bed. A Manchukuo soldier is smoking. Müller remarked: "The 'Japs' have already opened three brothels here. That's the first thing they introduce, legal opium, but not for the 'Japs'. Funny they haven't got heroin traders yet, but that will come".

Anatoli is worried. "I have no visa." I laughed "Manchukuo? Indeed everyone knows this is Chahar - a Province of China". Then Müller said: "I've just heard that this became Manchukuo two days ago. The 'Japs' have also occupied Kangpao on the Kalgan-Urga road, Kuyuan and Pao Ch'ang. The innkeeper says they intend to occupy Kalgan on about August 15th; about 40,000 troops have assembled not far away from Dolonor. 28 lorries and more soldiers arrived today. 30 are expected tomorrow. Many troops have gone southwest".

<u>Friday morning, July 26th.</u> I got up late, walked the streets, and found them festooned with Japanese and Manchukuo flags. Müller said:

One is the Manchu flag, the old Republican flag slightly changed. That's why I think they want to hold China. Kalgan will be a preparation for an independent North China and an independent Mongolia and there will be very few Mongols here.

As I strolled through the town, there were more smells of opium. Everywhere in the streets was the smell of opium. Down by the river, I saw animal skins being dipped and soaked in the water and one was a fine dog skin. In one place, I saw rice or corn being stored, as a donkey with its eyes wrapped with a cloth and a horse were going round and round threshing the grain. The poor animals get blinded by the threshing.

On my walk, I saw that there were many troops on the road to Kalgan. On the walls were lanterns and everywhere these were papered with Manchurian and Japanese flags crossed on each other. The streets here are full of soldiers with fixed bayonets; I passed a geisha girl, showing the Japanese had arrived. Theatre crowds were on one side of the street. They were singing: "God save Manchukuo soldiers and officers". There were lots of sing-song girls and Japanese soldiers.

What luck! There are great events here. The streets are full of Japanese and Manchukuo flags. The Japanese have decided to make this Chinese town and region part of Manchukuo. The town itself has 15,000 soldiers. Thousands of Japanese soldiers are assembled here and many have left on the road to Kalgan over which we travel on tomorrow.

I am witnessing the changeover of a big district from China to Manchukuo. There are barbed-wire entanglements just outside the hotel. There are two roads to Kalgan to where we go back; over one 200 Japanese lorries have travelled; the other is infested by bad bandits.

These were the final words that Gareth wrote in his narrative before he was captured by bandits and murdered. The following two pages show Gareth's last diary entry (which he used as an aide-mémoire to create the faithfully reproduced narrative):

Chapter 1 – The Final Journey

Transcript of Last Diary Entry

Dolonor - 9.45 p.m. Thursday July 25th. Arrived over mountains. Streets guarded - each corner, - many houses, by soldiers with fixed bayonets. Mud houses - we came through the West Gate - (not guarded). Poppy field just outside, lanterns in streets.

Came to inn, room was papered with Chinese account books, smell of opium, fire stove in middle and opium boiling by man with hair shaven bald, who every now and then drained it through leaves or filter. Anatoli worried: "I've no visa". I laughed: "Manchukuo indeed. Everybody knows that this is Chahar Province, China." Then Müller said: "I've just heard that this became Manchukuo two days ago. The Japs have also occupied Kangpao, on Kalgan-Urga road, Kuyuan and Paochang." The Innkeeper says they- intend to occupy Kalgan about August 15th. About 40,000 troops have assembled not far away. 28 lorries and soldiers arrived today. 30 expected tomorrow. Many troops have gone southwest. "The Japs have already opened three brothels here". We looked at-opium, "That's the first thing they introduce - legal opium, but not for the Japs. Funny they haven't got heroin traders yet, but that will come".

Good supper, meat, omelette etc, but sickly smell of opium; opium smoking room next door. Inn - mud huts; broken down. Soldiers and barbed wire outside.

[Second Page]

<u>Friday July 26</u> – Müller: "Lucky you don't wear A. O. F. B. also, or the Japs would think you were the Anti Oriental Fighting Brotherhood!"

Up late; walk, streets full of Japanese and Manchukuo flags. Müller: "One Manchu flag is the old Republican flag, slightly changed; that's why I think they want to hold China. Kalgan will be a preparation for an independent North China, and an independent Mongolia. Very few Mongols here." Went walk, smells, to river, sand everywhere. Flags. Saw skins being dipped and soaked in river. One fine dog skin. One corn or rice place; donkey (eyes wrapped round with cloth) and horse going round and round, they get blinded; threshing.

Many troops on Kalgan road. Went walk on arriving, lantern on wall and papered with Manchurian and Japanese flags crossed. Everywhere Japanese and Manchurian flags with more Japanese flags than Manchurian. Heard music, went through room, smell of opium, opium smokers one room, making opium in the other room. Smell of opium in the- streets. Theatre crowds on one side in open air. God save Manchu soldiers and officers. Lots of sing-song girls. Saw Japanese soldiers.

PART 2

GARETH'S TRAVELS

The following section, Part 2 - "Gareth's Travels", makes use of his numerous letters and diaries to paint a picture of the long and fascinating journey through Asia that eventually brought him in July 1935 to Inner Mongolia. The account begins six months earlier in Japan where Gareth enthusiastically interviewed many of the leading politicians of the day. It is here in the opinion of the author that the roots of the mystery are to be found.

Part 3 – "Capturing the News" covers the newspaper reporting of Gareth's capture by bandits and his subsequent murder.

Finally in Part 4 – "A Man Who Knew Too Much?" the author conducts her own investigation into the circumstances surrounding Gareth's death. There it is argued that Gareth's murder, far from being an ordinary act of banditry, may in fact have been an event of greater import.

However for a clearer understanding of the historical and political background to the Far East in that era, the reader is very strongly advised to refer to Appendix I – "Historical Background".

Chapter 2

Japan

"The Emperor is the descendant of the Sun Goddess. All Japanese are the sons of gods." Amletto Vespa.

Early on the morning of October 26th 1934, Gareth's liner, the *SS Manhattan* steamed out of Southampton harbour bound for the city of New York, on the first stage of his 'Round the World Fact Finding Tour'. His final destination was the Far East. The evening before, his father, Major Edgar Jones, his sister, Eirian, his niece Siriol (the author), and his close friends, the von Dewalls said goodbye to him on the boat train at Waterloo station, London. As he left, Wolf von Dewall, the London correspondent of *Die Frankfurter Zeitung*, gave him a Chinese name of Yo Nien Sse (which translates as lofty mountains, studying and reflecting).

Two days after he arrived in the United States of America the American Congressional elections were held, resulting in a great victory for the popular Franklin D. Roosevelt's Democratic Party. Gareth forever the journalist, immediately telegraphed this news, at great expense, to the *Berliner Tageblatt* arriving in time for their next morning's edition. He then spent a very full and hectic month on the East coast of America lecturing on his Russian experiences, meeting influential persons, writing articles for American and British newspapers and speaking on the radio. On November 27th he left by Pullman sleeper for Wales, Wisconsin in the Mid-West with the intention of visiting the Welsh farming community. One of their famous descendants was Frank Lloyd Wright, the idiosyncratic architect of worldwide repute and Gareth spent a most interesting time with him and his wife at their home, Taliesin.[1]

---

[1] Lloyd Wright's maternal grandparents, Richard and Mallie Lloyd Jones left their home in Llandysul, Cardiganshire (Ceredigion) in 1843 at the time of the Rebecca Riots to find a new life in America. Wright was proud of his Welsh heritage and according to his biography by Meryle Secrest: "anyone named Jones was accorded preferential treatment there".

Frank and Olgivanna Lloyd Wright at Taliesin.

Gareth and Mrs Lloyd Wright at Taliesin. The photo was taken by Frank Lloyd Wright.

He returned from Madison, Wisconsin, for yet more energetic days in Chicago before he embarked on the Grand Canyon Railway line. From the train's observation car he described passing the frozen Missouri River, and dreary cornfields in Kansas. Stopping briefly in Santé Fe, he continued through the Arizona desert to California. The Christmas period was spent in Hollywood where he visited the Metro Goldwyn Mayer Studios and attended the preview of the film *David Copperfield*. Earlier in the summer, as a young journalist on staff of *The Western Mail*, Gareth interviewed William Randolph Hearst, at his Welsh home, St Donat's Castle, Llantwit Major and the newspaper magnate invited Gareth to stay on his ranch, San Simeon when he visited California. New Year was spent at this elegant home and Gareth sent photographs of the palatial estate to his parents. One picture was of Gareth braving the inside of the Royal Bengal man-eating tiger's cage at the Hearst's private zoo. As in the Eastern States he lectured on such topics as the New Commonwealth and the International Police Force and wrote articles on Roosevelt's Foreign Policy for the *Manchester Guardian*. He was fêted wherever he went and he described his time in California as fantastic and a very great success.

William Randolph Hearst's ranch, San Simeon.

Chapter 2 - Japan

Gareth wrote on the reverse side. "I took this photo inside a man-eating tiger's cage at the Hearst Ranch. The trainer stood by my side with a pitch fork." January 2nd 1935.

Gareth's bedroom when he stayed at Hearst's Ranch.

Gareth in the Mojave desert.

On January 20th 1935, in San Francisco Gareth embarked on the *SS President Monroe* for Honolulu. The sea was extremely rough - the old boat pitched and tossed and rolled continually, it constantly poured with rain.[2] He hoped that when he reached port he would have more enthusiasm for Japan and China. The company was very dull - so dull that he spent most of his time reading. The best-selling book, which especially excited his imagination was *One's Company* by Peter Fleming,[3] an account of the author's adventurous journey through Chinese bandit country in the previous year - this thrilling story subsequently inspired Gareth's choice of route from Hong Kong to Manchukuo.

---

[2] He wrote to his family: "I would give anything to be at home in front of a good fire or to go for a walk with Dada (his father) and Ianto (his dog) on the beach. I am homesick, but not seasick."

[3] Peter Fleming was probably the role model for Ian Fleming, his brother, in the James Bond spy thrillers. On account of his buccaneering lifestyle, Peter became a special operation executive in World War Two.

After a few days in Hawaii he boarded the *SS President Coolidge*. As the ship left port, thousands of coloured streamers were thrown from the ship to the pier and Gareth was presented with a lei; a wreath of flowers to put round his neck. It was a beautiful boat, such a contrast to the *SS President Monroe* and was about five times larger and very luxurious, having excellent drawing rooms, suites, a cinema, tea garden and an orchestra. In the dining room he sat with a charming young Chinese man who had a great sense of humour and his young son, aged three, called Pax. Mr Cheng[4] had been for many years at the League of Nations Secretariat, hence the child's name. Pax could only speak French and was always talking about Mickey Mouse and 'le grand méchant loup' [the (animated) big bad wolf from the Three Little Pigs].

Gareth with young Pax on the SS Coolidge.[5]

During the voyage they experienced one of the worst storms in the Pacific for a very long time. Many people watched the

---

[4] Mr Cheng was very worried about the banks failing in Shanghai on account of the American Silver Purchase Act and he sent a cable from the boat telling the bank to pay out all his account in cash to his father-in-law.
[5] In the Second World War, the *SS President Coolidge* was converted to a troop carrier. On 20th October 1942 it struck a mine in the Segond Channel off the island of Espiritu Santo in Vanuatu in the Southern Pacific with the loss of two lives.

mountainous waves for hours. Huge 'monsters' came towards the ship and the boat would go up and then down again. Sometimes the whole vessel would crash, while bumping on two waves. One night there was a fancy dress party, but just as the dancing began a wave made the boat lurch and a great many people were swept from the middle of the floor to one end falling on top of each other. The tables collapsed and chairs fell over. The captain said it was the worst storm he had fought in 25 years of seamanship.

Gareth was delighted to be on land again after days of violent storms. The immigration officials paid great attention to him when they learned he was a journalist. They asked what papers he wrote for and made him list every book and pamphlet that he had with him. With his companions from the ship, Gareth caught a bus from Yokohama to the Imperial Hotel in Tokyo (designed by Frank Lloyd Wright, and said to be the most talked-of hotel in the world). The yellow brick was not very pleasing - the overhanging stones were good, but Gareth thought that the building just resembled some big railway station.[6]

The Imperial Hotel in Tokyo built by Frank Lloyd Wright in 1922 and eventually demolished.

---

[6] Though the Imperial Hotel withstood the Great Kanto earthquake of 1923, which destroyed nearly half the city of Tokyo, some years later this architectural masterpiece was demolished because it had been neglected and had become unsafe.

After such a long period at sea, and having had no news of events from home, he was delighted to find a huge bundle of letters waiting for him. At last he was in Japan and, as he quickly felt more comfortable in Tokyo, his homesickness lifted. Spring was a fine time to be in the city with its beautiful blossoms and he thought he would stay in Tokyo until the middle of April when the Emperor of Manchukuo, Pu Yi, was to visit the country. Everything in the city looked very modern except for the rickshaw men who shouted and followed him persistently wherever he went. Many of the houses were lightly built of wood because there were so many earthquakes. There were well fed children everywhere, many in old padded costume with wooden sandals, and they swarmed all over the place looking most picturesque in their coloured garments.

One evening Gareth, together with some young American students (who had been on the boat and were also staying at the Imperial Hotel), were taken by a young man from the American Embassy to a Japanese restaurant. Maiko (apprentice geisha) girls entertained them. These girls were doll-like and little more than children, seeming not to be fully trained. On entering, Gareth's party had to remove their shoes before sitting cross-legged on the floor while dinner was cooked on the table. Gareth remarked that he found it very difficult to use chopsticks and was the clumsiest of them all.

Gareth had no intention of spending much time at leisure and was soon at work in his role as a journalist. The facts contained in his diaries are of historical interest and form a great contrast with the light-hearted letters he wrote home. He interviewed many of the most powerful men who dominated Japanese policy in the early thirties and the questions he asked might be the first pieces of the jigsaw of his very short life. These may have had some bearing on his death and their significance will become apparent as this story unfolds.

The Japanese Ambassador to Great Britain, Mr Matsudaira gave Gareth a letter of introduction to Amau (Amŏ) Eliji, the spokesman for the Japanese Foreign Office in Tokyo and he contacted him soon after his arrival in Japan. Gareth described Amau's office as being in a wooden shack just like the Buttrils (army huts in Barry) during the Great War. Amau had lots of black hair, a roundish face with big glasses, and a rather serious appearance. Gareth attended a number of Amau's press conferences, which enabled him to gain an insight into the Japanese Foreign Policy towards Russia and China. Amau put on record that the Japanese had no intention of interfering with Chinese internal affairs, but that if the Russians invaded Manchukuo then they would have no option but to fight to defend Manchukuo.[7]

Gareth with maiko (geisha) girl.

---

[7] One year previously he proposed the "Amau Doctrine" which stated that Japan had a special mission to maintain peace and order in East Asia and opposed any financial assistance to China by foreign countries. This statement was termed in China and elsewhere as 'the Japanese Asian Monroe Doctrine', which openly challenged the 'Open Door' Policy and 'Nine-Power Treaty' system. A summary of Amau's statements is in the endnotes. The State of Manchukuo is referred to in a later footnote.

After the first press conference Gareth discussed Outer Mongolia with the Russian correspondent for Tass and then a man of about forty-five introduced himself as Mr Cox, the Reuters' correspondent. Mr Cox was exceedingly helpful - he took Gareth into his office and introduced him to some journalist colleagues who were influencing world opinion about Japan including Mr Iwanaga, the head of Rengo (the very powerful Japanese news agency), Mr Byass of *The Times* and Mr Young, an International News Service correspondent.

In a private conversation with Mr Cox, Gareth formed the impression that co-operation between China and Japan was impossible. Gareth wrote in his diary that James 'Jimmy' Melville Cox believed:

> They're certain to annexe Manchukuo. They've only got old Manchu's in big positions there. What the Japanese Army wants is the possession of North China - they want Pu Yi to go to Peking, which could then be taken in a day. Defensively the Japanese could say that they are helping the Manchu's to their rightful empire. Of course it would be foolish, but the Japanese military are of that frame of mind. They are mad - they think they can do anything and have never been in the outside world. In the Philippines they are aiming for domination, while in China, the Japanese want a proposal to send military advisors to fight against the Communists. You might get a chance of going through in June and seeing anti-Communist raids. The Russians can help the Communists in Sinkiang and we are afraid that the Szechuan Communists will join up with them. China is being united by a hatred of Japan.[8]

Despite Mr Cox's and the American correspondents' opinions, Tokyo seemed so peaceful that Gareth felt disappointed that it was going to be a terribly quiet summer in the Far East because Japan and China would be out of the news. The Japanese he met led him to believe that Japan was 'making friends' with China and Russia; that war was out of the question and he felt he was in for a dull time.

---

[8] In 1941 Jimmy Cox died in the custody of the Japanese Secret police. See endnote.

After a few days at the Imperial Hotel Gareth moved to the Bunka Apartments and wrote in his next letter home that:

> The time has rushed along so much that I'd better leave my experiences in Japan to another letter. I am having a great time and am most happy. I found a journalist friend, Günther Stein, whom I knew in London.[9] He is Jewish, formerly of the *Berliner Tageblatt,* and we are living in the same apartment house. He is good company. When I arrived I found that there were no sheets, towels, pillows or restaurant and that I was supposed to supply everything. I borrowed a cushion and blankets and put a coat over myself. The trams made a horrible din and I found it hard to sleep. I read poetry and tried to go to sleep, but it was very hard. I woke early with the noise of the trams. It is now very quiet and I overlook a number of Japanese houses. It is a beautiful crisp day - just the kind of day for a walk with Ianto down the Vale of Glamorgan. The sun is setting and I have been all day working. It is difficult to realise that I am in Asia, because everything is so modern. Nearly all the food I have is European, though I do like some of the Japanese food - the fish, lobsters and prawns are lovely. This place that I stay in is quite European - in my room I might be anywhere, London, Berlin or Vienna, except that every night I hear the watchman in the street beating two sticks, which sound a hollow ping-ping to show that all is well - like the 'Maestersingers' of Nüremberg. He comes carrying a Chinese lantern. The other night an earthquake awakened me. I felt the bed shaking back and forwards and the room was trembling. I could not quite understand what it was. It lasted for three minutes. A fellow traveller Mr Pickering, the Liberal M.P. from Leicester, said that it was a quite a fair-sized quake.

Gareth made an appointment to meet the British Ambassador, Sir Robert Clive, and walked to the Embassy for his interview. It was a lovely two mile walk from the Bunka Apartments passing wonderful

---

[9] Günther Stein was a colleague of the notorious double secret agent, Richard Sorge. See endnote.

trees along the moat. They discussed many political issues.[10] Having bid the Ambassador farewell he walked back to his apartment through the streets of Tokyo and came across what he thought was a fine temple. He saw people taking off their shoes and going through a doorway. He looked in, removed his shoes reverently and followed the women going in when he was stopped and told to use the other entrance. He took off his hat, was given a piece of wood, which he thought was a prayer stick and went in. To his great shock and surprise, inside a number of people were taking a bath!

A few days later Gareth interviewed Baron Shidehara[11] who seemed to be afraid of saying anything except that he desired peace and that it would be impossible to conquer China. He did however ask Gareth what had impressed him most about Japan and Gareth replied immediately saying: "The fascinating trees with their grotesque and poetic shapes". He noticed the ex-minister's eyes fill with tears and the older man said: "I am moved by that. It is curious that Lord Grey said a similar thing when he came to see me and when we looked out at the trees near the lake".

Though Gareth wrote affectionately of his home and family he was not lonely, and led a very full social life. His diaries and letters are full of innumerable invitations to lunch and dinner. He seems to have made quite an impression on the English community in Tokyo who found his conversation lively, and were particularly

---

[10] See endnote for a summary of the interview.
[11] Shidehara had been the Foreign Minister of Japan up to the end of 1931. He became Acting-Prime Minister after the attempted assassination of the Prime Minister, Hamaguchi. After the conquest of Manchuria he played no active part in government, as his policy towards China was considered weak. An acquaintance, Mr Kumasaka, told Gareth that when the Prime Minister Hamaguchi was mortally wounded on the station at Tokyo, he was standing near with Baron Shidehara. Hearing a bang, he rushed over to the Prime Minister and then went and stood near Shidehara. He guarded the Foreign Minister from behind as his life was in great danger, because of his politics, which, however, reflected the modern public opinion at the time. For three months, a "would–be" assassin lived in a house nearby in order to kill him. Fortunately, Shidehara had a heart attack, which kept him at home for a very long time and he was not assassinated. In 1945 after the Second World War, Shidehara was briefly the first Prime Minister in the period of the American occupation.

impressed that he had been foreign adviser to David Lloyd George. In his next letter home he gave an account of his invitation to dine with Sir Robert Clive, the Ambassador; Sir Leslie Wilson, the Governor of Queensland; Captain Vyvian, Colonel James and ladies. His recollections of the conversation at the meal were that it had revolved around whether Japan wanted war or peace.[12] This mix of journalistic investigation and high social life was something that Gareth relished:

> I am enjoying myself exceedingly. I've been busy seeing heaps of people and being invited out all the time. All is going well. I am amazed at the freedom of expression in Japan. There are many attacks on the military. The description of the famine here is in the papers and in Parliament continually.

He wrote from Bunka Apartments that he had decided to go to Siam and gave details of his journey. There were three reasons for his plans - journalistic, climatological and financial. He felt very few journalists went to the Philippines, the Dutch East Indies or to Siam and there would "be masses of new and valuable material":

> On Friday week, March 15th, I sail for the Philippines via Shanghai and Hong Kong. I shall stay a week in the Philippines, then go to Batavia in Java, to Singapore and then on to Bangkok. I have decided to go from Siam through French Indo-China to see the ruins of Angkor Wat in Cambodia, then to Hanoi and on to Hong Kong. It will be new material. I can't think of many British journalists who have written about Indo-China. In the late autumn I shall go to America to lecture and give radio talks where I have had some splendid reports last year, then HOME for Christmas.

> The summer in the Philippines, South China and Singapore is <u>terrible</u>. The only liveable place in the Far East

---

[12] Sir Leslie ridiculed the idea that Japan wanted to attack Australia, Dutch East Indies or India saying that he believed that they wanted good relations with China. He thought General Hayashi, the War Minister, had common sense and calmed the other ministers; that Baron Takahashi (an ex-Prime Minister) was a "wonderful old boy" and General Araki was now in the background, but was still revered by the young officers.

in August is in the mountains of Japan. All the diplomats and journalists go to Karuisawa where it is cool because there one has contacts and can work. Knowledge of countries like Siam will be helpful if I give talks in America.

Life was full and exciting and Gareth obviously enjoyed every minute of it. On March 7th in his next letter home he wrote that:

This is going to be an exceedingly interesting week, because I am going to have interviews with four of the outstanding personalities in Japanese life: Matsuoka, who took Japan out of the League of Nations at Geneva,[13] General Araki, the firebrand who was Minister of War, General Hayashi, who is now Minister of War and Admiral Osumi, who is the Minister of the Navy. These politicians are the men who play such a big part in modern Japan.

The first of these interviews was with Mr Matsuoka Yosuke, a stockily built man with broad rough features and Hitler-like moustache. He received Gareth wearing a black silk kimono. Gareth met him on a previous occasion, when dining with Mr Iwanaga. At this dinner party, Mr Matsuoka told the assembled company that he could not understand why Britain had suddenly deserted Japan at the League of Nations. He considered that Sir John Simon, the British Foreign Minister, had been on his side up to the very last and believed, but was not certain, that America had used pressure on the question of the war debts. When Matsuoka, who had been educated in the United States, travelled through America, was asked by the Americans: "When will you return to the League of Nations?" he sarcastically replied, "Why did you never join?"

---

[13] Matsuoka Yosuke took Japan out of the League of Nations on February 24th 1933, following the Manchurian (Mukden) Incident (September 18th 1931) and the Shanghai Fake War (January 28th 1932). On March 1st, 1932, a manifesto announced that Manchukuo was founded. The reference is to the time when all the members of the League of Nations, except Siam, voted against Japan following the Lytton Report, which condemned Japan for having invaded Manchuria and annexing the territory from China. Matsuoka was then instrumental for Japan withdrawing from the League. See endnote for a summary of the interview.

The following day he interviewed General Araki Sadao.[14] From a narrow side lane, passing the miniature trees in a few yards of garden, Gareth reached Araki's small humble wooden home on the outskirts of the city. He took off his shoes at the threshold, donned slippers, and was taken into a modest room with European furniture. In one corner, there stood a medieval suit of Japanese armour with a golden dragon on the helmet. In another stood the statue of General Nogi, who committed hara-kiri with his wife on the death of Emperor Meiji, grandfather of Emperor Hirohito, showing the type of courage that General Araki admired. The tiger skin on the sofa and the picture of a wild tiger with staring eyes about to spring were perhaps symbols of the sudden attack favoured by the Japanese Army in the past. As a contrast, underneath a picture of a tiger there was an oil painting of apples and grapes - Victorian and in Gareth's opinion, very amateurish. Near the window a bullet had the place of honour. General Araki, dressed in a black kimono, his head shaved like a Buddhist monk, entered quietly. His voice was quiet. His eyes were sharp and keen; his moustache was long and tapering to a point. His movements and welcome were more those of a priest than a military man.

Gareth recorded that the interview with General Araki was a great success:

It is curious that the firebrands of the world should be small in stature and meek in manner. The personality of General Araki, the "Tiger" of Japan, the prime mover in the conquest of Manchuria, former War Minister and it is rumoured the future Prime Minister bears this out.

Gareth's next important interview was with Admiral Osumi Mineo,[15] the Navy Minister. The admiral was a jolly gentleman with a round chubby face, sparkling eyes and laughing countenance. In the waiting room at the Naval Department there was a grand piano with a bronze statue of General Foch. The furniture was Victorian with chairs decorated with gilt flowers and with a dressing table and mirror. There were four ebony elephants, a Samurai suit of Japanese armour,

---

[14] See endnote for a summary of the interview.
[15] See endnote for the interview in full.

and in one corner stood a statue of an eagle with claws. He gave Gareth a typed reply and his answers were negative and guarded. The admiral though, expressed a wish to see Gareth again on his return to Japan later in the summer.

LEADERS IN AFFAIRS OF COMMERCE AND STATE

ADMIRAL OSUMI
Minister for
the Navy.

ADMIRAL OKADA
Prime Minister in the
new Government.

GENERAL HAYASHI
Minister for
War.

Photo taken from the 1934 Daily Telegraph supplement on Japan and Manchukuo.

The first of Gareth's three interviews were successful but on this fourth occasion, General Hayashi (the War Minister who had ruthlessly deposed General Araki) was only prepared to give him a written reply. It was no secret that Gareth intended to visit Manchukuo and then return to Japan in the summer to follow his journalistic investigations. He asked the General Hayashi very leading questions and these may have had some bearing on Gareth's fate. The first he posed was: "Some Chinese fear that Japan will attack North China. Has this fear any significance?" to which Hayashi replied that: "This is mere rumour. Japan will never attack North China unless we are provoked to do so". He questioned whether there was any significance in Major General Doihara's visit to Nanking and Canton. The Japanese officer, Doihara, figured prominently in the current newspaper articles and it was reported that he was endeavouring to bring autonomy to the Northern Provinces of China. Hayashi replied: "The Major General is travelling in a purely private capacity through different parts of China. He is an expert on China and has a large number of friends among the Chinese with whom he has held conversations. He has no official mission." Hayashi concluded stating that co-operation with the Chinese was difficult to foresee as anti-Japanese sentiment was deeply rooted in the Chinese heart.

March 15th was Gareth's last day in Tokyo. He went to see the War Exhibition of the Russo-Japanese War of 1905 in the big store opposite Maruzen. On display were pictures of General Nogi.[16] Crowds, including a number of children, were pressing to see scenes from the battle and the exhibits including his boots, bags and handwriting, which were on show in the exhibition.

On that last day Gareth lunched with Iwanaga (formerly station master on the South Manchurian railway) and sat next to Baron Tanaka Tokichi who was formerly Japanese Ambassador to the Soviet Union (1925-30). He attended Amau's press conference for the last time where he met a Hungarian, Metzge, who took him to see Kozo Yamada, the head of a commercial information bureau. Metzge said Mr Yamada had a great influence behind the scenes. Gareth was to send a telegram to Mr Yamada when he arrived in Manchukuo. He was given a visiting card to see Mr Tsutsui, the First Secretary of the Japanese Embassy in the capital of Manchukuo, Hsinking (Changchun) as well as a letter of introduction to see Major General Itagaki when Gareth arrived in the city.

His last letter home as he bade farewell to Japan is, with hindsight, poignant:

> Today I sail for the Philippines via Shanghai and Singapore. A year ago I was in Ireland interviewing De Valera. Don't you think I have an interesting life? I like Japan immensely. The people are courteous and kind. They seem to grin and laugh without stopping. Everybody giggles! It is most clean

---

[16] General Nogi was a dedicated general who lost both his sons in the battle for Port Arthur in the 1905 Russo-Japanese War and who expected a very high standard of discipline of his troops in the true Samurai tradition. The vanquished Russian Commander presented his white horse to General Nogi in respect of his high moral character.

here - spotless. People seem to spend their time having baths. When I go to visit Matsuoka or Shidehara I always take my shoes off at the threshold. Nobody dreams that there will be a war here - out of the question for a long time - if ever.

A postcard sent by Gareth from Japan sent to his niece Siriol (the author).

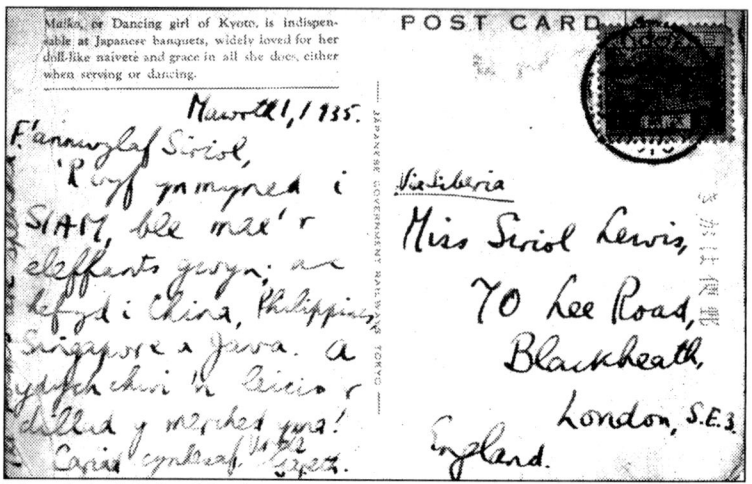

[March 1, 1935. My dearest Siriol, I am going to Siam where there are white elephants and also to China, Philippines, Singapore and Java. Do you like the clothes of these girls? Warmest love. Uncle Gareth.]

Chapter 2 - Japan

ENDNOTES

JIMMY COX.

Cox held controversial views and asked awkward questions at the Japanese Foreign Office press briefings. Raymond Lamont-Brown's book *Kempeitai, The Dreaded Japanese Secret Police* states that: "He made no effort to cover up his contempt and growing animosity for the Japanese militaristic state". In his book he also says that James 'Jimmy' Melville Cox, the *Reuters'* correspondent in Tokyo: "was arrested on 27th July 1940 by the Kempeitai on the usual non-specific charge of espionage". Two days later he was seen falling from an open window on the third floor of the Kempeitai Headquarters. They claimed that he had committed suicide because he was guilty of espionage. The foreign community very much doubted this and was fully convinced that he had been thrown out of the window to conceal damage done to his body by the Japanese secret police. "The mercurial Gaimu-daijin (Foreign Minister) Matsuoka Yosuke issued a report exonerating the Kempeitai."

GUNTHER STEIN

Günther Stein was a known socialist, but Gareth was probably unaware that he had become a committed Communist during his time spent as a correspondent for the *Berliner Tageblatt* in Moscow before 1933. During his period in Tokyo he became associated with Richard Sorge, the double agent. Stein allowed Sorge to use his house as a base for radio transmitting and acted as a courier for him by taking microfilms to Hong Kong. In 1941, Richard Sorge was tried by the Japanese and found guilty of spying for the Russians, for which crime they executed him. The case against Günther Stein was never proven. (Deakin, F W and Storry, G R (1966) *The Case of Richard Sorge*. Chatto and Windus.) Though Gareth had been David Lloyd George's foreign affairs adviser, he gave no indication in his diaries that he had any strong political affiliations.

THE FINAL FIVE ENDNOTES ARE TAKEN FROM GARETH'S DIARIES REFERING TO HIS INTERVIEWS WHILST IN JAPAN.

SUMMARY OF AMAU'S PRESS CONFERENCES

At his first press conference there were about fifty journalists assembled to talk with Mr Amau. Amau introduced them to young Japanese diplomats who appeared very embarrassed. They bowed to the journalists; some went to the English and some to the Americans. Amau stated that:

"The Japanese policy to China is to maintain peace and friendly relations. It benefits to Japan to keep the peace in East Asia. Japan has been standing like a watchdog in East Asia. We have fought several times for that. Other powers have an interest in China, but ours is more vital. The Chinese question to us is a matter of life or death. The British have a considerable interest, which is not necessarily vital. The U.S. is interested but only economically and commercially. China is a vast country. At the beginning of the Washington Conference (1922), Briand asked, "What is China?" China failed to answer this. In 1920 Soviet Russia compiled a Treaty with Outer Mongolia, by which each control ports in respect of recognising the benefited Government. Since then Outer Mongolia has sent an Ambassador to Moscow and Moscow sent to Korea Government representatives.

In 1924, our Government commanded a Treaty at Peking and Mukden with the authority of China by which the Government respected temporary integrity of China. Our Government was helping the Sun Yat-sen Government in Canton. Borodin represented the Government in Canton, and Canton government was dealt with independently. Therefore at the time Canton was the Facto authority. In 1920 Mongolia concluded a treaty with Soviets. In 1924 Mukden concluded a Treaty with Government. Today Sinkiary is virtually under the influence of the Soviet Outer Mongolia. The other day a Chinese Consul in Novostrik, who was returning home to China had to apply for visa from the Soviet authorities.

In the time of the Tsarists, there was a conference in the presence of the Tsar and it was discussed as how to find a way to penetrate the Far East and reach the ports. A railway route was finally decided upon through Siberia, Manchuria, Harbin, Dairien and Port Arthur. In 1895 we fought with China for the lease of Liaotung peninsula. In 1895-1905 China concluded a secret alliance with Russia. China promised materials for building of the Russian Court. The Russians promised to help China in the war between China and Japan.

"…We have been endeavouring to maintain peace in the Far East. China has had a civil war for 25 years, but we desire China restored some day.

We expect equal opportunities for foreign powers. League of Nations attacked Japan, because Japan closed door on China and made the China Sea a closed sea. But it is not Japan, but the League of Nations who closed the doors to Japan.

At the time of the Manchurian Incident it was resolved by the League of Nations (Feb 24th, 1933) that the China boycott since September

18th 1931 is recognised as a reprisal. The China boycott is legalised by the League of Nations decision and the principle of open door was closed to us. It was instigated by the Euro-American powers.

We are concerned about any communist presence in East Asia, but we have no intention of interfering with Chinese internal affairs. Manchukuo will separate China and Soviet Russia. We estimate there are 200,000 Soviet troops on the border. We have no intention to fight, but if the Soviets interfere with Manchukuo affairs, we will fight. We must defend Manchukuo".

At a later press conference Mr Amau discussed British dominions attitude to racism. In South Africa the restriction of the Japanese immigrant was strictest. There, even the consul had the greatest difficulty in entering a restaurant or finding a hotel. Australia was very much better. Japan only wanted free entry of their merchants. Japan was not going to invade Australia. In the Far East, Japan cannot compete with American but only the German goods, especially toys and sundry goods. "We import more from Germany than we export. Germany is restricting Japanese goods, and in banking and shipping they have a number of regulations by which they impose many different conditions on Japanese traders (shipping) e.g. currency. Germany proposes to buy soya beans from Manchukuo and wants to sell more to Japan. There is no political arrangement with Germany."

At the final press conference Amau reviewed the current aviation situation in Japan. It was different in Japan compared with Britain and U.S. owing to the mountainous and atmospheric conditions. In Manchukuo aviation was proceeding very rapidly, because there were plenty of landing places and atmospherics was good. The Japanese Army and Navy made great progress. They were one of the five largest aeronautic powers, but civilian aviation was very poor. There was a lot of rivalry between civilian, some of whom were without jobs, and army and naval aviation. In Japan it was difficult to find landing places as the land was over cultivated. He emphasised the quality of the pilots, the number of planes and aircraft carriers and the faith in German airships. He informed the journalists that the Pacific Aviation Co. would be organised in June or July to fly from Tokyo to San Francisco, via the Aleutian Islands and Alaska using Zeppelins. Since the Manchurian and Shanghai troubles, the military flying corps had improved greatly and they had increased their equipment. In the recent Jehol conflict in Manchuria the corps took part in the battle by bombing and carried ammunition to the advancing army. In this region, where the transport by land was very difficult, the supply of goods and arms to the advancing army by aeroplane was the only means available at the time.

SIR ROBERT CLIVE, BRITISH AMBASSADOR

1) The recent British economic mission was a success, and reversed the grievances that Japan had against Britain.
2) The Americans were withdrawing from the Far East as they had no great interests in the area compared with those of the British.
3) The Australians were pro-Japanese in that they were exporting millions of pounds worth of wool to Japan
4) Canada was diametrically opposed to the Australian point of view. (Canada insisted on a strong pro-American Policy.)
5) Japanese Foreign Policy aimed to show they were peaceful and co-operating with China and with Russia.
6) Sir Robert was amazed by an interesting change of relations with Soviet Russia - he had received an invitation from the Soviet Ambassador to dine with Prince Kanin, the Commander-in-Chief of the Japanese Army. He could not recollect a Japanese Commander-in-Chief socialising with the Russians since Iswolski's day, (Russian Minister to Japan, 1900) before the Anglo-Japanese alliance.
7) The Japanese Army was behind the Foreign Minister, Hirota, in his Chinese policy, because of their need for raw materials. Hirota saw the world shutting out Japanese goods and believed that the future market would be in China.
8) They were very disappointed with Manchuria, as the resources were not so rich as they were hoped to be. The invasion was mainly strategic against the Russians, as the Japanese feared Communism. The Russians were experts in oil and were going to set up a refinery in Kharatorovik for their own use in the Far East to refine Sakhalin oil. This, the Ambassador thought this might effect British oil interests. The recent British economic mission which had been a success, and which had reversed the grievances that Japan had against Britain.

MATSUOKA YOSUKE

Matsuoka had faced the world for his country at Geneva. When asked about his political aims, he replied that he was agitating to abolish political parties as the West was already doing. The disappearance of parties in Italy, Russia and Germany was too obvious to mention. In Japan, due to their racial traits and their history, they could never introduce Fascism similar to that of Mussolini and Hitler because it was not in their temperament to allow a dictator to control the whole country, and therefore such a thing would never happen in Japan. He believed that they should get away from the Western democracy that bred corruption and return to the rule of the Emperor as this was true Japanese democracy. The Emperor was the mainspring of their country, he was responsible for all that happened in Japan and ruled according to the "Will of Heaven". (They had a saying that the will of the people was the Will of Heaven.) The State Ministers were solely responsible to the Emperor, and through the Emperor the ministers were responsible to the people. For 3000 years they had the idea that Ministers who were responsible to Parliament could have no place in their history. Western civilisation was facing a kind of catastrophe as it had become too individualistic and egoistic. The Japanese were obliged to care for their parents; their notion was that children would even offer their lives for their parents. Gareth pressed his interview further and asked what was meant by 'Asia for the Asiatics'. Matsuoka replied:

> If that means the conquest of Asia, you cannot do it, even if we could it would take 100 to 200 years. It must mean a step towards finally establishing peace through the world, to let all and every nation have its own place and be satisfied.

GENERAL ARAKI SADAO

General Araki was held to be the greatest opponent of Communism in Japan and had been a supporter of war against the Soviet Union. He was the leader of the militarists and a champion of 'Asia for the Asiatics', a national figure in Japan revered by the young officers. He kept at his side, until he died at the age of 90, a file on Emperor Hirohito as an insurance against untimely death. He was opposed to many of Hirohito's policies and was his last domestic adversary. After a mutiny in February 1936, he and other supporters of the Strike-North faction were retired from the Army leaving the Emperor a free hand to plan to strike south. Bernard Shaw met his match with Araki telling him: "If you had been born in Russia you would have become a politician greater than Stalin. I should like to stay here talking with you until the Chinese land on the Japanese mainland".

Gareth interviewed Araki through an interpreter and he told Gareth that he thought that Communism might succeed in China, as conditions there were anarchical. If Chang Kai-shek could unify China the young Communists might rise against him and drive him from power. Gareth asked very directly whether a struggle was inevitable between Japan and the Soviet Union to which Araki responded that it all depended on the attitude of the other side and that he found it difficult to continue this line of conversation. He considered it futile to help the Chinese against the encroachment of Soviet influence when asked what Japan should do to counter-act the growing Soviet influence in Inner Mongolia. Gareth continued his searching questions and asked what would he advocate for Asia rather than Communism. Would it be Pan-Asianism, that is 'Asia for the Asiatics'? The conqueror of Manchuria pondered and then replied that he was firmly convinced that the fundamentals of Asiatic civilisation are just as good as European.

He ended the interview by saying that: "Unless all the peoples of the world get together, disaster will befall humanity. May the Twentieth Century be the century of transition from national separation to international harmony".

Gareth remarked that it was not these last sentiments, however that attracted many of the young Nationalists to the personality of General Araki.

ADMIRAL OSUMI MINEO

Admiral Osumi, the Naval Minister served Emperor Hirohito faithfully though even he opposed him during time of controversy. Gareth asked Osumi very pertinent questions about what his attitude to America developing bases on the Aleutian Islands and Alaska was and whether the Japanese Navy would be prepared to maintain the independence and neutrality of the Philippines if that neutrality were guaranteed by an international agreement. Osumi replied that he had nothing to say on either subject. He did however express a desire for a new Naval Treaty between Japan, Great Britain and the United States, the three leading sea powers of the world. Gareth had worked hard on a brief for Mr Lloyd George when the Naval Conference was convened in London in 1930. He wrote in his diary that Lloyd George said that: "The Conference is a farce, an absolute farce!"

Chapter 3

From Kobe to Manila

The Ghost ship takes Gareth from Kobe to Manila (via Shanghai and Hong Kong).

Gareth left Tokyo by train to join the American Mail Line ship, the *President Grant* at Yokohama. His final plan was to travel to Manila, Singapore, Java, Siam, China and Manchukuo, then return back to Japan in the late summer when it was cooler. He considered it was the only real way of studying the Far Eastern situation and everyone he spoke to in Japan thought it was a brilliant idea. He would have admirable material for articles and hopefully a fine post later either in London or with the *Manchester Guardian* or Reuters. On his return, there would be more chance of a job in Europe than in Asia, as there were few correspondents in Asia on account of the high cable rates. In his weekly letter home he wrote:

> My interviews were a great success. Think of it; I interviewed the Naval Minister, Mr Osumi, a fine jolly laughing old boy, General Araki, the leading militarist, a courteous dignified man with a long moustache, Matsuoka who took Japan away from the League, Baron Shidehara who was Foreign Minister and I had a written interview from the War Minister, General Hayashi. The military men in Japan are men of fine simple honest character. Mr Asano's superb dinner put me into touch with Japan's leading industrialists. You'll have been amused to see myself, a young man of 29, being asked to talk after dinner to the great figures of modern Japanese banking and shipping and factory life. There were 15 present and they were all at least 20-30 years older than I was. The contacts will be most valuable when I return in the summer.

In a brief postcard written just before he boarded the ship, he spoke longingly of his home at Eryl and he thought the park in Porthkerry would soon look fine in the spring. He was so very much looking forward to letters when he arrived in Singapore.

The liner taking him from the port of Yokohama, with its modern semi-skyscrapers, passed the great broken breakwater, many of whose massive stones had been hurled into the sea by earthquakes and skirted the Japanese coast. It was like a ghost ship and he scarcely saw a soul on-board until the dinner bell rang. When he entered the dining room, he found a German and an American at table vigorously discussing the Japanese:

> "Oh! They just copy, copy, copy," proclaimed the German "but we Germans were too clever for them once, when they tried to steal some of our plans" and he chuckled. "A Japanese firm wanted a boat to be built by a German firm", he continued, "So the Germans showed the representative the blueprints." The Japanese said: "We want to study the plans before accepting. May we take them back to the hotel?" "Certainly", said the German. "After a few days of study the Japanese brought the blueprints back and said they did not wish to order the vessel. They returned to Japan and built themselves a boat on exactly the same lines that they had seen in the German blue prints. The day of launching came, but at the dramatic moment the vessel overturned. The Germans, suspecting that the plans would be copied had omitted, on purpose, one or two of the essential details.

It was not the first time Gareth had heard the anecdote. Not to be outdone by the German, Mr Grunberg, who came from New York, commented: "I'm in the silverware business and there is not much about cutlery which your little friend does not know". Then pausing for a minute, he nodded proudly: "But the Japanese nearly put one over on me. I went to the Hotel Imperial, Tokyo, and at dinner I looked and remarked: 'if that isn't 1847 Rogers silverware! That's swell!' I looked again and on the back of the silverware was 'Tokyo'. It was a wonderful imitation."

The ship docked at Kobe and amongst the other passengers picked up some American YMCA leaders including a Mr Hammond. He was General Secretary to the International Council of the YMCA for the United States and Canada - a 'big shot'!

Chapter 3 – From Kobe to Manila

Gareth made the most of the short time while the ship was in dock and immediately made for the *Japan Chronicle* office, where he had had a long talk with the editor, Mr Young. He hated the Japanese and gave Gareth quite a different opinion from that which he had formed in Tokyo. They were building up their navy in order to bring pressure on China and might send troops to the Philippines to protect the Japanese living there. There was no doubt that they were heading for war. He believed that the Japanese intended to expand throughout Asia and that they could and would be absolutely ruthless about it. Their police were terrible, their legal methods were medieval and there was terror in the prisons. Gareth was most puzzled about the editor's views on Japan because most observers in Tokyo considered that Japan would be peaceful for quite a long time. Gareth thought that he had better wait until he returned in the summer before coming to any conclusions. With his proposed tour of the Far East in mind, he felt that it would place him in a far better position to assess the political situation of the region and as to whether the Japanese had designs on further territorial expansion.

The ship left Kobe to continue on the next part of its passage through the Inland Sea and in his next letter home he wrote:

> We have just gone through the Narrows and I have seen the port with the grey low lying houses, where George Strong brings light and cheer to the poor Japanese. We have passed the boat the *President Wilson* and we saw a lot of sailing vessels. It has been a bright sunshiny day and I have been going through my interviews in Japan, reading them out to Mr Hammond, whom I met at Tokyo and who is at my table sitting next to me. He learned a lot at Tokyo and has interesting views. He believes that Shantung [Shandong] Province will be persuaded by the Japanese to join with Manchukuo and that Peking will also go to Manchukuo in time.

Another American passenger prophesied future events in North China and said that a Japanese told him that the next step would be an independent movement organised in Shantung, which would be very strongly influenced by the Japanese. Tsing Tao was already Japanese controlled. They were bribing politicians in Shantung for the masses of goods that were entering without payment of duty. Though the Shantung authorities would declare that they wished to join Manchukuo, it would in fact have been orchestrated by the Japanese.

Despite these views Gareth was not convinced of their veracity and with an air of disappointment he wrote in his letter home to his family: "Things seem to be most peaceful now and this year promises to be disappointingly calm here in the Far East".

He had a most pleasant cabin on the upper deck. It was quiet, had a comfortable bed and every convenience. The weather was perfect: sunny and warm and he woke on the following Monday morning to see the magnificent inland sea with its islands, hills and slopes covered with picturesque Japanese pine trees. He had breakfast in bed - grapefruit, wheat cakes, rolls and butter, honey and milk and read the Japanese weekly *Chronicle,* which he found to be wittily written and full of 'hits' against Japan. He then had a bath and later sat and talked with Mr Hammond in the sun. Nearby there was a man who was rather drunk and as they were talking a rain of whisky descended on poor Mr Hammond! The drunk had tried to throw the rest of his whisky into the sea, but it missed the sea and hit Mr Hammond instead. The drunk apologised and Mr Hammond said: "I do not object so much to your throwing your whisky at me as I do your profanity!" Gareth said he would have rather chosen the profanity.

Sailing through the Straits of Shimonoseki, he said good-bye to Japan. The coast slowly disappeared and they entered the Straits of Tshushima. After three days at sea the ship arrived at Shanghai and he wrote:

> It was very dull and misty when I woke up this morning and found myself at berth in Shanghai. The boat was stationary in a yellow, muddy river. I looked out of the porthole and saw hundreds of Chinese junks and sampans floating lazily past. Then I descended to breakfast and went to catch the tender, which took me through the mist into the city with its modern European buildings as the ship is lying on the other side of the river some distance from the Bund. On the tender, I watched

the many junks with Chinese people working hard on-board. Disembarking, I strolled past fine-statured Sikh policemen, passing the beggars and the little women with their deformed feet. Rickshaw drivers were there by the hundred. I walked to the French Concession, which borders on the International Concession. I found the address of Mr Cheng's father-in-law in the Rue du Consulat (Mr Cheng was on the *Coolidge*) who is a silversmith and I was told that Mr Cheng was in a bank building nearby in a skyscraper. I went there, met a Chinese family and the little boy Pax, but Mr Cheng had gone to Nanking. I was told that business in Shanghai was terrible. "Crash! The crash is still to come. President Roosevelt by his silver policy has drained us of silver and we are suffering for his madness." The family do not like the Japanese. They consider that Chiang Kai-shek is very powerful, that he is trying to bring unity to China by crushing the local Governors, suppressing the warlords and defeating the Communists in Kiangsi.

Having visited the family of friends he had met on the *President Coolidge,* Gareth called on the editor, Mr Haward of the *China Daily News,* with whom he had lunch at the Cathay Hotel. The conversation revolved around Japan and how she was ruining the foreign trade in China in cotton as well as in silk. The machinery of the Chinese industrialists was out of date. The Japanese wished to send 3,000 officers and non-commissioned officers to China and to send away the German advisors. As yet, the new Dalai Lama had not been found and the editor, Mr Haward, believed it was likely that China would extend her influence over Tibet.

He then called at Reuters where the chief editor for the Far East, a surprising young man, Geoffrey, invited him out to dinner. As they went to find a taxi, a little Chinese beggar girl came up with a red face and a pigtail tied back with a ribbon and repeated with a mischievous smile in true Cockney accent, "Gimme copper. No Papa! No Mama! No whisky soda!"

They went to the Reuters' correspondent's flat in the Majestic Apartment for dinner where they talked, went to see the film *Casanova* and then Gareth was taken to a Shanghai dancing place where there were dancing partners provided at 6d a dance, which was three times more expensive than at Bindles, a café in Barry. Geoffrey said: "Chiang would be against this. He is all for the New Life Movement". After this pleasant and very sociable evening, he caught the tender for the *President Grant*. He wrote in his diary that he had gathered quite a lot of material on politics that day. Chiang Kai-shek seemed to have almost conquered the Communists and had them cornered in South Szechuan. He was in a very strong position and according to the Reuters' correspondent was rapidly unifying the country.

The voyage from Shanghai was not very interesting; the weather was a little overcast, the sea choppy, the skies dull and the ship rolling a little. The *President Grant* was two and half days at sea before she docked at Hong Kong, and he was fortunate to have at his table Mr Hammond (of the YMCA) and his wife.

The Inland Sea on route to Shanghai.

At Hong Kong Gareth went ashore about 10.30 a.m. on Friday March 22nd. On this rocky, mountainous island, which at the beginning of the last century was a famous pirates' lair, the great city of Hong Kong had been built. The place teemed with life. Hundreds of junks were on the river. He took a ferry to the island of Hong

Kong, landed on the waterfront, and felt a very British atmosphere. He immediately walked along the waterfront until he came to Reuters. There he had a letter of introduction to a Mr Gerald Yorke. He went to the office and met Mr Henry, the chief person there who said that Yorke was working in the library: "But won't you have tiffin?" He said: "Come back at one o'clock". At one o'clock, he took a rickshaw to Reuters and lunched with three correspondents. They were Varsity Blue types who were huge big-shouldered fellows. From their flat, there was a grand view over the battleships in the bay and they saw an American cruiser firing a salute (at £5 per shot) to greet the British Governor-General who was on-board for lunch. There was a great deal of activity in Hong Kong. Volunteer soldiers were preparing for all-night route marches. Destroyers were speeding past the Islands. It was a time of manoeuvres in case there should be conflict in the Pacific.

Following a drive to the magnificent Repulse Bay, whose deep blue waters lie between high wooded hills, Gareth called to see a Mr Barrett, the editor of a Hong Kong weekly, *The Critic* and known to Tom MacDonald, formerly of *The Western Mail*. He was out, but an Aberdonian with a 'whisky loving' face and good humour called Thorpe was in. Gareth discussed the Island's attitude to Japan with him. Japan was absolutely ruining British trade there. Thorpe took him and introduced him to Mr Owen Hughes, a trader, and then they had tea (or at least he did and Thorpe had whisky!) in the Hong Kong Hotel. Next to them at a nearby table was an oldish man with a monocle and a sharp but dignified face. He was none other than General von Seeckt who at one time was the Commander-in-Chief of the German Army and who for two years had been a training advisor to the Chinese Army under Chiang Kai-shek. A Chinese General in mufti accompanied the German.

After the tea in the Hong Kong Hotel, Gareth rounded off his full day by going to a cinema. It was quite exciting to hear "God Save the King" being played at the end and to see everybody standing to attention. After having dinner, he felt he had an evening so British that he could have imagined being in London. Finally, he found Gerald Yorke's address and knocked at the door, which was opened by his Chinese servant. He entered Yorke's room and found a very tall dark-haired Old Etonian smoking a cigar and surrounded by 19th

century documents and volumes. Yorke was a freelance journalist who wrote books and occasionally went into the interior of China for Reuters. He was the 'Gerald' who accompanied the author, Peter Fleming in *One's Company* through Communist areas. The other companion of Fleming in Manchuria was none other than Gareth's old Trinity College friend, Viscount Clive. Yorke's conversation was full of interesting material and he talked and talked. To Gareth's great delight, it was all very informative.

Before leaving the island, he had tea with the Barretts. Mr Barrett was a journalist, a little man with a beard and a big red nose and was an excellent raconteur. Gareth was a great hit with the children who wanted more and more stories and insisted on coming to see him sail at six o'clock. They were most excited when he threw down coloured streamers to them as the ship slowly moved out of harbour and continued its journey. Gareth wrote fondly of his memories of home:

> I wonder how Ianto is? I should enjoy a walk with him in the Vale of Glamorgan, especially now that yesterday was the first day of spring. I had a grand time when I was home especially the summers. I think they were the best summers I have ever had and I did enjoy *The Western Mail* experience.

Writing briefly home, 10 days after leaving Yokohama, Gareth imagined that he would be on United States soil again. He had had a quiet voyage with lovely weather to Manila and was looking forward with pleasant anticipation to a week in the Philippines.

Chapter 4

The Philippines

"Mao Tse-tung considered that Japan aspired to seize the Philippines, Siam, Indo-China, Malaya and the Dutch East Indies." Quote from 'Red Star over China' by Edgar Snow, 1937.

"Thousands of islands with sandy shores lined with palms, a land where every sunset is a Turneresque splendour ... and where there is a nucleus of civilisation in the capital, Manila." Such was Gareth's description of the Philippines in the initial paragraph of his article entitled: 'The Colony Fears Freedom it has Won'.

Gareth landed on a most historic occasion. Two days previously, on the 23rd of March, President Roosevelt had signed the Constitution granting the island independence. For 10 years, they were to be a Commonwealth and thereafter they would become a Republic. Soon the Commonwealth would hold elections. Gareth expected great rejoicing throughout the island but he found there was no joy in the coming of 'freedom'.

He was most impressed by the Philippines and he liked Manila very much. He intended to stay for one week so he booked into the YMCA, noting in his weekly letter home that he had been away for five months and that over half his absence had elapsed. He was sitting alone singing 'like a lark' when a Mr Robb came and invited him to stay at his home. Gareth was introduced to Mr Robb, a journalist, by Mr Ifor Powell[1], a man from Barry. So he left the YMCA and for the rest of his visit he stayed in the Robbs' big house on the outskirts of Manila. The Robbs' were grand people and everyone joked a lot. He had wheat cakes and maple syrup for breakfast and each morning Mr Robb woke him up reciting something out of Omar Khayyam: "Awake for morning in the bowl of night", or a quotation from Milton.

---

[1] Mr Ifor Powell was one of the leading authorities on the Philippines and had one of the best libraries ever collected about the islands.

Immediately he arrived in Manila, Gareth was met by reporters who interviewed him, much to his surprise! (Apparently, they interviewed almost every newcomer who arrived in the Philippines.) A Mr Zaragoza of the *Bulletin* phoned, called and questioned him amongst other things about Hitler and the International Police Force.[2] Mr Zaragoza told him that the Filipinos would like to have been an American protectorate. They 'rejoiced' that independence had been granted, but the majority still wanted to have the American connection. It was their finest market which the Philippines would soon lose. 'At present they have Free Trade with the America and send 86 percent of their exports to the United States. … gradually high tariffs would be placed upon Filipino goods until it found the markets were closed.'[3] The sugar industry was faced with doom, because it depended entirely on the American market. The Filipinos considered that the American politicians had treated the islands with 'ruthlessness and unscrupulousness' and that Congress merely passed the Act of Freedom on the Philippines in order to remove Filipino competition in sugar, cordage, coconut oil and other products. Throughout the U.S.A. there was a wave of isolation and it was felt was that the United States had abandoned the country. It would throw the Philippines into the arms of the Japanese who would control them. The Japanese would send advisers; they were already trying to get hold of their land and were capturing their fishing trade. The inhabitants of the Philippines were very afraid that Japan would invade the islands.

"We will be giving up the dependence upon America and merely exchange it for dependence upon Japan" stated one Filipino to Gareth and continued his explanation:

The Japanese will dominate us, even if they do not conquer us in a military way. There will be Japanese commercial penetration,

---

[2] Lord Davies of Llandinam was prominent in the demands for the establishment of an International Police Force.
[3] Coconut was exported to the United States and this yielded two basic war materials; coconut oils from which glycerine was a by-product and coconut shell charcoal was used as a filter in gas masks. The coconut oil was an essential for margarine. Manila hemp made the best ropes and cables for ships.

which will be so thorough that we will not be able to call our souls our own. The British in Manila and in the Far East share this fear of Japan. The British are alarmed at the Americans leaving the Philippines. It will mean that Japan will have complete mastery of the Western Pacific and will control the routes to Australia and to the Dutch East Indies. It will place the Japanese only a short distance from the rich oil fields of the Royal Dutch Company and from those in Borneo. It would be better for the Americans to stay for the peace of the world.

Everyone shrugged his or her shoulders when asked about the Japanese. "Après nous le déluge", they said. The Filipinos believed that the Japanese had designs on the Philippines, because it was so rich in raw materials. It had chromium, which was necessary to give unusual toughness to steel such as in the armour plating of battleships. Even if the Japanese did not enter the Philippines, the Filipinos feared an economic catastrophe if they were left to their own resources. The United States might realise before it was too late, the immense wealth of the Philippines; the recently discovered vast deposits of chromite - so valuable for war materials - the uses of coconut oil in making bombs and the richness of the iron ore, which was said to be of the highest quality in the Far East. There was a chance that America, rather than let these essentials for war be controlled by Japan, would still keep her grip on the Philippines. The decision depended on Washington's answer to the question: "Will the United States remain in the Far East?"

Gareth's talk with the Japanese Consul, Kimura, was very revealing. He told him that Japan would not be averse to coming to the Philippines:

> If there were chaos in the Philippines, then it would be the duty of a civilised nation to step in and use force. We could conquer the Philippines in two or three weeks if there was war. There is room for a million Japanese to immigrate commercially. There is no need to come in any other way on condition the Filipinos are courteous and peaceful, but if they are not then we cannot say what will happen. We will want the Philippines to grow cotton as a raw material for our textiles. We will need the Filipino iron ore, which is the best

in the Far East, for our steel industry and we will also need the chromite and the manganese.

Though Gareth liked Kimura very much, he had the distinct feeling that Japan had the upper hand in the domination of the Pacific: "I gathered good material on Japan's expansion from him", he remarked.

Gareth with his keen sense of the newsworthy found the Philippines were packed with interesting material for his articles and he was "most busy getting dozens and dozens of viewpoints dashing from one leading politician to the mayor, then to a judge and to a founder of the constitution". Much of his time he spent studying the politics of the islands and researching for his book. He spent very little time seeing the countryside and so he wrote very little about the country itself.

On April 4th, he sailed on a Dutch boat, the *Tgisadane* to Celebes, Macassar and on to Java via Bali, to Surabaya and thence to Batavia (Jakarta). Gareth would have preferred to travel on an American boat, but the Dutch had a monopoly of the shipping along this particular line. Much to his disappointment the boat only stopped a few minutes at Bali. After he had called at Batavia, he planned to sail on to Singapore and to reach there at about the end of April. It was typical of his social life in the course of his journey that Mr Robb, his very hospitable host, came to see him leave port. The very colourful departure was something he dramatically described in his weekly letter home:

> When we sailed there was a wonderful picture. Along side, we had an escort of three submarines. The decks were brilliantly decorated, there was a masterpiece on the stern; the stars and stripes were linked, the stars merging into the Union Jack in the white ensign - a marriage - with the searchlights playing on them making the rustling banners looking like silk: The Union of U.S. and Britain. I strolled on deck, bathed and dined with middle-aged Americans going around the world.

Typical Filipino homestead.

Filipino rural transport.

Chapter 5

Java

Opium is prepared for the King of Cambodia.

From the capital of the Philippines, Gareth embarked on another slow voyage to Batavia in the Dutch East Indies (Indonesia). The route passed through the Macassar Straits and his ship, the *MS Tgsidane,* called at the port of Macassar in the Celebes (Sulawesi). It stopped briefly at Bali and then called into the ports of Surabaya and Semarang on the north aspect of Java before reaching Batavia. Here Gareth was to spend another week. He intended to arrive in Singapore by late April, where he looked forward to receiving letters from home.

As in the Philippines, he continued to question the intentions of the Japanese and write articles on his views and those of the locals. The Dutch East Indies was particularly concerned because the Dutch feared the loss of her colonies and the rich resources of oil, rubber, sugar, tea, coconuts and minerals. Japan had little oil for herself and it was felt that she would seize Borneo to secure the commodity. The Dutch residents considered that the Japanese were imbued with idea of empire and as soon as Europe was distracted by war, they would strike just as they had done previously in Manchuria when there was a financial crisis in Britain.

On-board ship, he heard a Frenchman in conversation with a Dutchman and went over to talk to them. The gentleman from France regaled Gareth with an account of his experiences in Japan:

> I was arrested. I had been wandering over Japan, walking, travelling on little boats and on horseback and I was taking lots of photos. I arrived in Kobe and there the Japanese water police came on-board my ship. They made me stay in my cabin and asked me for my film. They took me ashore as a prisoner and then put me in a cell. I got in a panic when I saw the dark tiny cell. I shrieked: "French Consul". They wouldn't listen. I just stood still and yelled and yelled until they let me use the telephone. The French Consul said to

wait, but I was so excited and yelled over the phone. He sent his son. What a relief! They spent a long time examining me and then my photos. The Consul's son told me to be calm. As soon as I was calm on the next day, the photos were developed. When I showed no desire to keep the photos they said: 'alright' and then finally, they said I could go.

On Thursday 11th April Gareth wrote in his diary that whilst in Surabaya he had had an interesting talk with the British Consul. The Consul was most intelligent and had whispered to Gareth:

> I must be like a clam about negotiations with Britain. It is in Holland's interest to maintain neutrality, because they know that the British are obliged to defend them in any case. The Dutch are scared stiff of the Japanese and believe the Japanese want their oil. They are increasing their fortification in Borneo, have an air base for defence against the 'Japs' and a naval base in Surabaya. Holland cannot defend the East Indies any more than the British can defend Hong Kong. The Dutch are beginning to thank God for the British Empire.

One of the ship's passengers whom Gareth recognised was a Cambridge man from Caius College, a Mr Fletcher. He invited Gareth to stay on his estate at a Javanese rubber plantation

The next morning, having changed ships, Gareth woke up on the *Op de Nook* in Semarang. After breakfast Fletcher and he went ashore in a launch. They took a car and had a beautiful drive through central Java to the ninth century Buddhist Temple of Borobudur. The carvings in stone were magnificent.

On the following Sunday he wrote in his letter home addressed from a sisal and rubber plantation in Soekamandi, Java, Dutch East Indies:

> Here I am on a vast plantation employing 14,000 Javanese. There is tropical rain pouring down outside. I am in the comfortable house of Mr Fletcher, my host. I bought a second-class ticket to Surabaya by boat to Batavia, because it was £8 first-class. When I told Fletcher that I had a second-

class ticket, he was profoundly shocked that a white man should go second-class. Therefore, when I got on-board I changed it to a first-class. Everything is terribly expensive here. On-board they gave no soap. I had to buy one little piece that cost 2/-, so I must leave for a more moderate place like Singapore.

Gareth at the magnificent site at Borobudur.

We sailed from Semarang in the afternoon on Friday. The weather was fairly cool. I have not had the slightest trouble with the tropical heat; the only thing is that it makes one a bit drowsy at times. Nearly everybody has a sleep in the afternoon, but I can't get into the habit. We arrived at Batavia early yesterday morning. I had talks with the British Consul and others and had coffee at the Hotel des Indes with Fletcher and his friends. Then we motored out about 80-90 miles past rice fields to the Soekamandi plantation, which is capitalised at two and a half million pounds. There are 50 white men here and they live very comfortably. We can see volcanic mountains in the distance.

Chapter 5 - Java

Soon I shall have been away six months and there won't be long to go before my return home. Fletcher has finished his leave and can't go home for three years! Most people out here in the East can't go home for five years. So I am lucky. On Saturday 20th I sail for Singapore and I shall be glad to be on British soil again. Then I sail for Siam or go by train. On Tuesday, I shall go to Batavia and have conversations with the local bigwigs.

There he met Mr Zentgraff, a local newspaper editor, who chauffeured him around in his grand car. Mr Pekema took him to see the Acting-President of the Legislative Assembly, a dignified old Javanese nobleman who was regent at one time. He wore a brown, black and white turban, a white coat and a brown, black and white sarong. "Don't call him Malaysian", said Pekema: "He's proud of being Javanese". Mr Pekema went through the Legislative Assembly, bowed to the Acting-President and then went to his room. The Javanese asked Gareth about his journey and told him about the Assembly of which there were 60 members.

Returning to the capital, Gareth saw the Prime Minister of Java, Mr Pronk, who was very secretive and who seemed terrified to say a word. "The negotiations are not over, we do not want anything to appear in the press which might endanger our negotiations. I am very, very sorry to disappoint you, but our policy must be one of silence." Gareth did not glean what these negotiations were in his interview, but the following day when he went to Mr Zentgraff's office, he found him in very excited state:

Japan! I had most important talk with the Procurer General. It was very secret. We know that Japan has plans to come in as soon as war breaks out in Europe. So, we are working hard on the problem; that is the Japanese, as soon as Europe is preoccupied, will strike Java. We have given up our traditional policy of neutrality. The Japanese can do anything they like if there is war. They'd attack the Philippines and the Dutch East Indies. They know they could do it easily; they've got the power in the Far East. Just look at Ishihara's book.

Mr Zentgraff pointed out to Gareth a map that had Australia and the Dutch East Indies drawn in as colonies of Japan:

> I have a lot of Japanese friends and have lived a long time with the 'Japs', but there is not a single Japanese I'd trust if any motive of patriotism came in. There is not one who would not poison me if their country were at stake. What is more they would poison their families. The Japanese have a proverb: 'duty knows no family'.

He gave Gareth the example of a wife committing suicide before her husband went to Manchukuo. Another was of a boy in a burning school who protected a picture of the Emperor with his body. The children wept when they heard this and thought: "If only I had the opportunity". Then there was the wife whose husband was killed in war who was happy and was congratulated by her friends, which showed that the Japanese would risk all.

On Good Friday 1935, Gareth recalled that he had a very 'Consular' day. In the morning he had a long conversation with the German Consul-General, Herr Vallette who was a fervent Nazi especially in his racist views. Herr Vallette was a very nervous, serious man and gave Gareth his thoughts on possible German co-operation with the colonial nations in the event of any Japanese invasion:

> 'White races'? Why should we, the Germans, help them? What have they done for us? They have sent their coloured troops to ravage our children and even old women. The white races have condemned us to starve, they regard us as an inferior nation and surrounded us with troops and made us feel guilty for the [1914-18] war. When I went to fight in the trenches, I had opposite me the Ghurkha's; they were coughing all night. 'White races'! Let them give equality to Germany and then we will see. I believe, we should have an alliance with Japan, then if Russia attacked we'd have our back covered. The allied nations took away our colonies, took away our rights to extra territories and gave our land and our islands to the Japanese. Unity of the white races does not exist. We Germans hate mixed races. It is a blow to the pride

of our race. The Dutch are different from us. They marry native women. Take Zentgraff and Rittman, the great newspapermen, both have pure native wives. Rittman was telling me: 'I suppose your Adolf Hitler would call my wife a monkey'.

Well I said to Rittman: 'Hitler would never call your wife a monkey. She is a most charming woman; what we do and think only applies to Germany.' It is tragic to see the crash of Germans here, fine men who have lost all and had to be sent back to Germany. If only we had the colonies! What a tragedy for all these men that they can't get on.

As in the other ports of call, Gareth called on the Japanese Consul-General who wished to defend his country in the light of the local opinion:

Some of the accusations against the Japanese are absurd. Now they say we have wrecked the tourist trade at Bali. In the past, the women used to go half-naked and their beautiful shaped bodies attracted the visitors. But the cheap Japanese goods came in and the Bali women started covering their breasts and the tourists do not want to come any longer!

It is absurd to think that we want to attack. We have a peaceful policy - Peace in the Far East. Some of us resent Singapore, but there is no need, for we have a policy of peace. We would like an understanding with Great Britain. We'll import a lot from the Philippines. Our goods are of benefit to the natives; otherwise, they would go naked. We buy more from the world than we sell. The world is ruled by suspicion. There were rumours that Great Britain and Holland had a military understanding and the Dutch have fortified parts of Borneo. But this is wrong!

As usual, Gareth's time in Batavia was mostly taken up with talking to politicians and economists, but again he managed to secure a very full picture of the local life. He had lunch with Mr and Mrs Pekema, the head of the opium administration in Batavia. Mrs Pekema, a tall handsome Dutch woman – with (it was whispered) a dash of native blood, believed in black magic and practised it. She said at lunch: "I can break up any marriage in Batavia by black magic if I want to. I can separate the most devoted couples".

The following morning Mr Pekema, the head of the opium administration, invited Gareth to see an opium factory. "What an exciting job he has!" Gareth wrote. "Mr Pekema has to fight the import and smuggling of opium, but he controls an opium factory by which the state supplies opium to addicts in small quantities in order to wean them off the habit gradually." The visit to the opium factory was intensely interesting. Gareth arose early and at eight o'clock was in the office of the head of the opium administration. A taxi then took him out to the big factory on the outskirts of Batavia.

He was introduced to an Austrian who first showed him the raw material, which came in small blocks like dark peat from British India, Persia and Turkey. British India was growing fewer poppies. The factory employed about seven hundred men and children. Gareth saw how it was smoked, then watched huge machines preparing it, until it became a thick blackish-brown sickly smelling liquid. He watched it being driven into little tin bullets and then packed. In one corner, there were a number of boxes on top of each other - not very big and they were worth £70,000. All the boxes in the room must have been worth £300,000 to £400,000. The government sold one and a half million pounds worth a year; formerly they sold about five million pounds worth - all made in that factory.

The most exciting part was the place in the factory where all the investigations against smugglers took place. There was opium being concealed in medicine bottles, in doorknobs, in jugs with false bottoms, in eggs from China and other places. It was even hidden in 'cough pills'. He witnessed the preparation of opium for the King of Cambodia ordered by French Government administration in French Indo-China. He was told that there were 50,000 licensed opium addicts in Java.

After seeing the factory, he had lunch with the editor of one of the great Java newspapers - Mr Rittman. Then it was farewell to Batavia and once more Gareth's letter home noted his departure and plans and as usual he ended with his affectionate greetings:

Before long I must take a taxi to the *Ophir*, the Dutch vessel, which takes me to Singapore, where I arrive on Easter Monday. The Japanese Consul-General has promised to come to the boat to see me off, which is very kind of him, because the pier is five to seven miles away. Before coming to Singapore, I shall be crossing the Equator again. And now I must go off to the boat. Cariad Cynhesaf, Gareth.

Further photos of Bas-reliefs taken from Gareth's negatives at Borobudur.

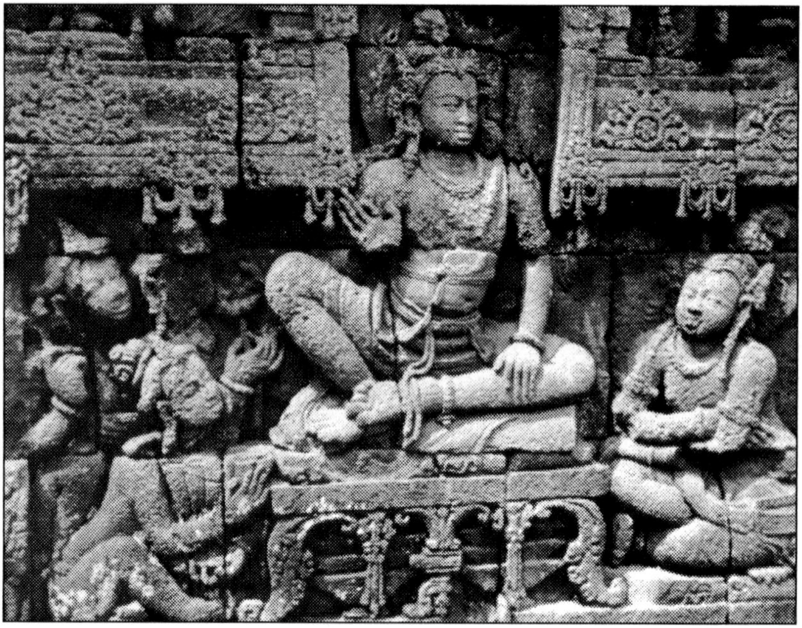

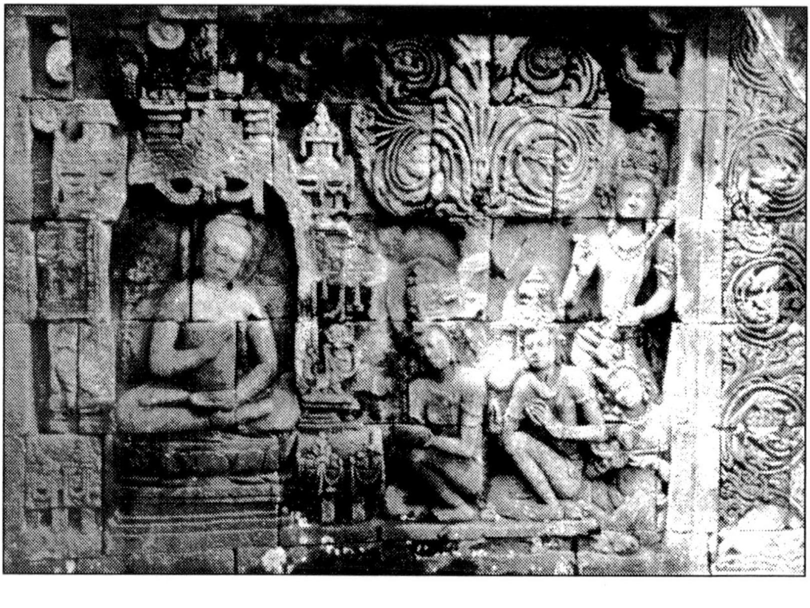

Chapter 6

Singapore

The Bulwark of the East.

The quayside in Batavia was bustling with activity when Gareth boarded the *SS Ophir* to continue the next part of his journey. The dock was decorated with masses of flowers including orchids. Nazis on the quay saluted each other with their right arm held high shouting: "Sieg Heil". There were many different languages to be heard - German, Russian and Dutch. One American complained he had to pay too many guilders and called the locals 'crooks'. An English 'gent.' sported a monocle. There were dozens of Chinese girls in long yellow dresses with a high neck and a slit skirt who waved. One of their handkerchiefs flew and landed on Gareth's shoulder.

The ship sailed through the Straits of Banka. To the east, some islands could be seen. Before long, she would stop at Munhok, a port on the Island of Banka, famous for its tin. Gareth was getting quite excited about the prospect of receiving a lot of letters, which would be full of news from home, on reaching Singapore. It was good fun on the ship, the company was pleasant and he sat at the table with the novelist, Vicki Baum, author of *Grand Hotel*. After coffee at dinner on the first night, he and his companions heard singing and clapping in the second-class and went to watch a travelling group of actors perform. Each night there was entertainment for the passengers, which Gareth thoroughly enjoyed.

For all the excitement of his journey so far, Gareth felt a pang of disappointment and he wrote expressing his feelings to his family at home:

The Far East will be rather quiet this summer, so my hopes for a scoop have been dashed, but I shall have grand preparation for knowledge of the Far East. I shall have covered a lot of ground by the time I am 30! I have my notebooks packed with material - it's all pretty technical and hard to summarise

Chapter 6 - Singapore

into a letter. I have received no confirmation of my terms with International News Service and Americans often do not keep to an oral contract. So perhaps I won't have much money left by that time - Oh yes, I've got £350 with me now and about £250 at home. So, that's all right.

On April 22nd, Easter Monday morning, Gareth woke to find the boat steaming into Singapore. There were plenty of ships in the harbour bearing the British flag. His first destination was the Dollar Line where he was overjoyed at finding a package of letters. He took them back to the YMCA where he read them for hours. After having lunch at the YMCA, he started talking to an American teacher who was sitting next to him. He was a Baptist and to quote Gareth (who was the son of a Welsh Nonconformist): "What more could be said of any man?" This American had to stay in Singapore for four years without going home. One Englishman from London had to stay here five years without going home and a third man four years. In retrospect, Gareth's comment was so poignant, for with dramatic irony he remarked: "Poor Fellows! If I were in their position it would mean I should not be in Barry until 1940. How would you like that?!"

The American teacher and he decided to hire a car to go and see the Sultanate of Johore, which was about 15 miles away. They drove on perfect roads along miles upon miles of rubber plantations and here and there was a rubber factory. Suddenly a tropical downpour came with thunder and lightning and terrific rain. The road became in parts like a river and from the sides of the roads torrents came rushing down. Soon they crossed a causeway near which there was a British gunboat dominating the residence of the Sultan of Johore and the town. Entering some shops they were amazed to see Japanese goods were two thirds or even half the price of the British goods of about the same quality.

After returning through the rubber plantations, Gareth treated the American to a good tea and Welsh rarebit in Singapore at the Capitol Hotel. Then with his usual great energy Gareth went rushing about seeing people and making arrangements. He had some inoculations and got a boat ticket to Bangkok. As in other major cities that Gareth visited in the Far East, he presented a letter of introduction to the local Japanese Consul-General[1] (although no record of this particular interview was made in his diary). It is however the author's opinion that an account of each of Gareth's Japanese consular meetings would probably have been dispatched back to the appropriate intelligence department in Tokyo, which was keeping a dossier on Gareth's movements and findings.

The next morning with the permission of the Commodore Mark Windlaw, the officer in command, Gareth went to see the naval base. It was 15 miles away. He was given a special pass at the naval office and was told not to take a camera. Taking a taxi he drove past rubber trees and noticed there were cuts in the trunk. From these trees, he watched the white juice of the rubber resin flow slowly out. On the wayside there seemed to be thousands of Chinese. Then finally Gareth arrived at a gate where a tall Sikh policeman was standing who took his admission pass. Before long Gareth's driver, a Hindu from South India, a Malabari and he were in the most strictly guarded fortress of Britain in the Far East, the bulwark in Asia. Driving past some well-built houses standing on columns like lake dwellings he noticed that underneath the living rooms on the upper floor there were motor cars parked. Eventually they arrived at the offices of the establishment and there he met the Chief Civil Engineer and one of the civil engineers, Mr Kneave who took him around the establishment.

It was a vast place and cost many millions of pounds. Gareth was shown the great dry dock, which would hold the largest vessels in the world. It was very deep about 80 to 90 feet and looked beautiful with fine symmetrical lines - deep and long like a Roman structure - absolutely white granite and cement. Some of the granite came from Scotland. Underneath were the engine rooms placed there to avoid

---

[1] "In July 1934 [British] codebreakers uncovered a major Japanese Spy network centred on Singapore. ... He [Harry Shaw] deciphered a telegram from the Japanese Consul-General in Singapore to his bosses in Tokyo which revealed that the Japanese had two 'top agents' at the heart of the British Government in Singapore. They were apparently providing their masters in Tokyo with details of all the secret plans to build up the colony as a bulwark against Japanese expansionism, a 'Gibraltar of the East'." © Michael Smith 2000. Extracted from *The Emperor's Codes* by Michael Smith, published by Bantam Press, a division of Transworld Publishers. All rights reserved.

being bombed by enemy planes. The big floating dock had been hauled all the way from England. This huge amazing dock was built in an area that had been a few years ago a mangrove swamp.

The Hindu chauffeur drove Gareth quickly back to Singapore, because Commodore Mark Windlaw was anxious to see him. They had a short talk in which the Commodore pointed out the importance of Singapore in naval defence and Gareth asked him: "What are the strategic advantages of Singapore?" The Commodore replied:

> Advantages! It's essential. Just look at the map. We command the East here. Aeroplanes cannot defend the trade routes. Just take the trade route between Africa and Singapore. That could be cut off by cruisers and submarines. What you have to do is to send a fleet to clear the waters. Aeroplanes would be no use out there and submarines could interrupt the trade far away. An essential for good old England!

At midday, he had lunch with Mr Peet, Acting-Editor of the *Strait Times,* who had a pleasant house with a garden.[2] His wife was a Texan and they were most kind to him. They discussed the American situation as well as Japan's expansion in the Far East. Then Gareth called on the German Consul who put him in touch with a German journalist, Herr Ries, who had been at Cambridge and who had spent a long time in Siam. They went to tea together at the Adelphi where he was given an outline of the Siamese situation.

Whilst Gareth was at Cambridge, he had once had breakfast with Prince Arthet who had subsequently been made a Regent. He hoped he would be able to get into close touch with this Siamese prince whom he was told had become a dominant figure in Siam. Ries advised him not to mention the name of another Cambridge acquaintance, Prince Chula, who had fallen into disgrace.

---

[2] Gareth was told to look out of the window into the garden of the next house. There he saw the tips of two big leaf fans from the banana trees moving up and down above a screen. "That's where the Prince of Siam who started a revolt lives," his host said "and some of his eight concubines are fanning him."

Chapter 6 - Singapore

Before Gareth boarded his ship the *SS Kistna* he dined with Commodore Windlaw, a frank jolly naval fellow, who took him to see some wonderful Indian dancing with Menaka, the Pavlova of the East, who was the star of the show. It was beautiful dancing, very graceful, lovely colours, but the music was weird. The theatre was full of Indians. After the concert he took his luggage down to the docks and found the *Kistna*. It was such a contrast to his luxury travel on the *President Coolidge*. The *SS Kistna* was very old and Gareth described her as the funniest boat he had seen for a very long time. She was so ancient and it took him back to the days when he used to sign on, whilst working on tramp steamers. He was the only passenger and had a cabin with two bunks and two portholes and an old fashioned kind of washbasin. When he had seen his cabin he left to go on-board a German liner to visit the German journalist. What a contrast this ship was. An orchestra was playing, there were mountains of flowers, hundreds of people flocked around and many were drinking champagne. It had bookshops, other luxury amenities and a magnificent swimming pool. He returned to his old boat, the *SS Kistna*, a little after midnight, wearily put on an electric fan in his room, climbed in to the upper bunk and tried to get to sleep. Then plonk! Plonk! The cranes started dropping machinery into the hold early in the morning. He heard clang! Clang! Through the porthole he could see Chinese coolies loading oilcans on to the *Kistna*.

They sailed that day at nine o'clock through the Keppel Straits, but a few miles out the boat had to wait for about two to three hours for the tide. There were three islands near by, each full of petrol tanks; one was full of British Anglo Petroleum Company aviation fuel. The middle island was Standard Oil of New York and the third a Dutch island with Dutch oil. They headed for the island of Sebarok for American oil and there they were stuck for many hours loading thousands of tins of kerosene that was being taken as cargo to Bangkok. What a rattle and din these made. The boat did not sail until nearly sunset and then they made their way through the Straits of Singapore; where Great Britain dominated the shipping of the East.

During the afternoon he had a glimpse of the P&O mail liner with black funnels looking a very sombre vessel appearing from behind an island and steaming into Singapore. She had come from London and was bearing mail for the Far East. Gareth realised how many homesick people from Britain would look forward with anticipation to receiving letters from their relatives at home.

When the boat *SS Kistna* was halfway between Singapore and Bangkok at 8.45 a.m. on Sunday morning on April 28th 1935 Gareth wrote, heading his weekly letter home with:

> On a tramp steamer, the kind you see in Barry Docks, about a couple or three thousand tons - and myself the only passenger. It is such a change from luxury liner. It is now six months since I left home. The second officer is from Aberystwyth, but he has not been home for 14 years and cannot speak Welsh. As well as him there are nine white or Eurasian officers on-board and the crew is a mixture of Chinese and Indian. The Chinese boys (waiters or stewards) are very efficient. I have meals in the saloon with the officers and the food is good and ample.

It was dark when they steamed past Singapore. The weather was cool and he spoke with the first officer on the bridge who was certain that there would be war with Japan. "That's what the people fight for," said the officer philosophically, continuing with:

> That's what the 'Japs' want. It is oil. The Japanese fishermen come here with diesel vessels and capture the fishing trade. They are spies, they know the country inside out and they have taken soundings. They even have rubber plantations opposite the naval base. Take it from me they know as much about the naval base as the British and on their fishing vessels they have naval officers. It won't be so quiet here in two years time. Japan is sure to fight; she has to fight. She could blow up that naval base to smithereens.

With an air of resignation he continued: "Well, the Japanese are doing just what we did. They are over populated and they have to expand". Gareth considered it was a silly idea. He could not see why Japan and Great Britain should not come to an understanding.

That night when he went to bed there was a very sudden and violent squall. In a second it was blowing about his room and a sharp rain started. He rang for his Chinese boy who closed the portholes. He had never experienced such a sudden squall and yet the sea remained perfectly calm. However the next day it was rough and the boat was pitching somewhat. The sky was overcast. It was pouring with rain, but he was sitting under the bridge and was protected. It was cool, when a violent storm blew up and his story breaks off, to be taken up after reaching Siam.

Postcard sent by Gareth of the Sultan of Johore and his wife.

Chapter 7

Siam

Gareth meets the young revolutionary, Luang Pradit.

The rough sea, which had appeared to be insignificant by comparison with the awful storms in the Pacific, developed into one of the worst storms he had ever experienced. The little craft was tossed about with the result that Gareth did not feel at all well nor did the second officer from Aberystwyth. The next day also was rough so he could not work and was delighted when he saw the first Siamese lighthouse about eight o'clock. There was a strong wind that night, but he woke the next morning to find the *SS Kistna* going up the river Menam to Bangkok. They landed at the Standard Oil of New York wharf. A customs officer came on-board and he asked Gareth: "Any opium, morphine or firearms?" Gareth was hurried into a launch filled with fat Indians, Chinese, Malays and a couple of Siamese and had a most interesting journey for about three miles up the river. Finally they landed, he found a taxi and drove through narrow, overcrowded streets packed with Chinese. Arriving at the YMCA Gareth met the secretary, Mr Zimmerman for whom he had a visiting card. There were no vacant rooms so he was taken by car to a very good hotel, the Rajdhani Hotel, moderately priced at three ticuls (the currency) a day for a room. Amusingly to Gareth in Siam one paid for everything in 'tickles'.

It was Tuesday April 30th and on his first day he introduced himself at the Legation where he met the Consul-General. Gareth enquired about the revolution that had occurred three years previously. An idealist, Pridi Panomyong had studied Law in France and there he was strongly influenced by Marxism. On his return from Europe he had lead the coup d'état. State Socialism was his goal. He had been given the title of Luang Pradit. It was basically a revolt of the disgruntled middle-class, who were dissatisfied with the arrogance of the Royal Princes. The Consul told Gareth that: "There is a lot of corruption, but a complete absence of any principles of democracy. Heaps of people are being arrested and imprisoned and there is no freedom of the press. There is an awakening in Siam but all ideas are mixed up and nothing is clear". After visiting the Legation he went to see a Chinese theatre. The play as far as he could understand was probably about bandits.

Returning to his hotel at about 10 o'clock after a Chinese dinner he found a man in shorts looking through the names in the hotel register. It turned out he was Elwyn Davies, one of the Davies families of Pennorth (Cynghordy) and he immediately invited Gareth to his home, driving the young man there in his car. Next morning there was a bible at the table; the Davies family were very religious and said grace before meals. Gareth, who loved children, immediately made friends with their son David. During the daytime they were most serious and grave, but in the evening when they were invited out the Davieses enjoyed jokes and they had a great time singing Welsh songs. On one occasion they listened to the repetition of the King's Speech and stood up to 'God Save the King'. The Davieses were very kind to Gareth showing him the sights of Bangkok.

He thought that the splendours of Bangkok outshone any city he had seen, but at the same time he had never seen such squalor and such dirty canals. It was the most magnificent centre of a city that he had yet seen in Asia and he was anxious to know whether or not Peking would beat it. Mrs Davies took him to the Palace of Prince Damrong, a great royalist statesman, an educationalist and a member of the Council of the ex-king. At the time of the revolution he was seized from his palace and had gone to live in voluntary exile in Penang. As was becoming the pattern, Gareth was invited to dinner with Whittridge, Vice-Consul who had been at Fitzwilliam House, Cambridge until 1931. He was good company and took him to see graceful Siamese classical dances, which were developed from old Hindu dances.

On Friday May 3rd, he went to the Royal Palace with Mr Davies. It was by special permission and included a visit to the 'Temple of the Emerald Buddha', one of the greatest treasures of the East over which wars had been fought. Gareth was amazed by the richness of the royal precincts, the throne rooms with all the gold, the jewels and the brilliant colours. On the card of permission was written: 'Visitors wearing knickerbockers, plus fours, blazers, sweaters, shorts are not allowed in the royal precincts. Ladies must wear stockings'. When they were waiting in a room filled with pictures of recent kings (including the abdicated King) an American came in without a coat and behaved abominably, because the Royal Guards said that he should wear a coat to see the Royal Palace. Gareth noted in his diary that the American regarded this as 'impudence'. Mr Davies said to him: "Surely you would wear a coat if you went to the White House". "Say", replied the American: "This isn't the White House. And what is more the White House is air-cooled and this isn't. Besides this isn't a real king. The British rule here!" A former American Minister was a great joke in Siam. Once in a most dignified State function he was seated behind the King when he suddenly hit the King's shoulder with a bang, darted his hand from an inside waistcoat pocket and shouted "Say, King, have a cigar!"

Gareth's stay in Bangkok was a round of entertainment as Elwyn Davies and his wife invited many guests to meet him. He enjoyed staying with a family. He dined on one occasion with a German doctor and his wife. The Davieses were most impressed when the Germans (with whom he spoke German) thought he was a fellow countryman and would not believe he was British. A few days later he was taken for a Frenchman by a Frenchman in Indo-China!

He had a private conversation with the American Minister, Mr Baker, a pleasant gentleman who remarked:

The newspapers are greatly influenced by Japan. All the news comes from Rengo, the Japanese news agency. The country is a sound [economic] possibility except for the ineffectiveness of the regime, the deterioration of the administration. Many of the best men of the old regime are in prison or exile. The most fantastic ideas and mixture of all theories and all philosophies, badly digested have been thrown on the government. They simply have not got an economic program. Pradit is very, very vague, doesn't know what he is talking about, he can't argue, just grins and remains obstinate.

One morning Gareth drove to see Pra Riam, the Vice-President of the Legislative Assembly. He appeared to be a clever man with very sharp eyes. Gareth asked him about Pan-Asianism:

No, we are nationalistic, but Pan-Asianism does not attract

many. We realise in our situation between Great Britain and France that we cannot adopt a movement that is antagonistic to foreigners. We are moving towards a moderate type of State Socialism. We want state control, but not state ownership. One reason the people want state control is to prevent our industrial life being dominated by the Japanese.

Pra Riam took them to see the Royal Elephant. It was a white elephant. The elephant's keeper went to the elephant and made him sit on his hind legs and then go down in prayer. It was captured in North Siam and the capture of a white elephant was considered a good omen of happiness during the King's reign.[1]

Monday May 6th was the Silver Jubilee day of King George V and Queen Mary. Gareth enjoyed the celebrations very much. The Davieses and he motored to the Legation and listened to the band of the Royal Siamese Navy. In his letter home he described the scene:

> They played 'Britain Never shall be Slaves' and 'Bay of Biscay' and other tunes wonderfully well. The navy is a great joke in Siam as it was nearly all composed of admirals. When it got dark hundreds upon hundreds of lanterns were lit and it was a beautiful sight. The native British population came. All our fellow countrymen as well as Chinese, Malays, Burmese, Hindus, Tamils and Sikhs; came pouring in their hundreds and they swarmed with their children through the Legation grounds. They *did* enjoy themselves, for a Chinese Theatre, a Siamese Theatre, and a Burmese Theatre (the Burmese women wore lovely flowers in their hair) and a Tamil Theatre were provided in different parts of the grounds. So if one stood in the middle under the Chinese lantern one could hear the Chinese laugh and clap in one corner, see the Siamese in a strange garb dancing in another, watch the Tamil comedians at a distance and listen to a Burmese band. The Chinese players were all children and had been brought from Amoy. Drums beat throughout the performance and the

---

[1] Tragically this was not the case as the young King was to die of gunshot wounds 10 years later.

sceneshifters moved and did their work while the actors went on acting.

Gareth with his usual keenness about the Japanese designs in the East interviewed the Japanese Minister:

The Siamese regard Japanese as the elder brother, Japan is an example to them that Japan has freed itself and progressed rapidly. In the last few years there has been an intercourse of students. The younger people look up to Japan and say: "If only we could do what they do". We have a link in religion. Buddhism is the national religion here.

In addition, Gareth had some most interesting interviews in Bangkok. One example was with the Prime Minister (who was also Foreign Minister and Commander-in-Chief of the Army). Elwyn Davies arranged it - he was a most valuable host. On the Tuesday afternoon, they were to meet the Prime Minister and took an early lunch accordingly. As they were eating, at precisely 12.05 p.m. a Siamese servant gave Elwyn Davies a note, which had arrived earlier in the day. According to Gareth, he got terribly excited and almost shook with nerves. "This note says the Prime Minister expects to meet us at 12!!" he shrieked. "Quick!" His host was a very nervy person. They leapt up, dashed to the car and at full speed they went, nearly knocking down Siamese, Chinese and Hindus until they came to the Foreign Office.

They saw the Prime Minister's motorcar and two soldiers with revolvers on a motorbike and sidecar nearby. They were just in time. It was all explained. The Prime Minister had changed the time to 12 noon and they had received the note very late. The Prime Minister was a plump old soldier in a green uniform and he grinned at Gareth who grinned back at him. He had an honest face, was bluff rather than intellectual with few ideas. The interpreter showered 'Excellencies' by the dozen. It was never 'The Prime Minister greets you...', but 'His Excellency greets...', 'His Excellency hopes...' and so on. The surroundings were sumptuous. The Kings of Siam looked down from the walls which also housed weapons of old Siamese armies.

Gareth had a long talk with the Luang Pradit[2] who had been the chief revolutionary, but who was now in the Government. He was a youngster and muddled in his ideas. It was the funniest revolution of which Gareth had ever heard. He described him as a very young man, with black hair, growing brush-like upwards, a round face like a moon and looking very boyish. On 24th June 1932 there had been a coup d'état, but before this there had been an absolute monarchy. A little before the coup it was felt that the intellectual classes were demanding reforms. After the coup d'état the King had signed a provisional constitution and in December 1932, he had made it definite. At the end of the interview Luang Pradit said: "People remain faithful to the monarchy, but only to the constitutional monarchy. Please do be careful [about what you write] - I do not want to hurt the King".

The Davieses had often had the young King as their guest to parties before anybody dreamed he would be King. Little David (aged six) was a little bewildered at his young friend, Prince Ananta Mahidon suddenly being made King after the abdication of King Prachadhipok Rama VII. "Has he suddenly grown up?" their son asked with childlike wonderment. Mrs Davies had tutored the young king in English and knew his mother who was a charming woman.

During his stay in Siam, Gareth met the Minister of Education, Pra Sarasatra Prabhard, whom he said he liked, but whom he thought got a bit muddled here and there during their long talk. He described him as being clad in the old Siamese dress of purple cloth. Gareth wanted to discuss the effects of the revolution on the education of Siam. The Minister stated he wished to base his education on Buddhism and wanted the youth to learn to live in their environment. The young journalist remarked that the Minister: "seemed to have read niblets of European ideas, mixed them up, shook them like making plum pudding and a funny mixture came out".

Gareth considered the Siamese qualities to be those of kindness, courtesy, hospitality, patience and charm of manner. His Cambridge Siamese acquaintance, Prince Arthet (Aditya), had become Regent, but on doctor's orders he was not allowed to see anyone and

---

[2] See the end of the Chapter for the full summary of the interview.

Gareth was disappointed not to meet him. Later he read in the papers that he had to be sent to the mountains. The Europeans told him: "Poor Prince Aditya. He has got T.B.".

Gareth agonised over whether to telephone his family in Barry from Siam as he had been dreaming about it for ages. It would have cost five guineas. Then he thought that if they heard Siam calling they would have heart attacks and think something had happened to him. He decided not to call, though he was disappointed not to do so. Instead he wrote to them saying that he hoped he would be in Manchukuo in June and therefore they should write to him c/o Poste Restante, Mukden.

Before he left, Gareth was fortunate to be in Bangkok at the time of a wonderful ceremony - the Ploughing Ceremony. Crowds had come to see the Royal Plough of Gold, but now it was time to say good-bye to Siam. On Saturday morning, May 1st, he rose early to motor to the station and the Davies', Mr and Mrs Aiken and Mr Moore of the *Bangkok Times* saw him to the train. Mr Moore said to him at the station: "Just heard that the Prince of Wales and Lloyd George are going to Cardiff". The train from Bangkok to Aranyi left at about 7.30 a.m. and he rode until 3.15 p.m. slowly, through very primitive little Siamese villages with palm leaf shacks raised from the ground.

Below is a summary of his interview with Luang Pradit:

In March 1933, Pradit presented to the Council of State his economic plan. The partisans of King Prachadhipok with the Council of State profited by this occasion and accused Pradit, who was Minister with Portfolio of being a Communist. The King signed a decree dissolving the National Assembly and suspended the Constitution. The latter told the sortie that it was the King and Council of State chosen by the old officials that governed the country. Pradit regarded this as a step towards an anarchist regime of absolute power and was exiled to Europe.

A few months later on the 24th of June 1933, his friends carried out further coup d'état, reopening the National Assembly and after applying their conditions, the King consented to them.

Chapter 7 – Siam 103

The new Government then recalled him from Europe. In October of the same year, there was a counter-revolution led by Prince Bovaradet, a cousin of the King and his former tutor. Before fighting the counter-revolution movement, the original revolutionists asked the King to return to the capital. The King refused. After suppressing the revolt, a delegate was sent to ask the King to return to the capital. At first he refused, but on the delegate's insistence, he returned for a few days to take part in the ceremonial celebration of the Constitution. A few days later he went to Europe on the pretext of needing eye treatment. There he abdicated and a Council of Regency was set up with Prince Ananta Mahidon being proclaimed King.

King Prachadhipok on his throne.

Ploughing ceremony.

Gareth in Bangkok.

Chapter 7 – Siam 105

Photo taken by Gareth in Bangkok.

The Emerald Buddha.

'Yaks' guarding the temple of Wat Arum.

Chapter 8

French Indo-China

Cambodia and Saigon: 'the most immoral place in the world'.

When Gareth arrived at the frontier station of Aranya and crossed the Cambodian frontier a very comfortable bus was waiting for him. The signs changed from Siamese to French. It was the end of the railway journey and the beginning of a 400 mile bus ride through flat open country to the Hotel Siemreap and to Angkor Wat. He was the only European and he got the front row all to himself, while the back part was packed with Cambodians who looked just like the Siamese. They stared at him and grinned. The children as in Siam and China wore around their necks talismans against the devils. The four hour bus journey started at 3.30 p.m. on a good road to Angkor. Along the route they stopped at a village where Gareth saw what he described as a "funny" shop. It had a narrow door and was a tiny office, carefully barricaded by wooden bars. A horrible old man with villainous eyes stood and stared through the bars. Behind him there were some strange pipes. Gareth went inside and saw two wooden tables filling the whole room except for the corridor. Behind, a Chinese man was lying at full length with his head near the wall and his feet near the corridor and he was inhaling smoke with a gurgling, lisping sound as if he were repeating – "Llanelli-Llanelli-Llanelli", but breathing inwards. Another man seemed half-asleep, but his eyes were half-open and he seemed very pleased with himself. Both men had skinny legs. Gareth had peered into an opium den, one of the many which swarmed in the main streets of French Indo-China. The bus then tooted and drove off with Gareth and his fellow passengers.

At 7.30 p.m. when it was dark they drove into Siemreap, which was about four miles from Angkor and Gareth went to the Hotel Siemreap where he found room and meals for seven piastres (about £1) a day. On Sunday May 12th after breakfast Gareth hired a boy who was: "very black with white teeth and who grinned all the time", to take him in his bicycle-driven vehicle to Angkor. Off they went out into the countryside through shaded woods, where the monkeys jumped from tree to tree alarmed at their coming. Suddenly they saw the grand, dark, grey towers or pinnacles of Angkor Wat near a beautiful lake where there were lilies and purple flowers. Gareth left the boy and explored inside Angkor Wat. He went further until he came to the great inner temple and heard intoning as if someone were reading an incantation. Peeping around a pillar he saw among the ruins 50 or 60 different stone Buddhas of all shapes and sizes, some covered in gold.

The boy who rode Gareth to Angkor Wat.

    Gareth saw a yellow packet on the table with the words: "Chang Kwong Hing, dealer in best quality joss sticks". He drew one out, lit it and placed it on a bamboo root. Smoke went up and the scent of incense carried him in thought to his first experience of Notre Dame in Paris. Gareth went back in the afternoon and went to the Bayon. It was absolutely silent; there was not a sound. At Preah Khan he fought his way through brushwood. Big trees had fallen in his path and he had to be on his guard against snakes. The hut in the middle was overgrown with branches and there were beautiful carvings partly hidden in earth, debris and leaves.

The magnificent temple of Angkor Wat in Cambodia.

The Giants Causeway leading to the southern gate of Angkor Thom.

Gareth returned to the hotel and to reality following a 'grand' day. Dinner awaited him and he conversed in French with the waiter at the Hotel Siemreap who said: "The cost of living is terrible, higher here than anywhere else. All must be imported from France and thus there is much suffering. If we had imports from Japan there would be a higher standard of living and the revolts might have been averted."

Gareth was up early next morning and left Siemreap at 6.45 a.m. arriving at Kampong Thum at 10.30 a.m.. He then travelled the whole day on the bus to Phnom Penh, capital of the kingdom of Cambodia. On the journey, four of his fellow passengers were captured bandits. They were shackled, manacled and guarded by two soldiers. Above the waist they were naked and each had only one hand free. They were tattooed and one had sores from some kind of disease. A Roman Catholic priest on the bus said: "Quatre pirates, probably guilty of robbery with violence and murder, and are being taken to Phnom Penh to be tried". He then pointed to the countryside and said: "There are tigers and panthers over there. There are many around Angkor". He arrived at Phnom Penh at 4.30 p.m. and went to the Hotel Manoli. Then Gareth took a rickshaw to the Royal Palace. On the way he saw 14 opium dens. He went to the throne hall where there was a magnificent throne. Behind the queen's throne were placed umbrellas. He saw a Renault car packed with children entering the palace. "Some of the king's children" a spectator volunteered. "How many?" he asked. "23, a few are the queens, two boys and two girls." "How many wives?" "There are 50 concubines and they are the dancers." He heard laughter outside and asked: "Who are they?" "Oh! They are the slaves of the concubines" was the reply.

The following morning, Tuesday May 14th at 6 a.m. Gareth left the hotel for his next destination. Through the early morning mist he could see the roof of the palace and above his head he described blue, swallow-like birds darting, hither and thither. As he walked to his bus station he stepped gingerly over a dead dog and he passed peasants and some convicts guarded by armed soldiers dressed in blue. Continuing his journey from Cambodia to French Indo-China by bus, Gareth remarked seeing maize planted along the road, banana trees and ponds with masses of lotus flowers. He crossed a huge, wide river by ferry and came to the 'Douanes'. He was in Cochin China. It was the end of the Siamese influence, the Indian influence and the beginning of China, the Annamites; there were many differences. The temples and tombstones differed; the peasants wore a strange headgear, a cloth rolled round the head and all the women were wearing black.

At twelve o'clock Gareth and his companions on the bus arrived in Saigon. His stay was very short, but most interesting. He met the British Consul who told him that:

The French were making great mistakes; they were closing the country entirely to themselves. All goods had to be French at the expense of the population and the displeasure gave rise to terrifying experiences. The country probably had the highest cost of living in the world and this was the cause of revolts and dissatisfaction though a few Japanese goods managed to come into the country. The French were bad colonists; they only came out to make money and then wanted then to rush home again. Trouble was coming from the anti-Europeans and the nationalists, but the French were ruthless and would suppress any revolt at once. As it was the Cambodians were fierce bandits and smugglers and they were prepared to shoot when provoked, but the local Annamites were mild and loved their families and the land.

Gareth met a Mr and Mrs Tanfield who confirmed that the prices were terrible in French Indo-China. It was probably the most expensive country in the world. The tariffs were terrific; this would ruin the country and it would lead to great suffering. The fear was that the Japanese would want to conquer them. And so many Annamites would prefer the French. Great Britain sent a number of battleships, perhaps to warn off the Japanese.

During Gareth's short stay in the country he gleaned from a lunch at the Chamber of Commerce that the Communists were very strong, but that it was a strange Communism. It was a mixture of Communism and Nationalism. It was directed from Canton, but Moscow directed Canton. All round the district there were Communist cells and they worked very hard indeed. He met a most hospitable Frenchman, Monsieur Dukson who took him for a ride, out into the country. He saw flat palm leaf shacks and the scene was very beautiful with palm trees and the moonlight reflected in the river Saigon. They talked of food and the Parisian restaurant 'La Patisserie Perigourdene' and Dukson exclaimed: "N'en parlez plus..." In Gareth's opinion, the French were always thinking of Paris and had no affection or loyalty to their colonies. Dukson then said:

> The French are smoke too much opium, especially the women. I had a petite amie. I took her for a journey; I did not know she smoked. First day nothing happened. Then on the second day she was nervous and irritable. "What's the matter?" "Nothing". In the middle of the night she woke me yelling, "I must have opium". We went to a little village and went to a rough place and she smoked. Opium calms the sexual desires of a man, but increases that of a woman. It makes the women mad about men. That's what smashes so many marriages here in Saigon. The husband and wife smoke. The husband loses his desire, but the wife increases her desire; she must have a man and she finds a lover.

They went to have dinner at a chic restaurant. A young man passed by and Dukson said: "He is a river pilot and smokes 50-60 pipes a day. He goes upstairs as there is an opium room above the restaurant." A woman chic in blue, with fair hair and aged about 40 years, passed by: "She smokes, but only about 10 to 15 pipes. A pipe lasts about 40 seconds and relaxes one for about 10 minutes". It wrecks character. It makes men steal and murder and they will do anything for opium. Dukson continued:

> I had a terrifying experience; we went by car with a friend from Annam and slept in the car in the forest. Next morning I read that the Mois had attacked a camp of French troops and had killed a French officer. We had a narrow escape. The Mois are primitive and still use poison arrows. The Government is terrible here; the papers live by blackmail. Recently the Government gave a subsidy to a company of a million piastres when only 20,000 piastres was necessary; a lot goes into private hands. Newspapers began a campaign of scandal and then suddenly a complete silence of news: "Not a sound!" "Why?" and Dukson declared "because this company had given a bribe to the editor".

They motored past a building where sometime ago there had been an uprising by soldiers who had killed their officers. Then they dashed full speed in Dukson's car through the town to Cholon to the ship, *D'Artagnon,* passing the river illuminated with brilliant lights and nearly knocking people down. Gareth had a large second-class cabin in the *D'Artagnon,* but it was very bare. They sailed at two o'clock whilst he was asleep. On Thursday, May 16th on-board ship he woke up late at ten o'clock and lunched at eleven with a chic French lady dressed in pink, a fat witty Frenchman, and an American and his wife. After lunch he discussed with the Frenchman that: 'Saigon was the most immoral place in the world'. On account of widespread opium addiction, it was often ill advised to ask: "how's your wife?" because many couples were either divorced (or with partners other than their own). A lot of the women smoked opium, as they had nothing to do all day. The Frenchman said: "You invite someone to dinner. At a certain time he or she gets irritable, shuffles on the seat and the face twitches. They just have to get their opium".

Gareth wrote that he had had a most interesting time in French Indo-China. He had enjoyed Siam and French Indo-China more than any other part of Asia.

Gareth quoted in his diary the beautiful message of *Subhadra Bhikhu:*

Nirvana is a state of mind and heart in which all desire for sensate life, all egoistic craving have become extinct and with every passion, every grasping desire, every fear, all ill will and every sorrow. It is a state of inward peace.

Happy are those who do not hate. Let us live happily then, free from hatred among those who hate.

Happy are those who are pure, let us live happily then, pure among the impure.

Happy are those who are free from all desires, let us live happily then, free from desires among the desiring.

Happy are those who call nothing their own.

Royal Palace in Phnom Penh.

The Royal Elephant of the King of Cambodia.

Chapter 8 - French Indo-China 115

The park in Phnom Penh.

Cambodian dancer.

Chapter 9

Hong Kong

Gareth makes his plans to travel through bandit territory.

Gareth's ship, the *D'Artagnon,* docked in Hong Kong on Saturday, May 17th and he was delighted to have many letters waiting for him. First he stayed at the Kowloon Hotel for 10 shillings a day for bed and breakfast. There he had a huge room, which was beautifully furnished with a fine veranda. Later he booked in at the Empress Lodge. He wrote: "It is seven months since I left home so I have been away more than half the period. I am looking forward so much to my welcome when I return, to Ianto's jumping and to a good dinner, with pheasant, partridge and boiled pudding!" It was little wonder that his thought turned to the gastronomic delights of home when his tiffin menu at the Chinese restaurant at the Hong Kong Hotel was crab and bamboo pith soup, prawn cutlet, fried shark's fin with scrambled egg, frog meat, bamboo shoots and chow fan. He continued his letter:

> The voyage from Saigon in the second-class was most enjoyable. At our table was a woman of mystery - a young Madame Andrefoutte - who was exquisitely dressed in the latest Paris chic. Her lips absolutely red; her eyebrows lined with some black stuff and her eyelids painted blue. She seemed nervous all the time and ill at ease, hardly saying a word, but she smoked 40-50 cigarettes a day. She is married to a Frenchman in Saigon. Monsieur Vaseille asked her where she was going to stay in Hong Kong and she replied that she was going to stay with a Chinese gentleman who was a friend of her husband's. "Oh! You can't do that," said Vaseille: "Think what the British will think of you. Why don't you stay with the Americans who are coming to meet you?"

Nevertheless, she insisted that she wanted to stay with the Chinese gentleman. Vaseille spoke to Gareth on the side and said:

I am sure she is an opium smoker. Most of the French women smoke opium in Indo-China and she is nervous, because she cannot get opium on-board ship. She wants to stay with the Chinese, because she'll be able to get opium easily there, whereas with her American friends she will be unable to get the drug.

Gareth also had the impression that she was an opium smoker because of her 'tell tale' large sunken eyes.

On the first evening after his arrival in Hong Kong, in the company of the jolly, laughing Frenchman, Monsieur Vaseille, he went to explore the colony. Next morning, he was delighted to have a fine welcome when he went to see a Hong Kong family - the Barretts - with whom he had tea on the previous visit. The children made him most welcome as they remembered the stories that he had told them on the last occasion they had met. They rushed around with glee and got extremely excited. The following day he was invited back for dinner and as Mrs Barrett was out, the children insisted on taking him as far as his elegant boarding house. On her return the Amah said: "the gentleman who came yesterday has taken the children away!" Gareth read Mr Barrett his notes of his travels from his diaries and the latter thought he had certainly collected the materials for one of the best books ever produced on the problems of the Pacific. In his opinion they threw an amazing light on the Japanese problem. He felt: "his revelations would be very startling with all the interest of Peter Fleming's book backed by a far deeper knowledge of political affairs."

The British Colony of Hong Kong was most hospitable to the young journalist and he had a round of dinner invitations including ones from the Acting-Colonial Secretary, the Chief Justice, the Commodore of Hong Kong, the Naval Intelligence Officer and many others. Mr Barrett who was a journalist on the Hong Kong *Critic* took him to Rotary for tiffin and he was asked to speak on how Lloyd George wrote his memoirs. He had no idea that it was being broadcasted on the radio until he was told later. He lunched with Sir Robert Ho Tung and Sir William Shenton. He dined on the Peak with the Acting-Colonial Secretary, Mr and Mrs Bratsman and remarked that the view was one of the most wonderful in the world as he saw

Kowloon from Hong Kong. On top a thick mist, like that in London, added further mystery to the scene. Following another dinner invitation he was driven along the frontier between British-leased territory and China proper and he wrote dramatically:

> We watched a number of smugglers openly carrying their wares across the frontier - on bamboo canes over their shoulders. Chinese gunboats in the Chinese navy do a tremendous amount of smuggling from Hong Kong to Canton and more than half the rest in junks and fast motor boats. We looked down on Bias Bay, the haunt of pirates and where they are so active in the proper season.

Gareth bought some Chinese paintings, which he thought were lovely. His excuse for buying them was he had used the money he had saved by not drinking and not smoking. "It was a reward for virtue."

Gareth's plan was to travel to see his American contacts in Changsha, and before he left he made his preparations for an epic journey with the advice of Gerald Yorke who was an old Etonian and a graduate of Oxford University. Yorke worked for Reuters as a freelance journalist and from all accounts had a private income. Gareth intended to make his way alone from Canton through bandit country to see his friends in the college, 'Yale in China'. Gerald[1] with his boy-servant Li,[2] had accompanied the author, Peter Fleming on the latter part of a similar journey, as described in his best-selling 1934 book *One's Company*. Gareth and he met again on the Friday night

---

[1] To quote Peter Fleming's book: 'He [Gerald Yorke] had an extremely distinguished academic career ... He had been to Mexico; and he was supposed to have lived for a time in a Welsh cave ... had come out to China to do some research work, travelling 'hard-class' on the Trans-Siberian Railway ... During the Jehol fighting he had been up to the Great Wall with the Chinese armies as Reuters' correspondent, and that he had been arrested, though for short time by the Chinese authorities behind the front ... He sounded like a potential companion for my [Peter Fleming's] journey to Canton.'

[2] Peter Fleming wrote: 'He [Li] had attached himself to one of the many generals and / or bandits who raised a so-called Volunteer Corps to resist the Japanese invasion of Jehol.'

after his arrival back in Hong Kong. They had an excellent dinner at the Peninsula Hotel and Yorke talked for four hours in a brilliant way about Buddhism, the Chinese and other topics. The following night Gareth returned the invitation by asking him to dinner as he enjoyed conversing with Yorke. Together they made plans for his adventurous journey to "Yale in China" at Changsha.

Gerald Yorke told him:

Be careful of footpads. I don't think there'll be bands of armed robbers, but some of the Sampan owners are in league with the village thugs and a white man travelling by himself is grand prey. They probably wouldn't kill you, just beat you up and take your money. So go to the magistrate before the river journey, ask for two armed guards, and pay them £5 each. Get a coolie to carry your luggage; otherwise you will lose face. They'll think you are an unemployed Russian looking for work.

After dinner in Gareth's room they went back to Yorke's rooms and woke Li, his manservant. He came sleepily, but smiling in a black silk gown, closely buttoned high, round the neck. "Friend want to go to Canton, Hankow. Want write letter", said Gerald. Li grinned. Looking at him no one would have ever thought that he was a keen Buddhist, meditated three hours a day and refused food where there might be an animal involved. He took the pen and wrote out the letters slowly and carefully. It was a work of art. He had to write his very best, as it was a matter of face. People were judged by the elegance of their handwriting. There was no doubt that Li's letter was excellent since he used to be a letter writer in Manchuria and even wrote to the former Governor, Chang Hseuh-liang.[3] Each magistrate had to pass an examination in which the handwriting was vital. It was an art and all officials were artists. One letter in Chinese characters was to show the way to the hotel, another was advice to the officials on the way, a further requested a sampan to take Gareth to Sherping and another to obtain a carrier coolie.

---

[3] Marshall Chang Hsueh-liang was the deputy Commander-in-Chief to Generalissimo Chiang Kai-shek and prior to the Mukden Incident was Governor of Mukden in Manchuria.

Gerald Yorke was full of good advice and Gareth's diary records the safe counsel that Yorke gave him:

> Get visiting cards with "Yo Nen Sse". Do not delay giving your card if someone gives you a card, because the man who gives you the card loses face. The most important gives his card last. Be careful, there are Communist bands in the area.

On the morning of Saturday 1st June, Gareth left for Canton and wrote a cheerful letter home:

> A happy June to you. I leave today for Canton. I've had an exceedingly interesting and enjoyable week. Wednesday, I entertained the little Barrett girls (Siriol's age), gave them pancakes and ice cream and took them to the cinema. I am off to catch the train in half hour's time. From Canton I shall go and stay in Changsha with an American friend in college there.

He met a fellow journalist, Brough, at the station and they found seats. Ruth and June and Mr Barrett came to see him off. Ruth said: "Please come and see us again soon Mr Jones, because when you come you make us all so happy".

He waved until the train was out of sight of the station and so it was goodbye Hong Kong.

HONGKONG & SHANGHAI HOTELS

TIFFIN

$2.00

Crab & Bamboo Pith Soup

竹 笙 蟹 拑

Prawn Cutlet

吉 列 蝦 球

Fried Shark's Fin with Scrambled Egg

炒 桂 花 翅

Frog Meat & Bamboo Shoots

大 地 田 鷄 片

Chow Fan

炒 飯

Tea

茶

Almonds

仁杏

Chinese Restaurant,
Hong Kong Hotel.

Gareth's menu at the Hong Kong Hotel.

Paintings purchased by Gareth in Hong Kong:

Minor Court Official, Chen Mingchu in the Qing (Ching) court.

Court official and his ladies.

Titled lady in robes of the Ching Court.

The Fukien women.

Chapter 10

Canton

Gareth is befriended by the Generals' daughters.

Gareth settled on the train for the three and a half-hour journey to Canton hoping to read, but a very lively man, Brough, the Reuters' correspondent from Hong Kong, joined him. Conversation was animated and the time passed quickly. They attracted the attention of a Chinese family, with whom they made friends. There were about six of them and only one of the two girls spoke a little English. Unbeknown to Gareth, by curious coincidence the pretty girl was the daughter of General Chen Chi-tang[1] and the plump one the daughter of General Tsai Ting-kai.[2]

It was early June when he wrote his next letter from the New Asia Hotel, Taiping Road, Canton and in which he described his journey in great detail:

> As soon as we crossed the border between the British New Territory and Kwangtung into China, soldiers with rifles came on to the train looking boyish and harmless. The hills around were covered with graves and big pots of bones that had been dug up. We passed an area where there had been floods and the rice fields were covered with water. Across the corridor of the train were two girls, one pretty and slim, deep brown eyes, pink dress with collar and slits in the dress below the knees, the other very plump and painted, laughing all the time like a plum pudding or the moon. Suddenly they got up and said "Change!" I went to their seat and they took mine. I pretended to read, when suddenly the pretty girl, in a hushed

---

[1] General Chen Chi-tang was the warlord of Canton. He was an adversary of Generallisamo Chiang Kai-shek and a sworn enemy of the Japanese. He was a leader in the Southwest Faction. See also the Historical Background in Appendix I.

[2] General Tsai Ting-cai was the General who fought against the Japanese in 1932 in what was later known as the Shanghai Incident. See also the Historical Background in the Appendix I.

voice, asked me in very poor English whether I lived in Hong Kong and we tried to make conversation. After this the girl went to sleep on the train, her head of black hair on her arms.

Arriving in Canton there was absolute chaos, everybody and everything going here, going there, coolies going everywhere. A car from Reuters, packed with papers inside, was waiting for them. Brough and Gareth saw the two girls waiting and helped them in as well, the pretty one almost sat on Gareth's knee. Quickly they drove, nearly knocking people down, going through disordered streets with bright signs and strange shops. They dropped the girls in what appeared to be a slum area and they disappeared down a narrow alley with high grey stone walls on each side. They had promised to come to Gareth's hotel at nine o'clock.

Later that day Brough came with a beautifully, chicly dressed girl and they dined with Gareth in his room. On the menu was bird's nest soup. At 9.10 p.m. there was a knock on the door, a procession of two girls and a brother - all smiles - trooped in and sat down. Gareth made several attempts to leave for the cinema and eventually they arrived. He sat next to 'Sylvia', to give her an English name, and she clutched his hand with excitement when they watched the film about Manchuria. There was plenty of noise with aeroplanes and bombs falling. His companions shouted: "The Chinese are being shot down by the Japanese." Gareth was taken aback because before entering the cinema Miss Sylvia spat - a Chinese custom which he disliked. As they sat inside, she said: "I am a poor girl." Gareth said "sorry no money" and she replied: "No, I am a pure girl". After the cinema she said: "Like walk tomorrow?" and he responded with: "Very much like walk tomorrow." She said: "Come at four o'clock". Then his new friends took him for a ride around the city. The rain was terrific. They went up into the hills and looked down upon the lights of Canton. It was a huge city and so 'grand'. He had never seen so much chaos in his life as in Canton. Everybody seemed to be tooting a motor horn or rushing about in a rickshaw.

On his first night in a Chinese bed at the New Asia Hotel he went into his room and found no mosquito net. He got into his bed which had a hard pillow, two soft pillows, a great red rug and one linen sheet. He could not understand why with each little move he slithered. He looked at his bed and found a straw mat under the sheet, much polished by wear! He slithered and slid on the bed and off went the rug and off went the sheet. Next the buzzing of mosquitoes disturbed him. Bite! Bite! He hit out. He had slithered so much that he tried the sofa. The buzzing continued and all the mosquitoes of Canton came at him like an air raid. Bite! Bite! Two o'clock, three o'clock, four o'clock struck. At last he found a mosquito net and got to sleep just before 5 a.m.. Then there were the noises; 'Canton beat New York for noise'. There was strange music until late, the bells of the sellers and the sound of beating sticks. There was a hooting like the sound of a ship similar to the blast of the sirens of the steamship, the *Majestic*, reminding him of the sounds he once heard when the ship left the harbour in New York.

The next day, the Chinese family whom Gareth had met on the train turned out to be the family - so he thought - of someone called General Choy, of whose identity and history he said he had absolutely no idea. They gave him a 'grand' time. Three young ladies and two young men called for him at four o'clock, the time they had agreed and took him by car to what he thought was the slum district with poor Chinese everywhere. They walked down an alleyway with grey walls and stopped outside a door with wooden bars. Sylvia shouted and a servant with a pockmarked face pushed it aside and they entered a hall with a marble floor into a rich house with big rooms. There were chairs of black wood and marble designs and on the walls were pictures in silk of flowers and gay birds. The entrance next to the hall was guarded by a huge, high iron grill and inside was a picture of Sun Yat-sen[3] and of a Chinese General, 'General Choy'. "My father, now in Hong Kong", said the plump girl. She took him into the drawing room where there were pictures of a tiger and mountains. There were many mirrors with modern furniture and a rather 'careless' aspect everywhere. He was led into a courtyard where there was a little fishpond, a statue of a heron catching a fish and several potted flowers. Trees grew up to the sky and therefore the courtyard was a little dark.

---

[3] Sun Yat-sen was the founder of the Chinese Republic in 1911 replacing the Manchu Dynasty.

The young people all grinned a lot at each other, because only one of the family spoke a little English. A 'slave' girl came in smoking a cigarette and offered them tea. They took photos in the courtyard, drank the tea and grinned again. The General's daughters spat a lot and there were spittoons everywhere. He noticed that Chinese men did not wait for ladies to go through the door first, as was customary elsewhere in his experience. The girls wore lipstick, powder and rouge and were most elegantly dressed with long Chinese gowns.

Despite the fact that the young people and Gareth seemed to enjoy each other's company, conversation was very difficult. Though Gareth was able to speak at least five languages, he had no idea of Chinese and Sylvia had very little knowledge of English. After having tea and eating oranges and apples, they went for a walk down a very poor alleyway where a woman wearing red headgear and making incantations, held her baby, while another woman burned pieces of paper and lit joss sticks. The baby was ill and the women were making incantations for the child to improve. Gareth and his newfound friends walked to Sun Yat Sen's Memorial which was a huge building with a blue roof. There were a few soldiers guarding it, but their idea of guarding was to look around with their rifles pointing anywhere, staring at everybody and grinning at the children. "General Choy's soldiers", said Gareth's friends.

They climbed a great hill and had a marvellous view over Canton. Then they walked through a park amid the stares of hundreds, interested partly by the ladies and partly by his strange looks. They took him by taxi to a restaurant and there they had a magnificent Chinese dinner. Gareth remarked: "Still Auntie's cooking will beat them all". At nine o'clock they dropped him at his hotel where he read about Confucius and Lao Tsu until he fell asleep.

The next morning as Brough and he motored to Shameen, they came to a bridge with barbed wire and a great iron gate guarded by a Sikh. The canal was packed with sampans. A stone pointed to the place where the Chinese had been shot at Shameen in 1925. At 2 o'clock Gareth was expected at the General's house to celebrate Sylvia's birthday. The General was in Hong Kong, and Gareth thought this was probably for his safety or because he was a very rich man. Gareth arrived on time at General Choy's home. They talked, laughed, took photos and then nine of them went off in the car. They drove through the hills covered with graves to Saho where the streets were crowded with soldiers in blue uniforms and schoolboy caps. They passed the camp of the First Route Army. Horsemen rode by on tiny horses. The horsemen stared at Gareth with open mouths and all the soldiers looked round and one even stepped out of rank. They drove back to Gareth's hotel in the city and where they all had ice cream and then his friends bade him goodbye.

That evening Gareth dined and then went to the theatre. The costumes were brilliant and there were drums on the stage banging away. The crowds were chattering and eating. Mothers were feeding their babies and boys were selling fruit. After this he went to the cinema and on coming out into a dark street met grinning opium smokers. One boy about 19 years old said: "Come. Smoke. Come sit down". He sat down and watched the boy and an old man. The boy who prepared the opium put thick black liquid on a needle, placed it over a flame and when it bubbled he twisted it and rolled it on glass. He deftly made it into a hard pellet and put it into the old man's pipe. He placed it over glass and the opium pellet bubbled. The old man inhaled and leaned back smiling. "You want smoke?" At that point Gareth quickly took a rickshaw back to the hotel. He had expected to have an uneventful and quiet time in Canton and possibly settle to write some more articles. Instead he was thoroughly enjoying himself in the company of Sylvia and the other young Chinese people. On June 4th Gareth wrote very briefly: "I am having a most enjoyable time. I lunch tomorrow with the Consul-General, but I find it difficult to settle down to write articles - no time. I am being taken to a Chinese film tonight. Love, Gareth".

As in all the other cities, Gareth had an introduction to the Japanese Consul who told him that the Province of Kwangsi was becoming more intelligent and understanding of the Japanese points of view about Manchuria. He had just returned from there after having a 10 day trip to the north. The Japanese had no definite policy except that they wanted good relations with the Chinese. The reason that the

Cantonese were anti-Japanese was because Chapei[4] was the Cantonese colony in Shanghai.

After discussing the current political situation with the Japanese Consul, Gareth must have been surprised when he called later on the Mayor of Canton. The Welshman found that the views that he had formed in Tokyo of the Japanese policies were so different from those in Canton. He must have been puzzled by the Mayor's truthful attitude to Chiang Kai-shek's strategy:

> Our policy is one of firmness against the Japanese. We are emphatic on that. We will not yield to the Japanese. In the troubles of 1931 we asked the Japanese to live in the concession of Shameen. Since then they have asked that they should reside in the city. We have refused. Then the Japanese have asked me to mitigate the effects of the boycott. I have replied that it is a matter for the masses over which I have no control. If they choose not to buy Japanese goods then I cannot force them to do so. Major General Doihara's visit was fruitless. As soon as I met him I asked him how he could expect friendship when Manchuria is still in foreign hands. One reason why we are against Chiang Kai-shek is that his foreign policy is weak. We regard Japan's advance as a result of Chiang Kai-shek's weakness. He should have made a defence of North China instead of retreating mildly. The Japanese have taken advantage of his weakness.

By now Gareth had made his careful plans based on the pattern of the journey undertaken by Peter Fleming. He wrote from the New Asia Hotel at 6 a.m. on June 8th 1935 that he was:

> Just getting ready to leave for Changsha by train, junk and bus. I shall stay in 'Yale in China' with Dick Weigle. I've had a great time in Canton. My Chinese friends whom I met on the train have been amazingly kind and have taken me out everyday for hours. What luck I have in meeting people! My young friends were none other than the families of General

---

[4] The Japanese indiscriminately bombed Chapei during the Shanghai Incident in January 1932, which was the first known air raid by Japan.

Chen and General Tsai; the latter was the national hero of the 19th Route Army and who kept the Japanese at bay in Shanghai. It was probably General Tsai I saw in Hong Kong with General Seeckt. You will remember the Chinese army keeping back the Japanese at the time of the Shanghai Incident and how the world applauded them.

Today, I shall be all day on a slow train. I shall look forward to letters in Shanghai where I shall be before the end of the month.

The daughters of General Tsai and General Chen.

Chapter 10 – Canton 131

The interior of General Tsai's house. Gareth is seated with Tsai Daosheng, the son of General Tsai. The inscription on the reverse side of the photograph translated loosely is: 'though we are journalists, far from home, we have the same fate and can understand each other.'

Chapter 11

Gareth's Journey to Changsha

By railway, wagon, sampan, walking, bus and by rickshaw.

A Chinese boy woke Gareth up early in the morning to embark on his adventurous journey to Changsha. He reluctantly got up, settled the bill, which was very high due to Roosevelt's policy of buying silver[1], got into a rickety taxi and rattled off to the Wongsha Station. He bought a second-class ticket to Lokchong, as there was no first-class on the train on the Canton-Hankow Railway.[2]

The train was awful. All the seats were wooden and the second-class was packed so Gareth spent the journey in the very primitive dining car. The train left at 7.45 a.m.. On the train were dozens of officers of General Chen Chi-tang's Army and a great many soldiers in blue uniforms, armed with revolvers or rifles who stared at him. The roof of the coach leaked, soaking Gareth, and water dripped down upon him until he changed his seat. Peering out of the train in one station he saw a Chinese General, looking very funny as he strutted up and down accompanied by his officers. In another he saw an anti-Japanese poster representing a Japanese soldier with a bayonet at the throat of a Chinese man.

All day long the train climbed slowly into the mountains, until five o'clock when, after nine and a quarter hours of travelling, it stopped at Lokchong. He had been told that the railway had not been built beyond that point and that he would have to find a sampan to reach his next destination, a town called Pingshek further upstream. He walked about a mile to the town where he was taken to a very primitive hotel in the dirty main street. At the entrance of each temple he passed there were Chen Chi-tang's soldiers, armed with fixed bayonets. The Chinese Hotel was like a barracks. It had one big room and the sleeping quarters were divided by wooden partitions.

---

[1] Silver Purchase Act passed by U.S. Congress in 1934.
[2] The railway was to be completed in 1936-37 and was expected to have a great effect on the unification of China.

Chapter 11 – Journey to Changsha

It had poured with rain en route and he looked at the flooded river, thinking it would be impossible to take a sampan to Pingshek. He showed his bit of paper with: "I want a sampan to Pingshek" written in Chinese. The boy and two other men made gestures to imply "no good - flood too high" by waving their hands to imitate the river and making noises like a flooded river.

Then he showed the written sentence: "I want a chair to Pingshek." They made gestures of a chair and seemed delighted. They intimated that he could get a chair to Pingshek for nine dollars and it would take two days.

At Lokchong, he went for a walk and wandered through the narrowest arcades until he came to a church with a cross. Entering the building, an Italian Dominican priest welcomed him and they spoke a mixture of French, Latin and Italian. He told Gareth that the railways had been built many miles into the mountains along the gorges and that Gareth need not go by chair. He should take the railway as far as it would go, but he should be careful between the railway end and Pingshek. 'Molto banditi!' said the priest. There were no bandits in Hunan, the Province beyond Pingshek. Reassuringly, one of the letters in Gareth's possession was to magistrats en route asking for two soldiers to accompany him should there be bandits between Lokchong and Pingshek, an area that had been recently infested by them.

At 5.45 a.m., the next morning, there was a banging at his door, hot water was brought in and soon the boy was carrying his luggage on a bamboo pole for the mile to the station. He was taken to a big coach crammed with people. There were 120 in one big coach, a number of them were soldiers of about 15 or 16 years old. Gareth was the only non-Chinese. Next to him was a little man wearing glasses and who had a tiny straw hat perched on the side of his head. For two days they were to be travelling companions, although neither could understand each other.

At 7.45 a.m., the train started, then stopped, then went backwards, went onward and then stopped again. At last the train puffed on to the new railway track, where hundreds of coolies were still working. It was a fine ride along the river, through the gorges where formerly bandits had a great time descending upon the sampans. The train travelled for about one hour and a half to a station called Kimma. Gareth's neighbour told him to follow the others out into a railway wagon and off they went again.

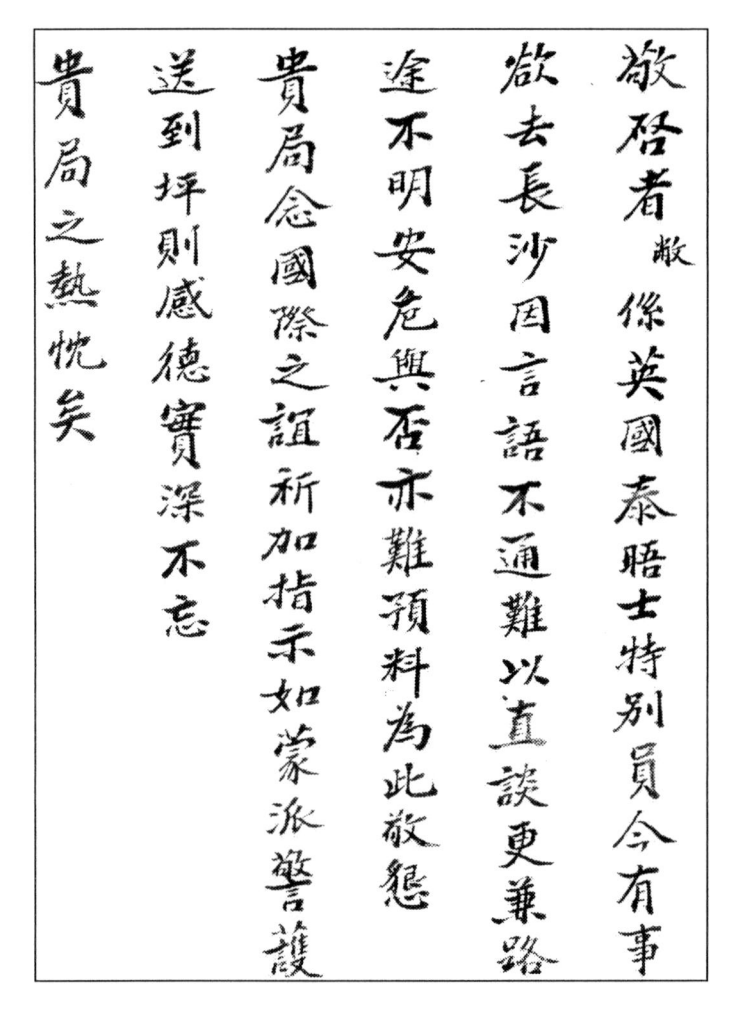

敬啟者敝係英國泰晤士特別員今有事
欲去長沙因言語不通難以直談更兼路
途不明安危與否亦難預料為此敬懇
貴局念國際之誼祈加指示如蒙派警護
送到坪則感德實深不忘
貴局之熱忱矣

This is one of Li's letters to the officials on the way. The general meaning is that Gareth was a journalist for 'The Times'. He wished the authorities to give him help in the language and safety on the grounds of international friendship. He would appreciate a guide or guard to accompany him.

Chapter 11 – Journey to Changsha

The occupants were amazed when he started eating bread, as they had never seen it before. Gareth gave them some to taste and they put tiny crumbs into their mouths: "as if it were caviar." Then he ate some chocolate and the passengers were amused. They tried to taste it and then kept the red and silver paper of a 1d Nestles bar as a memento.

The wagon jerked along the track, along the river and came to a stop. His companion indicated that they now had to walk to Pingshek. He got a coolie for his bags and they started walking. Gareth wrote from the Pingshek Hotel[3] on his arrival:

> This is one of the queerest places I have ever written my Sunday letter from. It is a small town on the Kwangtung-Hunan border. I am in a very queer inn and I had a 15 mile walk to get here. My room is very primitive and like a prison

---

[3] Extract from *One's Company* by Peter Fleming relating to Pingshek and the route that Gareth was following:

> Presently we climbed the last pass. Below us lay the village of Pingshek, squeezed in between the foothills and the river, and pricked by three little white forts, which stood on the knolls among the huddled houses ... The village inn was not a very good one. Li, for whom the linguistic problem now loomed larger with every step we took, was at sea with the local dialect. The feeling that he was losing face with us and perhaps being swindled by the inhabitants, made him very unhappy. "South man not good", he muttered and shook his head in a disconsolate way. His disgust was increased when the local soldiery came to examine our passports. Having few, if any foreigners before, they took us for Japanese and made an outcry. They were soothed only after an impassioned speech by the student, from Canton, whose ethnology was providentially more advanced than theirs ... Although the local wine was good the dinner was the worst of the journey - so bad that it took me half a minute's mastication to discover that a morsel, selected with chopsticks in an uncertain light was in fact the claw of a chicken. At this we lodged a complaint and the proprietress, a woman of spirit, beat her cook over the head with a stool. The dish was sent down again to the kitchen. On its return it was found to contain, among other things, the chicken's beak. After that we gave up.

cell with bars instead of windows and my oil lamp is very bad. I won't forget that walk. It lasted from 10.45 a.m. until four o'clock almost without stopping in boiling heat. My tongue almost seemed to crack from thirst and heat. In one village I got some boiling water to drink in an opium den, where a coolie was rolling his piece of opium just before smoking it, stretched out on a mat. In another place I got lemonade, but no sooner had I drunk it, then I got thirsty again.

A number of soldiers with small semi-automatic rifles and revolvers were marching along the track. We walked through unfinished tunnels, watched hundreds of coolies build up embankments. We saw sampans trying to go upstream, being tugged by about 10 coolies on the bank and moving about one foot a minute. Had I taken a sampan it would have lasted six-seven days to get to Pingshek!

My companion gave me his umbrella against the sun. Visions of iced drinks floated before me all the time until they almost became an obsession. We scrambled over embankments across hills and got carried by a ferry across a river. Then suddenly the sun disappeared and it poured. Afterwards the sun came out again and we boiled.

It was a pleasant Sunday afternoon when we saw Pingshek, a town on the river and on arrival I swallowed two bottles of orangeade at once.

The next day, two days after Gareth had left Canton, his companion woke him and he hurried through dim streets until they came to a mob of people fighting for bus tickets. Trying to buy a ticket he found his money was of no use. He had Canton money and the Hong Kong dollars were worthless. Luckily his travelling companion came to his rescue and he exchanged the Canton dollars for Hunan or Shanghai dollars. He bought his ticket and they were pushed into a lorry, resembling a prison lorry, with no windows except a few grills with iron bars. Inside were 21 people. At six o'clock, they went across the frontier into Hunan Province where they changed buses into another very uncomfortable lorry and yet again at Ichang.

His destination was Chenchow. The bus was stoned three times by local youths. They rattled along all day and at 3 p.m. they stopped after a nine hour bus journey. A coolie took Gareth's luggage and his bespectacled companion and he got into a sampan and crossed a very wide river to the most miserable town he had ever seen.

Gareth planned to go to the Presbyterian mission where Dick Weigle had told him to spend the night with the Reverend and Mrs Johnston. Hiring a terribly old rickshaw he said to the rickshaw coolie: "Meriko" (American) and made the sign of the cross implying he wished to go to a Church. The man nodded and said 'Yay-su' (Jesus). He said: "yes" and off they went. It was a terrible journey. His legs were perched over his luggage. The rain was pouring through the hide covering the rickshaw. The streets were so narrow that two rickshaws could hardly pass. The roofs gathered all the rain and poured threefold onto him and the rickshaw. The stones of the road were bad and he was bumped and bumped. They went on and on and on, never stopping. The rain never stopped either and he was getting wetter and wetter. At last they came to a river. He pointed to a church and Gareth was delighted to see a cross. They took a ferry across an angry flooded river. Then he went through flooded streets with water up to his ankles. Getting to the church he thought: "now for a lovely bath and a welcome from Americans".

From the church a Chinese man came out and glared at him. Then another came and scowled. It was a rotten welcome in the pouring rain. Gareth realised that it was a Chinese Roman Catholic church and that they probably mistook him for a White Russian tramp.

Realising it was the wrong place they went back into the drenching rain. "Yay-su?" (Jesus) said the coolie again. Gareth said: "Yes, Yay-su!" and he nodded, so they walked, splashing in the mud and water, past blind beggars and diseased people. They crossed by the ferry and returned to where they had left the rickshaw. It rained and rained. They bumped over cobbled stones, through narrow streets, nearly knocked over a few blind beggars and bashed into umbrellas until they came to a road full of debris, which was being widened by order of Chang Kai Shek. The rickshaw coolie stumbled in the street and fell just like a horse in shafts; Gareth's rucksack fell into a pool of mud. Recovering, they went on and on past the most miserable houses. At last they stopped by a grey wall, Gareth opened a door and looked in. It looked like a mission. Dripping wet, he went in and met a rather sad looking missionary lady.

"How do you do Mrs Johnson?" And Gareth continued: "Dick Weigle suggested I should stay here in Chenchow and has given me this letter of introduction to you". "But this not Chenchow. This is Henchow and I am not Mrs Johnson [she was actually called Mrs Birkle[4]]. You have come 100 miles too far!"

Gareth had a much-needed hot bath and a room for the night. He wrote from the mission that: "it is one of the most awful places that I have ever been in. I am dripping wet, hungry, tired. The town is flooded and full of miserable people". Next morning at 4.45 a.m. Mr Birkle called him. After a good breakfast, a rickshaw coolie took him for miles into the country until at last they reached the bus station. It was the fourth day of his journey and he left on a six hour bus trip from Henchow (Hengyang) to his final destination. The bus was a luxury bus with windows and front facing seats. Next to him sat a German missionary. Everywhere on the journey he saw soldiers, some of whom had curved swords and on the top of every hill there was a large tower or blockhouse. These had been built against the Communists who had ravaged the country in 1931. The mission where Gareth had stayed the previous night had been destroyed at that time.

One of the men on the bus could speak English. He was a keen anti-Japanese Nationalist. "We must have machines everywhere in China. We are building roads and railways. We will have railway right to Szechuan. The Canton-Hankow railway that will be finished next year will unify China. Chiang Kai-shek is a wonderful man."

"Why is he [Chiang Kai-shek] friendly with the Japanese?" Gareth asked. "Oh! That's a trick. He is pretending to be friendly to

---

[4] An American Bank had crashed in Shanghai. As a result of which Mrs Birkle had lost all her savings and the mission had lost a great deal of money.

mark time until he is strong enough to have revenge and regain Manchuria!"

Just before three o'clock the bus arrived at the gates of Changsha and soldiers came out of the towers and searched the bus for firearms. Then it drove to the centre, a city of half a million inhabitants. A rickshaw then took him to the big public school run by Yale University. Dick Weigle whom he met on the *President Monroe* gave him a very warm welcome. He had done the journey of 420 miles by railway, wagon, sampan, walking, bus and rickshaw!

Sitting beneath a tree in Yale, Changsha, Hunan on Wednesday, June 12th 1935 Gareth wrote in his typical fashion bringing his family up to date:

> Here I am safe and sound after an adventurous journey of over 400 miles from Canton into the interior of China. It was a journey. I think the Hunan Province will be very interesting to study, but I have so much I want to write about and I find it difficult to settle down. I haven't written up the Dutch East Indies for the *Manchester Guardian* yet. From here on is plain sailing, by train to Hankow, and then by boat to Nanking along the Yangtze.
>
> This is a beautiful place with trees and gardens and I am sitting in the shade. I am staying a few more days here. I went for a splendid picnic up a mountain yesterday and I am going to write some articles now. Sut mae Ianto? [How is Ianto?] I am looking forward to his welcome.

Chapter 11 – Journey to Changsha

These are a small selection of the items that Gareth bought in Changsha:

One of the pictures bought by Gareth and sent home from Changsha.

Chapter 11 – Journey to Changsha 141

Garment of a Han woman of the late 19th or early 20th century.

Chinese dress of a similar period.

Chapter 12

Journey from 'Yale in China', Changsha to Shanghai

Gareth's prestigious interview with Chang Hsueh-liang, Chiang Kai-shek's Commander-in-Chief.

Gareth spent a few days relaxing in Changsha following his adventurous trip from Canton to 'Yale in China'. He started to plan his next journey to Shanghai, a city that he had found so fascinating. Before he left this place of comparative tranquillity, with his usual energy he wrote five articles for various newspapers including the *Berliner Tageblatt*. He visited the market where he bought some pictures and some beautiful hand embroidered silks, hoping that there would not be too much duty to pay on them when they finally reached the destination of his home in Barry.

After a few days in Changsha, Hunan Province, he left by train for Hankow. En route he passed a place called Yochow where recently the Communists had been in control. Gareth made very few references in his diaries to the Communists and made no mention of Mao Tse-tung, Chou En-lai or Chu Teh. He probably knew nothing of the epic journey, which became known as the Long March, when in 1935, with amazing fortitude, the Communists from the south walked to join their brother fighters in the north. In 1927 Mao had retreated from Chiang Kai-shek taking refuge in the mountain ridge called Chingkanshan, which lay between the Provinces of Hunan and Kiangsi. Here he founded his first Red base and built up his guerrilla troops. The Generalissimo [Chiang Kai-shek] was determined to wipe them out and after many campaigns against them the Reds left their mountain base for the north. In this base Mao wrote his famous saying: "a single spark can light a prairie fire".

Very soon after Gareth's arrival in Hankow on June 20th he lunched with Consul-General Moss and Mr Gull, secretary of the China Association and a Chinese guest at the luncheon said to Mr Moss: "You English do not estimate Admiral Jellicoe enough. He was a great man". The host replied: "Yes, he was valuable in the

North Sea". To which the reply was: "No, not that, but his influence in the Pacific after his visit to Asia. It was Jellicoe who advised the making of Singapore into a powerful base".

During this journey, Gareth undertook one of the most prestigious interviews of his whole world tour. It was with the Deputy Commander-in-Chief of the Chinese Army, Marshall Chang Hsueh-liang. It took place at a particularly sensitive time for the 'Young Marshall' and during a critical period in the history of China.[1] Japan had just made a further move to dominate the Provinces north of the Great Wall and was demanding the demilitarisation of Chahar Province. Had Gareth possessed hindsight he would have realised that the questions he posed were most embarrassing during this period of crisis. Gareth was curious to know about the anti-Communist battles, remarking that they had been a great success and had been applauded. The Young Marshall responded that the Communists were bandits and that they had broken the main body of the corps. Some of them remained in bandit gangs that were scattered here and there. Seven thousand Communists had been put into reformation. They were however very desperate; they fought for their lives and were afraid of returning to their villages for there they would be killed by the villagers who knew them. The Young Marshall considered that the Kuomintang grip over Szechuan would increase as time went on. Not only did they have their military force there, but they also were spreading their ideas of unification. It was the same in Kweichow and Yunnan. Gareth continued his interview with Marshall Chang with the statement that in Canton there was opposition to unification and then asked whether the building of roads and the Hankow and Canton railway would be a help to the unification of China? Chang's response was that the roads and railway would be of help as it would facilitate the spread of ideas, and would also provide a cultural link with the South. It was the Government's intention to build a railway

---

[1] Following the Changpei Incident of June 5th 1935 when the Chinese apprehended four members of the Japanese Secret Special Service Agency, General Sung Che-yuan was dismissed by the Nanking Government from the post of Governor of Chahar and replaced by General Chin Te-chun. On June 27th he and Major-General Doihara met and formed what was known as the Chin-Doihara agreement. The terms of the agreement included the dissolution of anti-Japanese organs in Chahar, an end to Chinese immigration into the province and, significantly, the withdrawal of Sung's army.

south of the Yangtze, through Changsha to Kweichow and then up to Szechuan. Motor roads were planned to extend the grip of Central Government as far as Szechuan. He seemed pleased and 'tickled' when Gareth told him that the young students in Changsha wished to enter military institutes in order to fight Japan and stressed the importance of military training to strengthen the character of the young Chinese in general education.[2]

Gareth realised that he had obviously 'dropped a brick' when he asked whether Japanese aggression made any change in the Central Government's policy of co-operation towards the Japanese. The rather embarrassed Young Marshall replied very coldly in Chinese and to this the Consul translated: "I could reply, but that is a question on which I would rather not speak."[3] There was silence, then laughter. Gareth then asked if the Nanking Government had any plans for state industry as in every country in the Far East he had seen advances of State Socialism. Chang replied that they had the National Economic Council, which was going to consider plans for new industries, including state industries. Reconstruction work at the aerodrome was being undertaken at Wu Ch'ang. There was every indication that the Young Marshall was becoming 'air minded' though it was rumoured that this did not have the entire approval of the Nanking Government. Gareth, knowing the Young Marshall was keen on flying asked him whether he laid great stress on aviation. He replied: "Yes, there will be a new route to Szechuan. My second son is exceedingly keen and is going to become an aviator. He will have long years of training. I have my own aeroplane, a Ford Monoplane and I am keen on flying". Finally Gareth asked: "Mr Matsuoka said that China would, in this century, be filled either with the Bolshevism from Russia or with the spirit of Japonism. What do you think of that?" The Young Marshall replied with scorn: "Do you think that we, a nation with 4000 years, will disappear in such a short period as a century".

---

[2] The students said: " We must be friendly with Japan first. Be kind to your enemies, then you can learn their weaknesses and grow strong until the time comes to defeat them".
[3] Chang Hsueh-liang vehemently disliked the Japanese as they had murdered his father in 1928 and he, the Governor of Manchuria, had lost the province to the Japanese following the Mukden Incident of 1933.

After his interview with the Young Marshall, Gareth continued his journey by boat to Nanking, as this was the only means of transport. He boarded a fine boat, the *Wuilin,* which was on its maiden voyage and entered the huge river, the Yangste.[4] There was a terrific storm on the first night, but he soon made friends and chatted to a fellow passenger, Dr Outerbridge, who told him of the many people who were consulting him with diseases, due to starvation. The famine that he had seen in the south was due to the failure of the crops and the peasants were resorting to eating grass as a result. There were many beggars in the Province of Kiangsi.

From Nanking, he continued his journey this time by train to Shanghai and there he stayed a week. He had a very full programme and it is sometimes difficult to keep up with all his activities. He met many people and dined out a great deal. He had time to see some of the latest films including *Cardinal Richelieu, Blue Danube and Black Fury.* He also purchased the beautiful picture 'The Swallows' by Wong Ya Chun.

These activities left him little time for letter writing and so the letters over this period were very brief as were the diary entries. Invitations to meals came thick and fast and he was appreciative of the hospitality universally shown to him. He dined with Harold Abraham at the Country Club. One evening he had dinner with Mr Porter who told him that he feared the Japanese were trying to get a grip on Shanghai. That morning his car had been held up by six Japanese armoured cars in Bubbling Well Road. On another day Gareth met a

---

[4] While Gareth was on the waters of the River Yangste, a young Chinese girl sang this beautiful song, which he recorded in his diary:

"Sing to you. The sun is in the sky,
Can understand?
The sun greets the fish
Can understand?
But the fish under water
Can understand?
Not above water, but under water
I cannot get the fish
Can understand?
My boat no stay steady, go up, go down
Oh, I want to catch the fish and sell them, get money".

most remarkable man called Rewi Alley who took him to the mills and houses where the contract labour girls worked and the following day he went with him to see the Japanese factories and saw the boy labourers. Rewi was Inspector of Factories in Shanghai. He fought against the factory owners who allowed orphan children to work in the most appalling conditions. Some slept under their machine, were fed with gruel, and died of beriberi and starvation. The foreman beat children as young as eight years old. Girls were brought from the countryside and worked 14 hours a day some with a child strapped to their back or tied to their leg.

After his meeting with this exceptional New Zealander, Gareth wrote that he had had an extremely packed week in Shanghai and that he was off to Nanking that evening. He had had an exceedingly interesting time talking to everybody and people were amazingly kind, entertaining him wherever he went. He enjoyed seeing Mr Cheng again whom he had met on the *President Coolidge* and he was taking the little boy Pax, with his father to see the film, *Mickey Mouse*. The evening before he left, he had a good dinner with the Consulate men at the County Club. Shanghai, he found, was most interesting, but complained that it had such a rush there, seeing so many people.

On Sunday night he left Shanghai by the 11 o'clock train, took a sleeper and got back to Nanking at seven o'clock in the morning. Despite the momentum of his journey and the speed with which he travelled, on returning to Nanking he found time at the Bridge House Hotel on July 2nd to send the following letter to his parents:

> I'm off to Peking by the night express tonight. The letter I began on Sunday is somewhere in my luggage. It is a 36 hour journey to Peking so I'll be there on Thursday morning. In a few minutes Mr T.T. Li, the big man at the Foreign Office is coming to fetch me and take me to tea. I can't help laughing at his name. I had intended to write a long letter this afternoon, but the hot weather seems to have settled in and I fell asleep. I have been exceedingly lucky, because we have had rain and cool weather all June instead of the usual heat. I

shall look forward to letters in Peking where I shall try and stay about a fortnight.

Earlier in the day after his arrival on the night train from Shanghai he dashed off to the Consulate, Reuters, the Foreign Office and the Legislative. He continued to ask questions on the policy of these bodies towards the Japanese. He was told: "We know that the Japanese want to control Kalgan, an act of strategic importance, the route to Outer Mongolia. There is silent bitterness throughout China; the papers are not allowed to express it, but the resentment is there; there is a national feeling".

During his short stay in Nanking, Gareth succeeded in using his influence as a foreign journalist to gain an interview with the Vice-Minister of Foreign Affairs, Dr Hsu Mo. The Foreign Minister, Wang Ching-wei,[5] who was also Prime Minister, was away "ill" in Shanghai. It was either that he was taking a cure or it was a politically expedient measure to be absent. The Dictator, Chiang Kai-shek, was in Szechuan presumably fighting the Communists and Gareth was told he was a very sick man – bad teeth, indigestion and general breakdown and that he did not have many years to live. In which case if he died there would probably be chaos in China again. The Chinese were frightened of this. Chiang did everything himself, even gave commands to his sergeants, he gave no real power to others and there was no successor in view. He was afraid like Mussolini, Stalin and Hitler of having able men and was jealous of those with brains. He wanted to be the one and only!

Dr Hsu Mo informed Gareth that:

The Japanese military in North China seem to be able to do anything they like, nothing comes through diplomatic channels, the Japanese Embassy here only deals with small details and our Embassy in Tokyo has very little work to do. The Kwantung Army has the task of keeping peace in the north. What can we do? Nothing, our forces are being used against the Communists. We must wait; we will be able to

---

[5] Wang Ching-wei became leader of the Japanese puppet regime in China in 1941.

absorb the conquerors as we always have. Our enemies, the 'Japs', refuse to listen to reason, we cannot argue with them, they always point a pistol at our heads and say "Yes" or "No". There is no discussion at all. You've got to accept or be attacked. If we resist we lose more territory. They want to control the Yellow River. It is humiliating, but we can do nothing. Unity is coming. When Chiang has finished off the Communists in Szechuan and Kwangsi, Kwantung will come to the national banner. The Japanese think that unification will be bad for them, but I try to convince them of the contrary.

Gareth also spoke to a Chinese geologist, Ting, who said:

The Japanese Military want to make China their Empire and control China. There is iron ore and magnesium in Manchukuo. The U.S.A. is jealous; the Japanese will attack the Philippines, Borneo and later on Singapore. Why has the Government not even made a protest against Japanese action? Why have they acquiesced to her deeds? It is humiliating, but we are powerless.

Gareth had had a hectic day, but before he caught the night train to Peking (a 36 hour journey), he hired a car so that he and his friends might visit the nearby Sun Yat Sen Memorial and ancient Ming tombs. They drove out of Nanking through the city gates, which were flanked by massive city walls and later returned before dusk - as the gates were closed nightly as a means of defence.

This postcard was sent to Gareth's sister Gwyneth from Nanking wishing her a lovely time at the Eisteddfod. He was looking forward to going to Peking and then to Manchuria. It was signed with his usual affectionate words and his Chinese name of Yo Nien Sse.

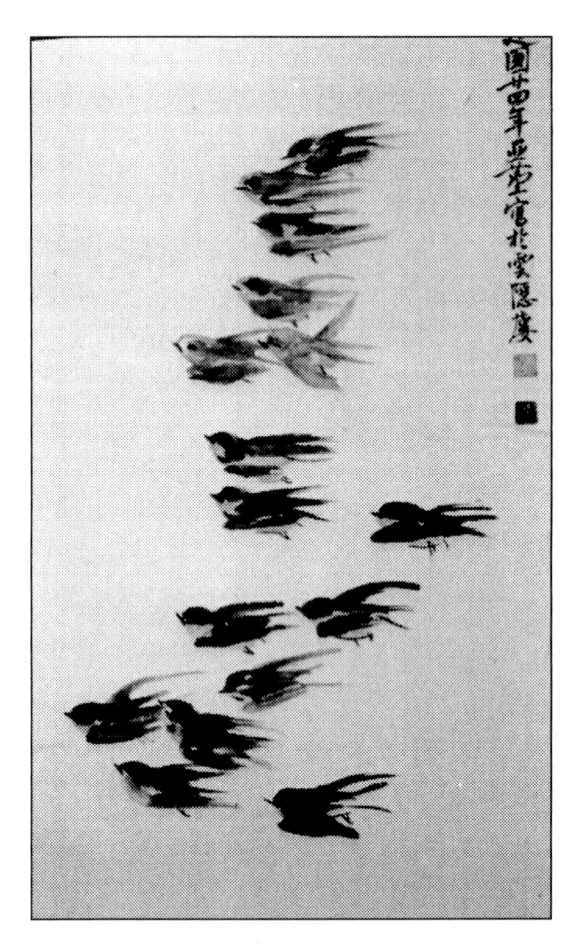

The Swallows by Wong Ya Chun (Ya Ying). The artist drew this picture on the 24th anniversary of the country (dated from 1911) at a place called Yun Ying Chu.

Chapter 13

Peking

An invitation to visit the palace of Prince Teh Wang.

Gareth arrived in Peking on the morning of July 4th on the penultimate leg of his fateful journey. He booked in at the Legation hospice, the German equivalent of the YMCA, for the week at $3.25 a day for a room. He said the scents in Peking were wonderful. Soon after his arrival he called on A.J. Timperley, the Peking correspondent for the *Manchester Guardian,* whom he found most helpful. Timperley shared accommodation with Macdonald, *The Times'* correspondent. They both proposed Gareth as a member of the Peking Club and gave him advice about whom to interview whilst in Peking.

The next day Gareth booked a rickshaw coolie named Pai and paid him a dollar a day. He took him everywhere, waited for hours, went huge distances and grinned all the time. The Welshman went to see Dr Müller to whom Wolf von Dewall, a London friend of Gareth, had given him an introduction. With a further letter of introduction from Von Dewall he called on Baron von Plessen at the German Embassy and he also visited the Japanese Embassy where he made an appointment to see the Consul. His final visit was to the Countess Lichnovsky, a sister of Prince Lichnovsky whom he had met at Cambridge. Pai took him to see the sights of Peking including the Temple of Heaven, the Lama Temple, the Temple of Confucius, the Hall of Classics, and finally the 'Thieves Market' (all stolen things) where he bought some silk. The buildings were beautiful, but in Gareth's opinion did not beat the splendour of Siam.

He made an appointment to see Sir Alexander Cadogan, the British Ambassador to China and the following day he called at the British Embassy. He noted in his diaries that he was bewildered at the Ambassador's replies and that they seemed confused and contradictory in content. In reply to the question as to how the British politicians should react to the present crisis of demilitarisation in the Northern Provinces, the Ambassador replied that it was a very difficult problem; people said they wanted a more positive policy, but this was not easy to define. If the British Embassy left Peking, they would lose face with the Chinese: if they did not it would be of no use having an Embassy in China in an area controlled by the Japanese. Sending gunboats had been suggested, but that would be impossible. As to whether Britain should come to an understanding with Japan, the Ambassador replied saying it depended how far an understanding would go. This would damage Great Britain's position in China and Britain would be considered pro-Japanese. Trade should be left to itself, except when the treaty rights were infringed. British interests in Northern China were not great though there were Kailin mines, oil and tobacco. The Japanese wished to develop North China economically. The Ambassador considered that everything was in the lap of the gods and that no one knew what the next step was.

Gareth wrote to his family on Sunday, July 7th 1935 and even recorded the time of 5.20 p.m.:

> Here is a grand stroke of luck. I heard that there is next Sunday a great meeting of the Mongolian princes in Inner Mongolia about 160 to 180 miles beyond Kalgan. I had been puzzling all day how to get there, because the railway does not penetrate into Inner Mongolia and it is hard and very expensive to get a car. It would be a wonderful opportunity, but difficult to carry out.
>
> Then suddenly as I am having tea near the swimming pool of the Peking Club, Baron von Plessen comes up and says: "Would you like to join Dr Müller (German correspondent and a friend of Wolf von Dewall) and me in an excursion into Inner Mongolia to visit Prince Teh Wang and the meeting of the Princes? There will be a car at our disposal". So I jumped at the offer. I shall be away about a week – Absolutely safe country. No bandits!

He remarked that the future in Peking was very uncertain and that there were heaps of rumours, but nothing else. There were some Japanese aeroplanes flying very low in the mornings, but that was the only excitement.

Chapter 13 – Peking

On the day after his letter, Gareth lunched with Baron von Plessen, Countess Lichnovsky and Mr Fischer of the German Embassy. The countess was a very serious woman who lectured on Aristotle and taught English and Philosophy.

The diplomat, Baron von Plessen, wrote from the German Legation on the Tuesday to Gareth giving advice for his trip to Inner Mongolia:

Müller tells me that you need an "Inland Passport" for our trip to Mongolia, as otherwise they will not let you out of Kalgan. You can get the Inland Passport through your Embassy and you had best apply to someone in the Chinese Secretariat there. (Sir Eric Teichman, Scott or Tuinal.) The train leaves Ch'ienmen Station (East station) on Thursday at 7 a.m.. I suggest that we meet at the train. I shall be there at 6.45 a.m.. Get a first-class ticket to Kalgan, which we reach at 3.45 p.m.. If you have time, could you drop in at my office in this German Legation sometime between three & five today? I have to leave my office for a meeting at the Peking Club at five o'clock. I must apologise for leaving our luncheon so abruptly yesterday, but it was on urgent business.

Gareth applied for a passport and visa and on the 10th July, 1935, Geoffrey Tuinal wrote this covering letter:

Herewith your passport with visa for Hopei, Chahar and Suiyan. You should be warned not to travel to disturbed areas within those places - e.g. the eastern borders of Chahar as conditions are constantly changing. You should consult and be guided by the local Chinese authorities, as to the safety of any stages of your route to Kalgan - Larsen's Ranch, Pai Ling-miao - Kueihua. The Chinese authorities here require $1 for the visa, which I have paid when applying for yours. Perhaps you will be so good as to send $1 along to me sometime. I hope you have a good trip.

In his next letter home Gareth wrote that in *The Times* dated June 24th it was reported that the crisis in North China had settled down.[1] China had acceded to the demands made of her and Japan stood as a dominant power in North China. The He-Umetsu agreement accepting these demands was signed on the 9th July and on the following day Gareth interviewed the Japanese Military Attaché, Major Takahashi Tan. This Japanese officer with Major General Doihara and Colonel Matsui were involved in the negotiations. In the light of the reports from *The Times*, Gareth conducted a comprehensive interview with Takahashi and as he bade Gareth farewell, the Japanese grinned broadly and showed his gold teeth[2]

Before Gareth departed Peking, he interviewed the Japanese Counsellor, Waktsugi asking further questions about the Japanese position in North China and Mongolia.[3]

---

[1] The crisis concerned primarily the demilitarisation of the province of Chahar. The report noted that General Sung Cheh-yuan, Governor of Kalgan was requested to resign and 40,000 of his troops were disbanded. *The Times* also stated that Prince Teh Wang was the leader of the autonomy movement in Mongolia and the Japanese military were also involved. Major-General Doihara had flown to the Prince's palace at Pai Ling-miao to make plans for an aerodrome and radio station and there were similar plans in Kalgan. Chiang Kai-shek was fully occupied in the south opposing the Communists and the Southwest Activists.

[2] Gareth asked Takahashi about the roads planned by the South Manchu Commission at Kalgan. Takahashi answered: "When the trouble comes we will need the roads for strategic purposes. The two systems, 'Bolshoi' and Japanese cannot live side by side. There will be trouble, the negotiations over the Outer Mongolian-Manchukuo frontier will fail and there will be frontier incidents. We may demand in Chahar that there shall be no Chinese colonisation. We must have control over Inner Mongolia for the purposes of defence."

[3] From Gareth's notes, Waktsugi stated that: "We wish to increase the economic prosperity of North China, Manchukuo and Japan and to stop the barriers that have been put up between countries. Our aim is to improve communications; it is only recently that the telephone service has been renewed. For our own reasons we want cotton to be grown here, especially in Shantung and we wish to set up Japanese factories in Tient-sin and Tsing-tao. We want to raise the standard of living, and also develop the raw materials. In the interest of defence we must maintain influence in Mongolia. It is against the Communist menace from the north. We want to help the Mongols in their autonomy. If the Chinese could defend themselves against the northern influence there would not be any need for us to do anything, but the Chinese are weak and therefore we must take measures of self-defence".

Chapter 13 – Peking 155

All this exciting activity and the travel preparations would not have left Gareth much time for correspondence, but before leaving for Inner Mongolia he sent a typical letter home from the Peking Club on Wednesday, 10th July:

Today I had an interesting talk with the American Ambassador and this morning with Major Takahashi, the Japanese Military Attaché whose name you have often seen in the papers. Peking is quiet now. Last night Mr Cheng, the Chinese Commissioner for Foreign Affairs invited me and four journalists to dinner and we had a most amusing talk, for all present had had lives packed with thrilling experiences. Mr Cheng looked very pale and worried, poor fellow, because the Japanese will probably throw him out.

It was good to have your letter of June 14th yesterday. A new Lanchester car! I hope Gwyneth enjoys driving it. Please note that airmail is so much slower than the Trans-Siberian Railway as it goes via Singapore - I have already read *The Times* of June 24th sent via Siberia.

Tomorrow I start off for the great journey to Inner Mongolia; up from Kalgan to the palace of Prince Teh Wang, the leader of the Mongols with whom I shall be staying. Do not be surprised if you do not hear from me for a very long time, because postal arrangements are not good there and I may stay more than a week - perhaps two if it is interesting. It is a wonderful opportunity and I shall have good company in Baron von Plessen and Dr Müller. I am taking a lot of films to Inner Mongolia. It is by the way a very safe country – <u>no bandits</u>!

Gobeithio cewch Awst hyfryd [I hope you have a nice August]. I'll probably sail from Yokohama on September 13th arriving in San Francisco on the 25th. I hope to get many radio talks, so do not be surprised if I do not return home until November.

"Sut mae Siriol a John? Bydd Ianto yn mwynhau chwarae gyda hwy. Cariad Cynhesaf a lots o gusanau. Gareth". [How are Siriol and John? Ianto enjoys playing with them. Warmest love and lots of kisses. Gareth.]

Siriol and her brother, John with Ianto, taken at Eryl in 1935.

It was into the newly demilitarised zone of Chahar that Gareth ventured with his companions, Baron von Plessen and Dr Herbert Müller, to visit the palace of Prince Teh Wang in Inner Mongolia. He had made it known in Peking that he was keen to investigate the political situation in the region and to find out "what the Japs were up to". [4]

Subsequent events were to answer the question...

---

[4] It would appear that Gareth wished to emulate Peter Fleming's journey. His Cambridge friend, Viscount Clive, was the 'M' in Peter Fleming's book *One's Company*. Together the two men joined a troop of Japanese and Kwantung soldiers on anti-bandits operation in Manchukuo. The foray was unsuccessful as the bandits were forewarned by their scouts. The Japanese soldiers afforded Peter Fleming and 'M' every consideration and respect. Gareth no doubt expected to be treated in the same manner.

Chapter 13 – Peking

Gareth's father with Ianto, his dog.

PART 3

CAPTURING THE NEWS

Chapter 14

Bandits

The press breaks the news of the capture.

South Wales Echo & Evening Express — ONE PENNY. MONDAY, JULY 29,

CARDIFF JOURNALIST CAPTURED BY BANDITS

TROOPS RUSHED TO HIS RESCUE

Mr. Gareth Jones's Ordeal on World Tour

£8,000 RANSOM DEMANDED

(From Reuter's Correspondent)
PEIPING (Pekin), Monday.

Mr. Gareth Jones, for two years on the staff of the "Western Mail" and "South Wales Echo," and now on a world tour, during which he is contributing articles to the "Western Mail," was captured by Chinese bandits near Paochang, 83 miles north-east of Kalgar and not far from Kuynan.

Mr. Jones fell into the hands of the bandits with a German correspondent, Dr. Herber Mueller, who was travelling through China with him, when their train was attacked.

LLOYD GEORGE'S ASSISTANCE SOUGHT

MR. GARETH JONES.

South Wales Echo & Evening Express – 29th July 1935.

Monday July 29th 1935 - *South Wales Echo and Evening Express* (seventh edition):

Cardiff Journalist Captured by Bandits

Mr Jones fell into the hands of the bandits with a German correspondent, Dr Herbert Müller, who was travelling through China with him, when his train was attacked ... They were taken to the bandits' lair and 500 troops had been sent to endeavour to effect their rescue.

It is understood that a sum of £8,000 has been demanded as ransom money. Mr Jones' father, Major Edgar Jones, of Barry, is seeking the assistance of Mr Lloyd George, to whom a wire has been sent asking if he would make representations through diplomatic channels to the Chinese Ambassador.

Meanwhile British authorities have made representations to the local Chinese authorities to release Mr Jones and the British Embassy has sent a telegram to Captain Scott, Assistant Military Attaché in Peking, who has been travelling back from Mongolia (with the High Commissioner for Tibet, Sir Charles Bell), instructing him to remain in Kalgan to endeavour to secure Mr Jones' release. It is understood also, that the Japanese military authorities have expressed their willingness to free him and his German companion.

Mr Jones and Herr Müller were captured on their way back from Dolonor to Kalgan. They had chartered a motor-coach called the "Gobi Express" at Pankiang the headquarters of the Mongol Prince Wang, about 160 miles northeast of Kalgan, on June 22nd. Dolonor is about 150 miles northeast of Kalgan, so it would appear that Mr Jones and his companion were making a circuitous detour on their way back to this city. To reach Dolonor they would have had to travel through country unsettled by the recent withdrawal of General Sung Che-yuan's troops many of whom, following demobilisation at the request of the Japanese, had become bandits. Dr

Chapter 14 – Bandits

Herbert Müller is a representative of *Deutsches Nachrichtenburo*, the German news agency. (Dr Müller's principal profession was dealing with curios. He spoke excellent Chinese and was apparently accustomed with dealing with the Chinese on money matters).

The following day the news hit the national newspapers and it was revealed that the men had been captured on their way back to Kalgan from Dolonor at a place called Pao Ch'ang. The Russian chauffeur who had been captured with them had been sent back with a ransom demand for the sum of £8,000 and 200 Mauser rifles. Apparently the bandits held up the vehicle at a range of 40 yards with rifles and a machine gun, two shots of which hit the engine. They then looted it and carried off the two passengers. The bandits were dressed in uniforms of the Peace Preservation Corps [local police].

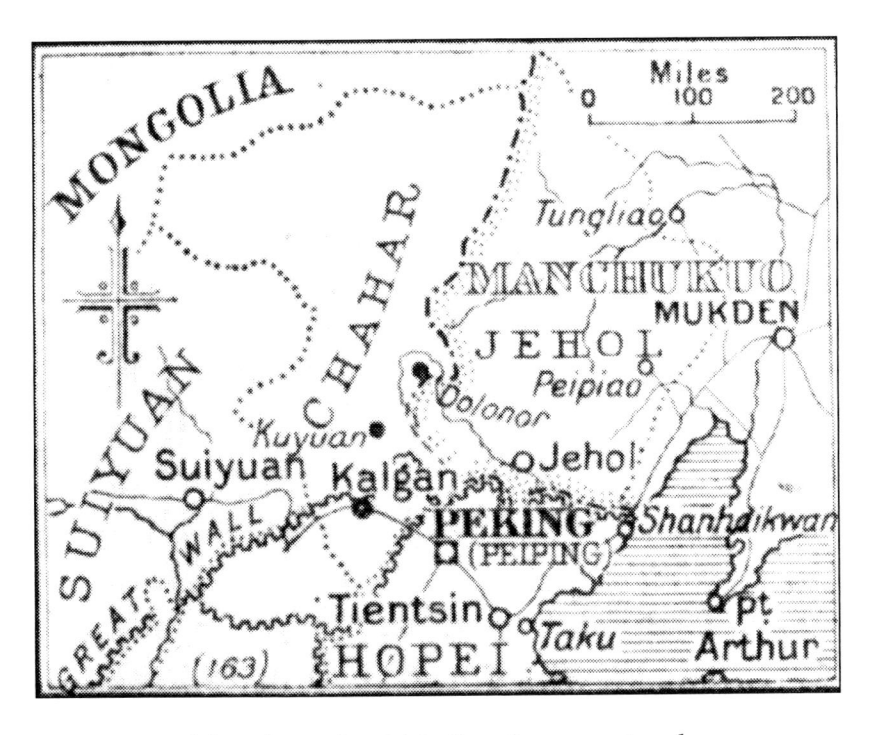

Map of area in which Gareth was captured.

Chapter 14 – Bandits

Tuesday 30th July - *South Wales Echo and Evening Express* (late edition):

Welshman Lone Prisoner with Bandits

Mr Gareth Jones is still in the hands of Chinese bandits, but Dr Müller, his companion, has been released. The doctor, who arrived at Pao Ch'ang today, telephoned a brief message to Kalgan confirming the news ... The mystery of why Dr Müller was released alone and Mr Gareth Jones kept in captivity is not explained.

Unconfirmed reports stated that Dr Müller was set at liberty at the instance of Chang Chung-Chi, a member of the Peace Preservation group, an ex-bandit and a friend of the bandit leader who had captured the two men and that Dr Müller was to obtain the ransom from the British and German Embassies on this condition.

Wednesday 31st July – Reuters' correspondent:

It was revealed that Dr Müller was released on 10 day parole ... it was presumed that Gareth Jones was being kept hostage for his parole.

Thursday 1st August - the family received a telegram from Changkiakow (Kalgan):

"Well treated. Expect release soon. Love Gareth."

Friday 2nd August - *The Daily Telegraph*:

On reaching Kalgan Dr Müller told his story to the Vice-Chairman of the government of Chahar Province. The latter telephoned the commander of the local militia, Chang Chung-Chi in Pao Ch'ang to keep in touch with the bandits and to endeavour to persuade them to release Mr Jones. As inducements the Chang Chung-chi offered to incorporate the bandits into the Chahar army and the Chahar government would pay the ransom money demanded. The bandits were believed to be over 200 strong. The commander of the militia at Pao Ch'ang made contact with the bandits and declared that they had now reduced their ransom from £8,000 to £3,400.

On his arrival in Peking Dr Müller stated that Mr Jones was in no personal danger and the government of Chahar Province would pay whatever ransom was necessary. He added that: "Gareth Jones was safe from bodily harm although once a rope was put round his neck and he was threatened with hanging. Although young and new to the country, he behaved splendidly and never lost his nerve".

Meanwhile Major Takahashi, the Japanese Attaché at Peking, gave orders instructing the Kwantung troops in Jehol and the Japanese military mission in Kalgan to co-operate with the Chinese in their efforts to secure Jones' release. These efforts included sending out Japanese search parties. Lieut. Millar, Assistant Military Attaché in Peking, left for Kalgan to join Capt. Scott, both of whom were expert linguists. It was stated that Jones had been warned not to attempt to go to Dolonor from Mongolia.

Friday 2nd August - a newspaper correspondent from the port of Dairen (Dalien), in the Japanese territory of Manchukuo reported in *The Western Mail and South Wales News* that authoritative sources considered:

Mr Gareth Jones is not being held purely for a ransom, but he is a victim of international complications. The British journalist was thought to be a secret agent with confidential material and had penetrated into secret territory. Chahar Province is a disturbed region on the Sino-Manchukuo frontier border in which the Japanese, Russians and Chinese are striving for predominance and his [Gareth's] presence as an independent observer is feared ... When all sides are assured that Mr Jones is not a secret agent, possessing confidential information, he will be released. The Japanese authorities explained to me that they secured a promise that Mr Jones would eventually be freed, though the ransom was not determined.

The week following the release of Dr Müller there was a period of uncertainty as to the whereabouts of Gareth and the family waited anxiously though still with some hope. Rumours of his release in one newspaper were immediately countered by another paper denying it. Reuters' reports were deemed to be accurate though many fictitious facts were printed as 'news' in the popular papers.

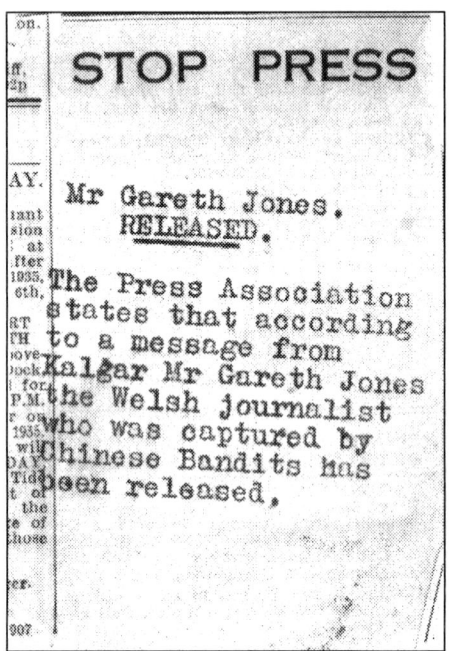

> **STOP PRESS**
>
> Mr Gareth Jones,
> RELEASED.
>
> The Press Association states that according to a message from Kalgar Mr Gareth Jones the Welsh journalist who was captured by Chinese Bandits has been released.

Incorrect stop press report from the Press Association printed in the South Wales Echo and Evening News.

<u>Sunday 4th August</u> – Reuters' Peking correspondent:

Torrential rains had held up the progress of the negotiations with the bandits, as travelling was very difficult, with the roads being streams of thick mud. However Jones' release was now expected at any time as the ransom money had reached Pao Ch'ang and that £800 [sic] had been paid to the men who originally captured the journalist. The money was sent by car from Kalgan yesterday with a protective escort of cavalry and those accompanying it had succeeded in making contact with the bandits.

Monday 5th August - Dr Müller's despatch to Berlin, (translated):

We approached a village called "The Great Tool House of the Family Ho" when Mr Jones noticed a man in Chinese uniform which did not astonish us and as we were indisputably in Chinese territory it was only to be expected that we would see members of the Chinese gendarmerie. Then in the houses, behind walls, on both sides of the road more men began shooting at us like savages. Bullets flew past my head and two went through the bonnet of the car. Finally after about 30 to 40 shots they stopped. They then apologised stating they thought it was a Japanese car and took me into a house for a cup of tea. I did not see that Mr Gareth Jones and the Russian driver had their arms bound and were taken into another house.

Whilst I was in conversation with the men, my servant arrived with the luggage from the car. At first I was assured that this was merely a formal examination, but at the sight of some silver dollars one of the men could not restrain himself and snatched the money. At this point they announced that they were bandits. Then Gareth Jones was brought into the small crowded room and threatened by the bandits with firearms. I now realised that I was a prisoner. Outside in the courtyard, my servant was given a list of demands to be fulfilled in 10 days at which time we would be released. I was bound and later heard how Gareth Jones had fared. He was taken into a Chinese house, made to climb on a bunk and the ends of his bonds were fastened to the timber rafters. A man came in with a noosed rope and Jones thought he was about to be murdered. "I felt no fear", he said with justifiable pride. We were then led out and everything was removed from our pockets, even to our handkerchiefs. Of our clothing they left us shoes, stockings, shorts and khaki shirts. We were prepared for our journey so that from a distance we could not be distinguished as foreigners. From curious peasants looking on, clothes were removed for us to wear and we were given dirty straw hats torn from no less dirty heads, which were rammed on our heads. At last the eventful journey on horseback began.

> Press Assoc. just phoned from London.
>
> The Emissary of the Chinese Government offered the Bandits the £3500 but the Bandits refused and demanded £8000. The Emissary phoned to the Government at Peking from Pao-chang and the Chinese government have made arrangements to send the £8000 to the Bandits.

Telephone message in Mrs Edgar Jones', Gareth's mother's handwriting.[1]

---

[1] <u>Press Assoc.</u> - Just phoned from London. The Emissary of the Chinese Government offered the £3500 but the bandits refused and demanded £8000. The Emissary phoned to the Government at Peking from Pao Ch'ang and the Chinese Government have made arrangements to send the £8000 to the bandits.

Chapter 14 – Bandits

<u>Saturday 10th August</u> - Dr Müller's second despatch to Berlin (later reported by *The Star*):

The ride with the bandits through mountainous country, which the two prisoners soon found very painful as their hands were bound. Despite this Dr Müller recalled the joy of seeing beautiful meadows and ripening corn around them. "The district through which we passed yielded little food - a few hens and pigs in the villages, a few vegetables and a little bad flour." After the first excitement of the capture they were well treated and they decided to make friends with the bandits. They made jokes with their captors on the first night and showed them how to wind up the watches that they had confiscated and how the camera, compass and photometer worked. His account continued to say that on the second day they repaired the gang's machine gun. Ironically, they probably owed their lives to the fact that the machine gun had not worked properly when they were captured.

On the evening of the second day, a man arrived saying he had been sent by the Chinese authorities to affect their release and on the next morning the bandits allowed Dr Müller to go with the promise that he would return with the ransom: "I bid Gareth a short but moving farewell and then I mounted my horse and a peasant followed to shield me in case I was shot from behind. A few hours later I reached Pao Ch'ang and I renounced my suspicions that my guides were bandits of another gang."

<u>Saturday 10th August</u> - *The Western Mail and South Wales News* (quoting Dr Müller):

When we were captured, the bandits were surprising harsh with Jones as he cried: "Do not touch me, I am British!" The bandits thereupon bound and gagged him. Later, however, Jones charmed his captors by singing songs in German, English and Welsh in the evenings; which he (Müller) claimed saved Jones' life. The bandits were particularly impressed when he sang the 'David of the White Rock' (Dafydd y Garreg Wen) in Welsh. Repeatedly they begged him to sing more and while their pickets watched the surrounding country the valley resounded with the Welshman's hymns.

His personality so impressed the bandits that they abandoned their harshness. One evening when there was only one chicken for 30 men, the bandits cooked the bird and laid it before Jones – whom they described as the singing Welshman while they ate cornmeal porridge. From this he was certain that no harm would come to Jones. They said: "We are poor and our only chance of riches is to obtain ransom for you foreign devils". They told them of the cruel destiny that had led them into the path of banditry, a path that they could not quit without endangering their relatives in Manchuria.

They should not think ill of them and should believe that they were not only good men at heart, but good Chinese as well. Dr Müller added that the bandits were avoiding contact with the Japanese patrols. Jones was forced to ride 50 miles a day. He was wearing shorts and his knees were badly cut by the saddle.

Nevertheless he was very cheerful, regarding the experience as stimulating.

Monday 12th August – Cable from Reuters' Peking correspondent:

It appears that the original gang of bandits that held Mr Jones have handed him over to another gang who have raised the ransom demanded to 100,000 dollars and are holding him somewhere near the Chahar-Jehol border. The authorities are now doing their best to start negotiations with the fresh gang.

Tuesday 13th August – Reuters' report:

Mr Gareth Jones had been taken across the border into Jehol (now part of Manchukuo and therefore under Manchukuo and Japanese control by his captors).

Tuesday 13th August - *The Daily Telegraph*:

Mystery of Gareth Jones Deepens. - Reported Safe, But Still Untraced

The Chinese assert that they are unable to communicate with the bandits, because they are in a demilitarised zone, where Chinese police are forbidden. The Japanese take refuge in the statement that Mr Jones is outside their zone of authority. The Chinese authorities assert that they paid £1,000 as a preliminary ransom whereupon the bandits demanded an additional £9,000 and 500 pistols ... Major Takahashi, the Military Attaché is leaving by plane tomorrow morning. He has advised the Chahar authorities to pay the £10,000 rather than experience difficulties with the British Government.

Wednesday 14th August – *The Western Mail & South Wales News:*

Japanese "Ultimatum" to Chinese Commander

CHANGKIAKOW [Kalgan]. A further attempt to secure the liberation of Mr Gareth Jones, the British journalist, kidnapped by Chinese bandits in the Chahar Province 16 days ago was made at this outpost today. Major Takahashi, Japanese Attaché in Peking, and Col. Matsui, Chief of the Japanese Military Mission, met Chang Chu-chang, commander of the Chahar Peace Corps, and said in effect: "We advise you in the strongest terms to find Jones by putting up the ransom." When Chang Chu-chang replied, "We have already made an exhaustive search," Major Takahashi said: "Now look in the right place."

The significance of this Japanese ultimatum was thoroughly understood. The bandits holding Jones wore Peace Corps uniforms. Therefore, either directly or indirectly, Chang Chu-chang's organization must know where Jones is. The Japanese authorities are confident that Jones will soon be delivered at Kalgan.

Chapter 15

The Tragic End

On the eve of his thirtieth birthday.

The Evening News

GARETH JONES FOUND MURDERED

FORMER SECRETARY TO MR. LLOYD GEORGE

Troops Chasing the Chinese Bandits Who Had Held Him to £8,000 Ransom Find His Body

THREE BULLET WOUNDS

Extract from Evening News, London, Friday, August 16th, 1935.

Friday 16th August – London *Evening Standard* (telegram sent to Berlin by Dr Müller):

Gareth Jones is no more. His body, pierced by three bullets, is lying in Pao Ch'ang. Details of his death are so far not obtainable. One thing is certain, that my dear comrade met death with the same fearlessness with which he stood up to his captors and to threats of death and imprisonment.

Chapter 15 – The Tragic End

Early on the morning of Friday 16th August 1935, the telephone rang in Gareth's home at Eryl, Barry. His father, Major Edgar Jones, answered the call from a Press Association reporter who told him that, according to a telegram from *The Daily Telegraph* special correspondent, his son had died.

Friday 16th August – *Glasgow Times* (from Reuters):

He [Major Jones] was almost too overcome to speak. "Oh! How terrible", he whispered after a long pause. "Thank you for letting me know." Then he went with heavy step to break the news to his wife. Mrs Edgar Jones, who was stunned by the blow, was comforted by her two daughters, all of whom had waited so anxiously over the past few weeks. Major Jones later told a reporter: "It is a terrible business. We were hoping against hope until the end".

An unfortunate misunderstanding between two Chinese magistrates during a critical period may have had something to do with the tragedy. While one of them was conducting the negotiations for handing over the ransom, the bandits moved into the jurisdiction of his neighbour. The neighbour had not been warned of the negotiations and had sent troops to intercept the band. This it was felt may have destroyed the bandit's belief in the sincerity of the negotiations and may explain why the bandits never got the ransom money that had been sent.

Saturday 17th August - *Daily Mail*:

From information obtained locally, the militia believed that Mr Jones was shot by the bandits last Monday – eve of his thirtieth birthday.

Saturday 17th August – *Sheffield Independent*:

On the Wednesday 7th August, the Chahar Provincial Government had sent a messenger to maintain contact with the bandits, but he himself had been taken prisoner. From that moment there was no news. The Chinese authorities were

Chapter 15 – The Tragic End

moved to action and decided to send out troops in pursuit and it was they who found the British journalist's body, today [Friday]. Though the ransom money had been offered in full, the bandits seemed curiously obdurate and had begun moving by rapid stages towards the Chahar-Jehol frontier.

Emissaries from the Chahar Government reported that the bandits refused to accept the ransom offered ... The Chinese and British authorities confessed themselves baffled and when the bandits were inside the Jehol border in Manchukuo, it was hoped that the Japanese authorities would have been able to secure Gareth's release.[1]

Saturday 17th August – *The Daily Telegraph*:

Verification of the reports are intensely difficult here [Kalgan], owing to the international situation. The Japanese authorities discount the report of the death of Mr Jones, and though unaware of the facts, said that the bandits who were holding him were last seen southeast of Kuyuan, many miles from the Pao Ch'ang district. Moreover, the Japanese asserted that the bandit chief had every reason to preserve Mr Jones in safety.

In Peking, despite the absence of identification, it is regretfully concluded that the body which was found is that of Mr Jones.

Monday 19th August - *The Daily Telegraph* (sub-headline from their special correspondent):

News held up for four days

I was the first to receive confirmation of Mr Jones' death. Although the Chahar authorities knew of it four days ago, they withheld the news from Lieut. Millar; the British Attaché here, until I had enlisted the help of Mr Hashimoto, the

---

[1] Also reported in: the London *Evening News*, August 16th, *Manchester Guardian*, August 17th.

Japanese Consul. The British Authorities are greatly angered by this procrastination, for at the time Lieut. Millar was urgently demanding permission to go into the bandit area. Lieut. Millar who was secretly smuggled out of Kalgan and managed to reach Pao Ch'ang at dawn.

<u>Saturday 17th August</u> – *Greenock Telegraph*:

And so ends tragically an anxious fortnight in the course of which varying reports concerning Mr Jones' whereabouts and safety came to hand.

PART 4

GARETH: A MAN WHO KNEW TOO MUCH?

Friday 16th August – London *Evening Standard* - Mr Lloyd George's statement:

Jones Knew Too Much

I was struck with horror when the news of poor Mr Gareth Jones was conveyed to me. I was uneasy about his fate from the moment I ascertained that when his companion, Dr Herbert Müller, was released he was detained. The so-called bandits fastened on to Mr Gareth Jones as the more dangerous of the two.

That part of the world is a cauldron of conflicting intrigue and one or other interests concerned probably knew that Mr Gareth Jones knew too much of what was going on. Mr Gareth Jones was a born scout, dauntless to the last degree. He had a passion for finding out what was happening in foreign lands wherever there was trouble, and in pursuit of his investigations he shrank from no risk. Doubtless he had notes in his possession that would have been of great interest to me or to many other foreign powers interested in Mongolia. I had always been afraid that he would take one risk too many. Nothing escaped his observation, and he allowed no obstacle to turn from his course when he thought that there was some fact, which he could obtain. He had the almost unfailing knack of getting at things that mattered.

Chapter 16

Dr Müller's Parole

The ill-fated journey.

Following his release from the hands of the bandits, Dr Herbert Müller gave a very full and colourful account of his experiences to the authorities and to the press representatives.

Anatoli, Gareth and Dr Herbert Müller.

The following is Müller's own despatched report to the Official German News Agency in its entirety:

I left Peking on July 11th with Baron von Plessen of the Germany Embassy and Mr Gareth Jones in order to profit from an invitation of Prince Teh of the West Sunnit in connection with the Sunnit-Mongol Congress. From Prince Teh's residence I started on a longer journey for the northeast part of Inner Mongolia, Herr Purpis, director of the Wostwag in Kalgan, having most kindly placed a motorcar at my disposal. Mr Jones travelled with me, also my boy Liang, and the Russian chauffeur, Anatoli Petrewschtschew. At midday on July 25th we were approaching Dolonor, our next objective. We were still about 100 Li (approximately 35 miles) from the place when we came across an ox-cart carrying, to my surprise, the flags of Manchukuo and Japan. The Chinese in charge of the cart explained to me that they had been presented to him by the Japanese in the village of Huang–C'hi, and that this place now belonged to Manchukuo. That was for me the first indication that the situation had changed since my last visit in August 1934 when I was reassured that it was Chinese territory.

This year, on the day after our arrival we saw the whole town bedecked with Manchukuo and Japanese flags, and we learnt that these had been distributed by the Japanese three to four days before our arrival with orders to raise them in order to salute the entry of new Japanese troops. I learnt from an old acquaintance that the Japanese had directed a mechanised brigade in the direction of Chahar on about July 22nd. About eighty armoured cars reached Dolonor on the first day of the advance, and that the numbers were increasing daily until the time of our departure. In Dolonor itself, we saw an enormous number of apparently brand new three axled heavy military lorries, tanks and staff motorcars, and learned that an appreciably larger number had left Dolonor travelling in a southerly direction.

I found that the Japanese officials had appreciably increased in Dolonor since last year. I heard, though I was not able to confirm, that the official annexation of East Chahar by Manchukuo had been proclaimed some days before our arrival. A proclamation of General Li Shou-hsin of July 17th posted up in every place stated that he had taken over responsibility for 'Peace and Quiet' in East Chahar and that the people would flourish exceedingly under the 'Kingly Principle'.

Having visited the headquarters of the Kwantung Army mission we were detained there for three hours and were cross-examined by a crowd of Japanese officers and were only released after a Japanese lama by the name of Hashimoto, whom I knew, had been summoned. The Japanese believed that we were after military secrets. We were allowed back to our inn and told to remain there until our departure. We were informed that there were three routes back. One was in bad condition due to rain, in another there

Chapter 16 – Dr Müller's Parole

was the risk of bandits and that the best route and safest was that passing over the River Shang-tu-ho. This we followed leaving at five o'clock in the morning on the 27th. In the course of our journey we came to a place we could not pass and some Mongols refused to help without the payment of an enormous sum of money. As night was falling they promised to come back the next day with planks and oxen. We spent the night in our tent and during the night four horsemen arrived and then made off, three northwards and one to the south. The next day another group of Mongols arrived and they managed help us get out of the sand. On the 28th July at 1 p.m. we were attacked by bandits.

We had passed through a village and saw men in the familiar blue uniform of the Pao An-tui [Chahar Peace Preservation Corps] when suddenly from both sides our car was shot at. About 35 shots came from service rifles, but only one from a machine gun, which jammed. Two bullet holes were visible in the hood of the car. They then ceased firing and said that they had taken our car to be a Japanese one. I was invited into a farmhouse to have a cup of tea, but while I was there, Jones was bound and taken into another house where the cord which tied his hands was thrown over a rafter in the roof and behind him came a man with a noose, Jones thought that they intended to hang him. He was then brought into the house where I was. The boy brought in our baggage and when I protested at one of the men putting into his pocket some silver dollars, saying it was hardly worthy of the Pao An-tui, one of them replied: "We are not Pao An-tui, we are just bandits".

Meanwhile the bandits had begun to dictate their list of demands to my boy as follows: $100,000 in cash: forty rifles with 20,000 of ammunition: twenty automatic pistols with 20,000 rounds of ammunition: twenty revolvers with 20,000 rounds of ammunition. I added a note to say that we were in the hands of bandits and the notes were given to my boy, who with the chauffeur proceeded to Pao Ch'ang Hsien and Kalgan. On reaching Pao Ch'ang Hsien they reported to the officer in charge of the Pao An-tui and the District

Magistrate. These informed by telephone the Provincial Government at Kalgan and also took appropriate measures to get in contact with the bandits.

There could be no question of using military or police to apply coercion for, apart from the fact that it could endanger our lives, the forces at the disposal of the authorities were in no way sufficient. In June in compliance with the notorious demands of the Japanese, the troops formerly stationed there under the command of Sung Che-yuan were withdrawn. On July 18th the commanding officer of the Special Mission of the Kwantung Army at Dolonor, Major Ueyama appeared at Pao Ch'ang Hsien in person with twenty motor vehicles and six tanks and demanded that the Pao An-tui should be limited to 150 men per district (Hsien) and 100 rounds of ammunition. He did this by frequent visits and intimidation of Chinese officials. Even the District Magistrate was maltreated by one of the Japanese officers. A sergeant of the Pao An-tui and three men were ordered by the officer in command to set off on our trail and found us on the afternoon of the following day.

Jones and I had been deprived of all our personal possessions including our spectacles with the exception of the clothes we were wearing and we were rigged out with long blue trousers with coat to match and a coolie hat simply taken from the peasants standing around.

In the meanwhile the bandits together with their horses had assembled, and we saw that they were about twenty to thirty men strong. Each man carried either a rifle, or a pistol, or a light machine gun. All were mounted, and in addition there were about half a dozen spare horses. We were each given a horse and compelled to ride with the bandits, proceeding partly along tracks and partly across pasture, arable and mountains in a northeasterly direction. In these and the following two days we went in a great bend towards the east, which brought us back again on Tuesday 30th July to the neighbourhood of the main road to Pao Ch'ang Hsien. The treatment they meted out to us was good, as soon as they had got over their first excitement, and the measures taken for our comfort were as good as could be expected in the circumstances. We lived in the wretched plague-infested houses of the poor tenant farmers of this neighbourhood, and for food were dependent on what they had in hand. The bandits took no provisions with them.

The emissary of the Chinese authorities overtook us on Monday afternoon. The sentries posted by the bandits shot at them, but after a white flag had been raised, they were taken prisoner and eventually, when the bandit chief declared himself ready for them, they were unbound and brought before him for an interview.

At about six o'clock that evening, knowing nothing of the arrivals, we met up with two of them and Chang Ye-chi approached us saying that he had come about our liberation. At first we distrusted him and with some scepticism we listened to his announcement that he had been sent by the authorities Pao Ch'ang and that he had not succeeded in securing the release of us both. The ransom was reduced to $50,000 and they were prepared to let me depart if I returned after the performance of my mission. At first they demanded that two of the policemen stay behind, but the bandits relented the next day. It was quite possible that these men were the representatives of another band in which there were Koreans and Japanese and with which after interrogation we would not have much time to live. But Jones and I decided that we did not warrant neglecting such a feeble chance of ultimate freedom. After the bandits had led us back to the village named Kotir on the road to Pao Ch'ang, I took leave of Jones and in three hours I found myself in Pao Ch'ang.

The main reason why the bandits assented to my liberation rather than that of Jones was probably because I had command of the language and that I could conduct negotiations with the Chinese authorities. Gareth Jones was also a better horseman. They themselves said however that I owed the fact of their choice falling on me was because I was a German.

The authorities in Pao Ch'ang received me in a most friendly way. It was decided that Chang Ye-chi should on the morning of August 1st return to and remain in contact with the bandits taking with him some food for Jones. I myself returned by motor vehicle belonging to the Wostwag to Kalgan. There, Lieutenant Millar of the British Embassy was awaiting me and we were joined later by Captain Scott. I reported to these gentlemen and they were both of the agreement that I should return to Peking and report to the British and German Embassies.

On the night of the 31st, I returned to Peking where I reported to the German, British and Chinese authorities and discussed with the Deputy Governor of Chahar, Mr Ch'ien and the representative of the Nanking Government, Mr Wang Keh-min, the measures to be taken for setting Mr Jones at liberty. Both governments declared their readiness to pay any ransom demanded. I returned to Kalgan and found that Chang had been in contact with bandits, that the ransom had been reduced to $8,000, but that he had not been able to secure Jones' release. The bandits then moved over to the Kuyuan neighbourhood and the captain of the Pao An-tui in Kuyuan not being informed of the negotiations set his gendarmerie against them. It seems certain that they were 100 strong moving in three columns. Their leader was Pao Fang-wu to whom were attached two Japanese and the second in command was "old rat Lo". The Japanese had proposed to despatch Jones, but Pao had not assented to this and had handed him over to a smaller group of former Chinese soldiery. A further negotiator was sent to the bandits who was known to me. Chang by now had lost the confidence of the bandits.

Over the next few days there was no information and I visited Colonel Matsui on the fifth. He informed me that the bandits had passed over the Jehol frontier into Manchukuo. He had contacted Jehol City and wished to call troops and aeroplanes into action. This made useless the plan that I should proceed in person to Kuyuan and I returned to Peking

Chapter 16 – Dr Müller's Parole

on the sixth. No information is at hand at present according to Takahashi the Japanese Military Attaché. On the 8th, Jones was seen alive and well, but while the Japanese authorities declare that they have lost contact with the bandits the Chinese assert that though they expected their demands of $8,000 to have satisfied the bandits, Jones was handed over to another group who insist on the original demand of $100,000.

While official reports mention only Chinese bandits, the truth must be somewhat different. The bandits into whose hands we fell made the following declaration: that they were pure Chinese from Manchukuo, that they had entered Japanese service and had received the commission from the Japanese to cross the Chahar border and make as much trouble as they could. They were furnished with uniforms, weapons, and bullion and to prove this they showed me brand new Manchukuo notes of the Central Manchukuo Bank. In Chahar they had found no one who was ready to accept these. They had crossed the Jehol boundary in different sections between the 20th and the 22nd of July, the sections being composed of two large bands of 300 men. They belonged to the first band but in the second band were a number of Koreans under the leadership of Japanese. Had we fallen into the hands of the second band we would have not escaped with our lives. They themselves hated the Japanese, but were compelled to obey Japanese orders for fear of retaliatory measures being taken against their families in Manchukuo.

Our bandits told us their first precise commission was to make an attack on a White Mongol banner [tribe] and kill a Mongol militia leader called Mao because of his strong Chinese propensities. Forty dollars a head was promised if they brought back the Mongol's head to the Japanese. On July 22nd, Sir Charles Bell, Erikson (the Swedish missionary doctor), and Captain Scott and party were travelling along the road towards Larsen's camp from the Dolonor area and in between lay the White Mongol Banner's territory. There they were warned of a previous bandit attack, which seemed to be the same attack of which our bandits spoke about during my capture.

How far the bandits were following orders to create trouble or following specific orders is difficult to ascertain with certainty, but it is very clear that our misfortune occurred on a route recommended by the Japanese and there is the possibility that the rider, who passed our camp on the night of the 27th, was carrying special orders to the bandits. The firing on us on the 28th took place in a way that led us to suppose that the bandits had more to do than merely hold up our car, for apart from the rifles, a machine gun opened fire (made by the Mukden arsenal) and only the circumstance that it jammed, saved us and our car from being hit by more than two bullets. The manner of our capture makes it indubitable that our visit to Dolonor coinciding as it did with preparations for important military action in Chahar was most unwelcome by the Japanese.

On August 20th I made a rebuttal to the Central News Agency on a statement of 'Nanking's Opinion on the Jones' Case' which could not be passed in silence by the surviving member of the party which travelled from Kalgan to Te-Wang-fu, Pei tze-miao, (Beidzemiao) Western Ujmutchin, Eastern Sunnit and Dolonor between July 11th and July 27th and which was attacked by bandits on the way back to Kalgan on the 28th of July.

At the time our party left Kalgan there were no reports of rampant banditry in any parts of Inner Mongolia. A large party of foreigners was staying at Mr Larsen's place and making long excursions into the country without being molested in any way. Others coming from Kalgan and Suiyan converged on the residence of the Western Sunnit Prince to participate in the Obo festival of that tribe, which took place on July 14th.

There was nothing adventurous about a trip in Inner Mongolia at that time and accordingly there was no special warning and the pledge relieving the Chinese authorities, as I, myself, had done it before for years, was a matter of routine. We got permission - valid for one month - to travel to Inner

Mongolia, Erhlien and Pai Ling-miao, but the borders of Inner Mongolia are not yet fixed, there was no warning given against proceeding to Dolonor and consequently the travellers showed no utter disregard to such warning. I am an experienced traveller and have known Inner Mongolia since 1913 and I have gone over thousands of miles there. I know the risks and hardships of travelling in those parts and, when approached by Mr Gareth Jones for advice as to a visit to Inner Mongolia, I recommended a more comfortable trip based on the Suiyan Railway although he was himself making preparations for an extended journey into Eastern Chahar. But advice from a third party prevailed and I consented, very reluctantly, to accept the company of Mr Gareth Jones, telling him quite openly that it was the first time I had taken another foreigner on such a trip and that by doing so I was acting against my principles.

My intention on this trip was to visit Eastern Chahar up to the Manchukuo and outer Mongolian boundary and to study the activities of Japan in those parts. This tallied with Mr Jones' plans, which were to travel in the East in order to study Japanese activities on the Asiatic continent in general. The route which the party took after leaving Dolonor and which has puzzled obviously a number of people, was not of our own choosing, but was recommended to us by the Japanese military authorities at Dolonor who declared all other routes to be impracticable and who dictated to the party the stations to be passed by us, which included Huangchitayingtze, Szelangcheng, Habarga and Pao Ch'ang Hsien.

Though Dr Müller gave this very comprehensive report, much of it was suppressed in the British press by His Majesty's Government (according to *The Week*), particularly the details relating to the presence of Japanese troops in Dolonor for this was considered to be of a politically sensitive nature.

Chapter 17

The British Embassy in China Investigates

Millar - The indefatigable young lieutenant.

As soon as the British Embassy in Peking became aware of Gareth's serious predicament, they immediately instigated on-the-spot support. They also set into motion all the necessary wheels of diplomatic influence that they could exert in order to bring a successful outcome to this unfortunate incident.

On 29th July, The Foreign Office in London telegraphed Sir Alexander Cadogan, the British Ambassador to China:

> According to a press telegram from Pao Ch'ang - British subject Gareth Jones has been captured by bandits. Please telegraph any information and report action being taken.

The investigation of events surrounding the kidnapping and eventual murder of Gareth was set out in a summary report by Mr R. Howe (acting as deputy to Sir Alexander Cadogan in his absence) and sent to the Foreign Office on 13th September:

> On receiving word of Mr Jones' capture, I immediately made representations both to the local authorities and to the Wai Chia Pu [Department of Foreign Affairs] in Nanking, requesting that speedy and effective steps be taken to effect his early release. It was also proposed to take advantage of the presence in Inner Mongolia of Captain Scott (with Sir Charles Bell), one of the military language officers attached to this Embassy, and I accordingly endeavoured to transmit instructions to him to return to Kalgan and make further enquiries into the case. On receiving word through Mr Baker-Carr, the British American Tobacco Company's Kalgan representative, from Dr Müller that he wished to be put in touch as soon as possible with a representative of this Embassy since Mr Jones' life was said to be in danger, I sent Lieutenant Millar another of the military language officers

Chapter 17 – The British Embassy in China

attached to this Embassy, to Kalgan on 30th July with instructions to take such action locally as might be possible to press for Mr Jones' release. At the same time I informed the local authorities and the Wai Chia Pu of Lieutenant Millar's mission[1] and requested them to offer him all assistance, and assurances to this effect were subsequently received. During Millar's stay at Kalgan from 30th July to 21st August he maintained close personal contact and put unremitting pressure on the Chahar Provincial authorities and the local special delegate for foreign affairs and was in constant telephonic communication with the Embassy.

As regards the Japanese authorities, it appeared at first desirable to deal solely with the Chinese authorities so long as the bandits did not cross the Jehol border, in order that they might be afforded no excuse for evading their responsibilities. On receiving word, however, that Mr Jones was in Chengte [Jehol City in Manchukuo] - I instructed the Military Attaché to this Embassy to make enquiries of the Japanese Military Attaché, Colonel Takahashi, as to whether he had any information, and thereafter Colonel Lovat-Fraser kept in close touch with his Japanese colleague.

With respect to the movements of the bandits subsequent to the release of Dr Müller, it appears that shortly after the Pao Ch'ang Hsien district authorities had established contact with the bandits the latter moved to the neighbourhood of Kuyuan Hsien near the Jehol border. Fresh steps were taken by the Chinese authorities to get in touch with the bandits and negotiations were opened with them through the Kuyuan Hsien magistrate.

---

[1] Millar was by no means inexperienced in dealing with kidnappings. Earlier that year while he was in Chungking, in Szechuan province (interviewing General He, the chief representative of the Nanking Government who was most optimistic in his forecast of defeating the Communists in the area). From Chunking, he made a most hazardous journey by sampan down the river Yangtze prior to negotiating the safe release of two missionaries, Messrs Hayman and Bosshardt from Communists in Changsha.

About this period (3rd / 4th August) the bandits moved over the old border of Jehol into Fengning Hsien and this news gave rise to the report that Mr Jones had been rescued by 'Manchukuo' troops and was being escorted to Chengte [Jehol City]. At no time however did the bandits proceed far into Jehol and the Chinese authorities remained in touch with them and continued confident of Mr Jones' eventual release.

On 6th August Lieutenant Millar filed the following status report from Kalgan to his Military Attaché in Peking:

Yesterday evening, Dr Müller informed me by phone that Colonel Matsui, Chief of the Japanese military mission in Kalgan had told him that news had been received that Jones had been taken to the Fengning area in Jehol. Dr Müller stated that the bandits were now a considerable distance inside the Province of Jehol. Matsui also informed Müller that the Japanese authorities in Jehol had been ordered to take all possible steps to effect the release of Jones, and he, Matsui, was of the opinion that this could be accomplished without resort to force.

Müller left for Peking this morning at noon, as he was of the opinion that the Chinese authorities would now be unable to do any more in the matter, and that Jones would be released and would return direct to Peking via Jehol. I understand that Müller intends to proceed to Jehol, if possible.

This morning I interviewed Mr Yueh, the Commissioner for Foreign Affairs, who asked my opinion as to the reliability of Müller, to which I replied that having met him for the first time a few days ago, and knowing nothing concerning his history, I was unable to form any definite opinion. Mr Yueh was of the opinion that Müller's story should be accepted with reserve, but he declined to be more explicit.

Apart from the statement of Nair (Secretary of the Pan-Asiatic League) it was generally believed that the Japanese were preparing to take some more definite action but whether or not this would take the form of military action, was not known.

At 2.30 p.m. this afternoon I interviewed Mr Yang, who as Chief Representative of the Chahar Government in Kalgan, is responsible for the conduct of this case. This interview, unlike its predecessor, was characterised by the greatest secrecy, only Mr Yang, a secretary, and myself being present. It took place in a small room, all the doors and windows being closed, and to which no attendants etc., were allowed access. In my very limited experience these precautions are rarely adopted by the Chinese, even if the subject under discussion is confidential. The following is a record of Mr Yang's statement:

The Japanese at Dolonor being incensed at Dr Müller's inquisitiveness (he had examined their cars, taken photographs, and made numerous enquiries concerning their intentions etc.), had deliberately advised him not to take the usual road on his return journey, and had then organised the capture of himself and Jones.

Pao Fang Wu, [the bandit chief, a former Chinese military officer living in the Japanese concession at Tientsin], then asked the Japanese how the two prisoners should be disposed of, and the Japanese agreed that Dr Müller, being German, should be released and that Jones, being English, should be retained. After Müller was released and had told his story in Kalgan and Peking, which tended to implicate the Japanese, the latter blamed Pao for releasing him and placed Pao under arrest - he is still in confinement. Jones was then handed over to another group of bandits under the leadership of Tuan - these bandits are mostly disbanded soldiers. The two Japanese advisors are still in attendance. The final demand for $8,000 was made without the knowledge of the Japanese, Pao being in a semi-independent position.

Yesterday, an emissary despatched from Kuyuan returned, having gained contact with the Tuan group of bandits. He stated that at the instigation of the Japanese the ransom demanded had been increased to $100,000, but that Jones' life was not in danger. These bandits moved continually, but were normally only a "few tens of li" within the Jehol country.

The Provincial Authorities were now negotiating for the release of Jones, outwardly, with Tuan, but in fact with his Japanese advisers. (A "face-saving" device.)

The Japanese military mission at Kalgan and Dolonor had recently both approached the Provincial Authorities asking if they could be of any assistance in effecting Jones' release - these offers have not yet been accepted.

There are representatives of three separate and semi-independent Japanese Military organisations in the Jehol-Chahar-Inner Mongolia area viz: The Kwantung Special Service Bureau, the Tientsin Protocol Troops, and the Manchukuo. It is uncertain as to which of these organisations the Japanese [advisors] belong.

Finally, Mr Yang said that he would like to ask my advice as to whether or not the Provincial Authorities should accept the Japanese offer of assistance, to which I replied:

1. That H. M. Embassy was concerned, not with ways and means, but with results.
2. That I was not in a position to offer any advice on such a subject not being fully conversant with the local Sino-Japanese situation.
3. That this was a question of policy, entirely dependant on whether or not the Chinese authorities considered they were in a position speedily to effect the release of Jones without Japanese assistance - a question they alone could decide.

I then asked Mr Yang the following questions:

Millar: Are you satisfied that the information you have received tending to implicate the Japanese is entirely to be relied on?
Yang: Yes, the evidence we have received that this outrage was instigated by the Japanese is conclusive.
Millar: If, as you say, the Japanese are responsible for this affair, do you consider it likely that they will cause Jones to be released merely on the payment of a ransom?
Yang: We hope so, and we are working on this assumption, should this prove incorrect, then we will have no alternative but to accept the offer of Japanese co-operation.
Millar: Apart from the most obvious consideration (implying consequent "loss of face") why are you unwilling to accept the Japanese offer of assistance?
Yang: Because we fear that such assistance would be granted only at a price which we could ill afford to pay e.g. in return for some political concession.
Millar: Why, if the Japanese were annoyed at Dr Müller's actions, and for this reason arranged his capture, do you suppose that they ordered his release?
Yang: Because he is a German and the relations of the Germans and the Japanese are very friendly.

This interview has been described at some length, in the hope of providing sufficient material to make possible an appreciation of the situation.

It would appear that the possibility of Jones' release being affected solely by the efforts of the Chinese authorities, is somewhat remote. On the other hand their methods are so torturous and obscure that they may be able to elicit "unofficial" Japanese assistance through the two Japanese advisers said to be working with the bandits.

If, however, this affair is of Japanese instigation, one has no reason to suppose that Jones will be released unless the Chinese make official representations to the Japanese, or the matter is taken up with the Japanese by the H. M. Embassy.

Again, it is more likely that the Chinese Authorities unaided, have little or no hope of affecting Jones' release, but are unwilling to admit this.

The period after Millar's above 6th August dispatch is taken up again by Mr Howe's summary report to the Foreign Office:

The bandits then moved west again into what is nominally Chinese territory and on the 9th August the Chinese authorities at Kalgan informed Lieutenant Millar that Mr Jones had been seen the previous evening at a place about halfway between Kuyuan and Tushih K'ou, and that he was thin but in good health. The bandits now split into two bands, the one going northwest towards Pao Ch'ang and the other retracing its steps southeast. It was not known with certainty which band held Mr Jones but it was thought probable by the Chinese authorities that he was with the latter. Difficulties hitherto unexplained occurred in the progress of the negotiations and the middleman sent to negotiate with the bandits is said to have been detained and later shot. Doubtless in consequence of this development the Chinese authorities decided to take action to surround the former band, no action being possible against the latter owing to their proximity to the Jehol border. The next development was that on the 16th August Lieutenant Millar received a report that a foreigner had been shot by bandits in the Pao Ch'ang area and on the following day he was informed by the Chahar Provincial authorities that the person in question was Mr Jones.

Then on the 22nd August Millar submitted his final report, including witness statements and a death certificate to the British Military Attaché in Peking:

Late on the evening of the 17th I was informed that I could proceed to Pao Ch'ang providing my departure was kept strictly secret. At 6.30 a.m. on the 18th, clothed as if paying an ordinary visit and without any baggage, I arrived at the Provincial Government Headquarters. I was there provided with a large "Japanese mouthpad", a long Chinese coat, and large goggles. Two lorries and an escort of about 17 men armed with Light M.G.'s [machine guns], pistols and swords were waiting, accompanied by Mr Chai Wei-chi, representative of the Provincial Government. I left Kalgan at about 7.45 a.m. and Mr Chai throughout the journey held up a large umbrella to screen me from the passers by.

Ten miles from Pao Ch'ang we were met by a Guard of Honour of about one squadron of Pao An-tui. A general salute was blown by two trumpeters - disregarding Mr Chai's protests, I discarded my 'disguise', descended from the lorry, and inspected the Guard.

We then continued on our way for another five miles, accompanied by the Guard of Honour, who galloped alongside the lorries, and encountered another Guard of Honour. The same procedure was adopted, and this Guard accompanied us to Pao Ch'ang.

We arrived at Pao Ch'ang at 4 p.m. in a very dirty condition and feeling rather shaken and tired, as the road in parts is very bad, and were accorded what might be described as a 'Civic Reception'.

Drawn up on either side of the city gate was a vast throng with several banners - mounted and foot Pao An-tui - all the notables of the district, many of them ancient and venerable old men - school children clad in their best clothes, marshalled by their teachers, the late District Magistrate, and his successor - General Chia the Commander of the Pao An-tui and his staff - and a crowd of Chinese and Mongol onlookers. On jumping off the lorry we were greeted by a trumpet fanfare, I was then introduced to the two District Magistrates, and other notables, and after attempting to say a few appropriate words, we entered the city.

Rooms had been prepared, and a Guard of three men with swords, remained night and day at the entrance of the house, another three men armed with pistols, were posted at the gate. On leaving the compound we were always escorted by a Guard of at least three.

Six men were detailed to act as servants and everything possible was done to make us comfortable. Immediately on arrival, I inspected the body [see Appendix IV – Identification of Gareth Jones' Body].

The examination of the various witnesses continued until midnight, and on the next day up to 8 p.m. (19th).

The first witness in the case, Chiang Yung Kui, was the ex-Pao Ch'ang Magistrate (until 12th August before taking up the post of Magistrate at K'an Pao) and said:

> On the 28th July, sometime after 12 noon, a Russian chauffeur reported to me in Pao Ch'ang that one German and one Englishman had been captured on that day by bandits near Kuan Ha Kou, about 40 Li northeast of Pao Ch'ang. He also brought a written demand from the bandits for arms, ammunition, and $100,000 to be delivered in ten days, in exchange for the prisoners. I immediately informed the Provincial Government by wire, and despatched Chang Yun Chui with three policemen to get into touch with the bandits and negotiate for the release of the prisoners. I instructed Chang to inform the bandits that if they doubted the good faith of the Chinese authorities, some would be sent to act as hostages. On the 30th these men returned with Dr Müller, and reported the bandits' revised demands. On the morning I again despatched Chang instructing him to ask the bandits if they would accept any kind of notes, as it was difficult, if not impossible, to collect in a short time so many notes of the kind they had demanded. I also wired the Provincial Authorities. Chang returned on the night of the 31st and informed me of the bandits' increased demands.
>
> On 2nd August I was informed that the bandits had gone to the Kuyuan area. I at once wired to the Kuyuan Magistrate asking him to do everything possible to effect the release of the captive, and at the same time despatched Li Yu to try to get in touch with the bandits. I informed him that

even if the bandits had crossed into Jehol, he must still endeavour to get in touch with them.

On August 2nd or 3rd I received a wire from the Kuyuan Magistrate, stating the bandits had crossed the border into Jehol. I received no further news until Li Yu returned on August 10th.

On the 11th, I was informed that the bandits had returned to the Pao Ch'ang area, so I despatched two police officers to search for them. One took with him 20 policemen who were to remain in the vicinity, whilst the other was to negotiate. On the 13th they returned saying that the bandits were divided into many groups, and that it was impossible to discover by which group Jones was held. Neither would they allow the police officer to approach.

(Note: on interrogating this police officer it was found that the bandits with whom he had been attempting to negotiate could not have been those by whom Jones was held - a question of times and distances.)

The second witness was Chang Yun Chi, a Lieutenant of the Pao Ch'ang Pao An-tui, who said that:

On the morning of the 29th July having received instructions from Chiang Yung Kui, then District Magistrate of Pao Ch'ang I proceeded with five policemen to Kuan Ma Kou. About 20 Li southeast of Kuan Ma Kou we encountered some bandits who fired at us, I waved my hand as a sign to them, and they stopped firing. On approaching them, they seized, bound and searched us. We were then placed in separate rooms in a small village. This was at about 4 p.m. on the 29th July. I discussed the question of the release of the two foreigners with them for a very long time - they appeared to have no particular leader, and seemed to be the ordinary rough type of bandit. They said that they wanted $100,000 and a quantity of arms and ammunition as a ransom for the prisoners. Finally they said they would accept $50,000 providing the notes were all of the "International Bank of Communications", were not of consecutive numbers, had no special marks on them, and were not new.

I saw both foreigners in the village, and was permitted to say a few words to the German.

Early on the morning of the 30th we all moved off towards the west, and after walking about 10-15 Li they stopped, and allowed the German to go away with us. They informed us before our departure that unless the ransom was produced in seven days, the Englishman would be shot.

We arrived at Pao Ch'ang at about 4 p.m. on the 29th. Having received instructions from Chiang Yung Kui, I again went in search of the bandits at 10 a.m. on the 30th and found them near Ch'a Han Nao Pao about 40 Li northeast of Pao Ch'ang at 6 p.m.. There were about 90 of them, the day before there had been about 30. They refused to extend the time limit, or alter their demands regarding the kinds of notes, and in addition they said that they again required arms and ammunition. I returned to Pao Ch'ang at about midnight 31st August and reported to the District Magistrate.

On the next day I was ill. I know no more concerning this case.

The third witness was Li Hsiang, of Meng Chia Ying-Tse, - the cowherd who saw Gareth being shot testified:

At about 12 noon, six or seven days ago (note: this would be on the 11th or 12th) I was about four or five Li east of Meng Chia Ying, looking after my cows, when 60 or 70 armed mounted men arrived from the north. They were not dressed in uniform. They came to within a few hundred yards of where l was standing, dismounted, and formed a circle, I was afraid, and so lay down. I then heard three shots in rapid succession. The men then mounted and rode away towards the south through T'ou Ta-kou. I then collected the cows which had strayed, and whilst doing so, saw a body lying on the ground. I went up to the body, which was laying face upwards, and found it was that of a foreigner with dark hair and blue eyes, wearing Chinese clothing. Blood was flowing from the top of the head and around the mouth. I returned to my village and told the villagers what I had seen, and then went about my business. I did not touch the body, but the foreigner appeared dead. At about 5 p.m. about one hundred Pao An-tui arrived from the north, they were mounted. One of them asked me if I had seen the bandits, I then told them the whole story, and led them to the corpse.

They appeared very agitated on seeing the dead foreigner, and cursed the bandits. Leaving a few men in charge of the corpse, the remainder went off in pursuit of the bandits. At about 7 p.m. I heard faint sounds of firing from the south.

I do not know how the body was disposed of, and know nothing more concerning the case.

The last witness was the Lieutenant of the Pao Ch'ang Pao An-tui, who pursued the bandits after Gareth was left for dead:

At about 4 a.m. on August 12th I started out with about one hundred mounted Pao An-tui in search of bandits. After several detours I arrived at Meng Chia Ying Tse about 4 p.m.. There I met a cowherd who guided me to the dead body of a foreigner, and he informed me of the circumstances of his death. Having left an officer in charge of the corpse, I went in pursuit of the bandits with the remainder of my men. I encountered the bandits about 40 Li south of Meng Chia Ying Tse and in the ensuing engagement four were killed and one seriously wounded. On questioning the wounded man, he said that the foreigner had refused to eat any food for three or four days and was unable to keep up with the bandits. On arrival near Meng Chia Ying Tse he had refused to mount his horse and had therefore been shot. The wounded bandit was unable to answer any more questions and died within a few hours.

It being already dark, we were unable to pursue the bandits any further, so returned to a village near Meng Chia Ying Tse, whence I despatched Chou-man, a local farmer with a written message reporting the incident to General Chia Tse Wen, Commander of the Pao An-tui at Pao Ch'ang. I gave this message to Chou-Man at midnight on the night of 12/13th, and he started for Pao Ch'ang at once. I remained until the 13th, and on the 14th A.D.C. Yu Yung Ling arrived. I handed the body over to him.

Lieutenant Millar ended his investigation by giving brief details of his return trip to Peking accompanying Gareth's coffin, including a description of a Chinese memorial service for Gareth held in Kalgan:

Owing to heavy rain on the night of the 18th/19th it was doubtful if the road to Kalgan would be passable on the 20th, as it is entirely unmetalled. The intervening period being dry, however, we started the return journey with the coffin at 9.30 a.m. on the 20th.

About two miles outside Kalgan we were met by a large police escort, and a band, from there we drove direct to a hall which had been prepared for the reception of the coffin. The hall was decorated with wreathes and silk hangings to which were attached Chinese characters in gold, indicating the good wishes of the Chinese authorities for the dead man, and sympathy for his parents. The ensuing ceremony was short, but most impressive. A table had been spread in front of the coffin on which were arranged lighted candles, incense-burners, and various fruits and flowers. The chief officials, civil, military and police of the Chahar Provincial Government were all present. Led by Mr Yang, the Chief Secretary, they walked passed the coffin, turned, and made three bows, murmuring some sentences in Chinese. They slowly resumed their places, and a short silence was observed.

A silk hanging was presented to me by the Commissioner for Foreign Affairs, with the request that it might be sent to the parents of the deceased.[2]

In short, everything possible was done by the Provincial Authorities to express their respect for the dead man, and deep commiserations for his parents.

All arrangements have been made for sending the body by rail to Peking. A representative of the Provincial Government was detailed to accompany me, and having telephoned Mr Howe on the previous night, we were met by the Embassy Constable on our arrival at Peking at 4 p.m. on the 21st.

---

[2] The banners were inscribed: "To the memory of the British journalist Gareth Jones. Cut off in his prime as by frost in the midst of high summer". "The valiant soul endures for ever". The Chahar Provincial Government: "Scorning the risks of death he attained perfect virtue". The Chahar Peace Preservation Bureau: "Regardless of personal safety, he placed duty first".

Chapter 18
Lloyd George Contacts The Foreign Office

Mr A.J. Sylvester, David Lloyd George's Private Secretary, investigates.

"If it were not for Lloyd George's secretary, who has been wonderful, nothing would have been done. Little do they care! So much for our Foreign Office!" - Mrs Edgar Jones, Gareth's mother.

If the numerous letters, minutes, reports and memoranda are taken into account, the Foreign Office cannot be said to have been negligent in Gareth's case. There are nearly 500 pages in the Foreign Office files kept secret in the Public Record Office Archives at Kew Gardens, London, until 1965 under the 30 year disclosure rules. Mr Sylvester instigated much of it and the fact that he was David Lloyd George's Private Secretary carried much weight. Gareth's father, Major Edgar Jones, notified the ex-Prime Minister as soon as he had heard of his son's plight and, through the latter's secretary, the Foreign Office was contacted on July 29th to the effect that a press telegram had reported that Gareth had been captured by bandits in Inner Mongolia. Sylvester telephoned the news to the Foreign Office who said that they had no knowledge of the fact and so would contact Peking. Later they informed him that bandits had abducted Gareth and a German named Müller near Pao Ch'ang. He was also told that Sir Alexander Cadogan had made representations to Wai Chia Pu (The Department of Foreign Affairs) and the local authorities.

Mr Sylvester acted as an intermediary and, when informed of events, he conveyed the news to Gareth's father. Much of this was reported in the newspapers, though the troop movements in Dolonor as well as Dr Müller's full account were suppressed by a self-imposed press censorship influenced by the British Establishment.

On 16th August, the press reported Gareth's murder and that his parents were asking to bring his body home as they wished to bury him in his beloved Wales. In a letter to Gareth's sister, Eirian, his mother wrote while discussing the final arrangements for their return: "I feel very sad about everything. I want the ashes with us at home. I

Chapter 18 – Lloyd George Contacts The Foreign Office

shall feel more at ease then." The casket with his ashes came home on December 19th in the steam ship *SS Rawalpindi* for burial in the Merthyr Dyfan cemetery in Barry.

Gareth's parents called to see Mr Sylvester on September 2nd 1935. They were particularly concerned as to what had happened to his possessions and in particular his diaries and notebooks. Some photographs appeared in *The Western Mail* on August 23rd and also in other papers which they believed had been taken with his camera. The camera was never retrieved, but the remaining photos were and the diaries, eventually, though unaccountably, and these were returned to his parents. The Embassy Officials had, however, read them before their return and remarked on certain entries.

On 3rd September, Mr Sylvester wrote to Mr C.W. Orde at the Foreign Office in order to clear up some points on their behalf:

> Mr Lloyd George would like a full enquiry to be made into the tragic affair of Gareth's death if the Foreign Office had not already done so in order to establish just how the whole tragedy had happened, and precisely who gave advice to Gareth Jones and what that advice was.

On the 7th September Mr Sylvester wrote to Mr Orde of the Foreign Office saying that:

> I have this morning received a letter from the person with whom I had an interview the other day, which sets out in large measure what I have already written you, but in some way amplifies it. I am therefore sending you an extract from this letter regarding Gareth Jones and should be obliged if you would have all these points carefully examined and incorporated in the full report from the Foreign Office:
>
> > ... I had passed on to you the suspicion that is in the minds of some of his [Gareth] friends that he may have been the victim of a plot to get him out of the way because of some knowledge he may have happened on that neither the Japanese nor the Germans would want to have published. She (possibly one Adelaide Hooker who was in Kalgan around

August 2nd) told me - what I had not heard before - that the chauffeur of the car in which he and Dr Müller were driving was Russian, if he was a White Russian that would fit in well with this theory. If on the other hand he was a Communist it might be that he had an interest in getting hold of Gareth Jones' papers from a different point of view. Or he may have had nothing to do with the affair. <u>But what happened to him?</u> And the car? In any case it seems to me that I have seen no mention of that. Every effort should be made, in the interests of the Foreign Office no less than of Gareth Jones' parents, to recover his papers, find out by cross-questioning Dr Müller just what happened to their belongings when they were captured, whether he (Dr Müller) brought all his own papers safely away, how Gareth Jones' telegram to his parents was dispatched (I have not seen any explanation of this in any of the press accounts); how it was that the brigands who are supposed to have captured them were themselves captured some 200 miles away from the place where Gareth Jones' body was found; whether any medical evidence was taken as to how long he had been dead. If I remember rightly it was an Englishman named Miller attached to the British Legation (and not Dr Müller) who identified the body?

There is much need for further information on a number of points. As I suggested to you in our talk I should think it would be quite worthwhile for the Foreign Office to arrange for a trained lawyer skilled at cross-questioning – or a detective? – to see Dr Müller, ostensibly on behalf of Gareth Jones' relatives, and see what light he can obtain on the whole affair. He should of course know German well – though apparently Dr Müller is at home in the English language.

Someone with expert diplomatic knowledge speaking at a private meeting at which I was present some months ago said that if the archives at the Japanese and German War Offices became accessible to the public they would probably reveal a very close and friendly understanding, if not actually a Treaty for Mutual Assistance, between those two war-minded Powers.

Chapter 18 – Lloyd George Contacts The Foreign Office

On 16th September, Sylvester sent the following letter to Mr Orde:

I am very much obliged to you for your letter of the 13th September which I am laying before Lloyd George. I shall await further communication from you when you receive the information. Meantime I enclose herewith a copy of *The Week* dated September 11th which has just come into my hands. The effect of reading this only increases one's suspicions of the whole affair, including Dr Müller.

The report in *The Week* alleged that:

It was on July 25th that they arrived in Dolonor. To their astonishment they found the place beflagged with the flags of a Japanese-controlled independent government, supported by the presence of a fully mechanised brigade of Japanese troops, composed of four thousand men[1] and four hundred automobiles, among which were included a number of tanks.

"They observed", said Müller: "that the crews of the tanks were in part made up of '*émigré*' White Guards". Astonished by these facts, they visited the Japanese headquarters. There they found an Indian gentleman named Nair who explained that he had once been a member of the Indian National Assembly, but was now head of the Pan-Asiatic League, the Japanese organisation for the extension of Japanese domination over Asia. Müller told those to whom he disclosed these facts that when the Indian was questioned as to why the town of Dolonor was so stiff with Japanese troops, the reply was that: "they had come to protect the population". It was after leaving the Japanese headquarters that the climax of their discoveries was reached. As they passed through the town they came upon a notice board, and upon the noticeboard was boldly written: 'Headquarters of the Autonomous Government of East Chahar'.

---

[1] The author notes that depending on the source this figure varies.

The significance of the noticeboard was unmistakable. They had stumbled into the very middle of an event designed to alter the history of Asia. They copied the wording on the noticeboard and it was at this point that they were arrested.

Back at Japanese headquarters, the Indian of the Pan-Asiatic League informed them they were under arrest on suspicion of espionage. They had been seen making notes and examining military transports. They were then grilled by a succession of Japanese officers, kept under arrest for several hours, and finally told that during the rest of their stay in Dolonor they must not leave the hotel where they were staying.

When they left Dolonor there were three roads they could take. The Japanese, so Dr Müller told our informant in Peking, 'strongly recommended' one of those roads. They took that road, and it was on that road that the bandits captured them. The bandits were not in the technical sense of the word bandits at all. They were Chinese nationalists from Jehol. The Japanese, who retained their families 'under control' as a form of hostage for the good behaviour of the 'hired' bandits, had recruited them.

Gareth Jones was at one time member of the Lloyd George Secretariat – and at the first news of the kidnapping Lloyd George went to the Foreign Office for information and, it was suggested, to stimulate action. A little later Lloyd George gave out a strange press statement wherein he suggested that Gareth Jones had been murdered not out of pure banditry, but because he had probably unearthed some dangerous political secret. And after that Lloyd George said nothing; and the newspapers wrote the customary obituaries of deep regret.

Why did Lloyd George, who had obviously 'got a sniff' of the truth somewhere – presumably at the Foreign Office suddenly shut up and say nothing? Is it, in other words, to be supposed that the imperial considerations

Chapter 18 – Lloyd George Contacts The Foreign Office

involved are of so powerful a character that the Foreign Office was able to persuade Lloyd George to remain silent? As for the Germans, their attitude was fully intelligible, since they had a military "understanding" with Japan, and in any case they could scarcely have been expected to be more active on behalf of a British subject than the British Government itself. As for the journalists to whom the Müller story was given, our information is that they did all they could; they cabled the right facts. And later the Foreign Office "advised" against publication.

This prompted the following comments from the Foreign Office on 17th September:

It is not clear why, if both Gareth Jones and Müller found out the secret of Japanese designs on Chahar (of which the whole world was aware at the time), only Gareth Jones and not Müller was murdered by the alleged bandits in Japanese pay. Otherwise the story is fairly plausible and certainly sensational, with the Foreign Office living up to its reputation for international intrigue.

Personally I do not believe that there is anything at all in these suspicions of Japanese foul play. But given that there were [suspicions] I suppose that it would be quite impossible to get at the truth. We can but act as suggested.

Following this letter 16th of September from Mr Sylvester, Mr Orde of the Foreign Office sought advice from a Whitehall colleague, Mr Kitson:

I have had several letters from Mr Sylvester regarding this case. We can give Lloyd George, as a former employer of Mr Gareth Jones, a great deal of information, which is of legitimate interest in the case. The basis that there is a German-Japanese conspiracy is far-fetched. I cannot help imagining that Mr Lloyd George is trying to make political capital out of this. We could tell Mr Sylvester that we are trying to get hold of Müller and take his story.

Mr Kitson wrote in reply:

> This story is very sensational, but there is just some possibility that there is some truth in it. We might send copy of the letter to Sir Alexander Cadogan and to the Berlin Chancery to see if they have any information on Müller.

In consequence of this note, the Foreign Office sent copies of Sylvester's letter to the British Embassies in Peking and Berlin.

The British Embassy in China denied the theory of a German-Japanese pact. "There is evidence that at least some members of the Japanese staff are in contact with the Germans, but no evidence to connect them." On 18th September, Sir Alexander Cadogan met Mr Hsu Mo (whom Gareth had interviewed in Nanking) at the Wai Chia Pu and pressed for further information regarding the murder of Gareth Jones, which His Majesty's Ambassador said he would: "like to receive in time for use in answering questions which would undoubtedly be asked in Parliament."

Mr Basil Newton of the Berlin Embassy was asked for information on Müller and was assured that the Foreign Office would not necessarily pass everything on for "internal political reasons". On 26th September 1935, he replied that:

> Unless General von Blomberg,[2] some officials at the War Ministry and Ministry of Foreign Affairs are the most arrant liars there is no treaty or entente between Japan and Germany today. What is more, in view of Hitler's peculiar views on racial questions - which are no joke as any German Jew can testify - it will take a good deal of persuading him to join with Japan or any other exotic race against the chosen Aryan stock.

These Embassy replies suggest that the Foreign Office was completely unaware of any German–Japanese negotiations and were not trying to hide any suggestion of an impending agreement.

---

[2] The German Minister of War.

Chapter 18 – Lloyd George Contacts The Foreign Office

On September 23rd, A.W.G. Randall of the Foreign Office stated that there was no foundation whatever to substantiate a German-Japanese Pact.[3] He noted that Messrs Jones and Müller made the trip against the advice of the local and British authorities and had signed a voluntary bond disclaiming the Chinese authorities of responsibility.

Autographed photo of David Lloyd George to Gareth.

On 5th November, Kitson produced the following report:

This is the comprehensive report referred to in the Peking despatch. It contains all the available evidence covering the

---

[3] Even by May 1934, the United States Military Attaché in Berlin, Lieutenant Colonel Wuest, reported that evidence was accumulating which tended "to show the existence of unusually close and friendly relations between Germany and Japan even to the extent of a possible secret alliance". Also see Endnote on page 213 regarding later U.S. suspicions of a German–Japanese alliance in 1935.

case from the time of Müller and Jones' departure from Peking to Jones' death and the identification of his body. After recapitulating all the facts of the case and assessing the evidence supplied by the enclosures to this despatch, Mr Howe reaches the conclusion that while certain Japanese elements may have been connected with the bandits and while the Japanese military authorities may have been responsible for their original presence in the area in question the Japanese authorities must be acquitted of direct connivance in the affair and that the actual kidnapping was the work of the bandits themselves.

In assessing this case we are largely dependent for the truth on the evidence of the only available witness of the kidnapping, and Mr Jones' companion, Dr Müller; and a perusal of his report, supported by the evidence contained in certain of the other enclosures, bears out to a marked degree the story contained in *The Week*. In his report, Dr Müller shows that the road taken by himself and Jones from Dolonor to Kalgan was recommended to them by the Japanese in Dolonor who had previously arrested them in the belief that they were after military secrets. Later in the same report Müller says that the bandits told him that he owed his release to the fact that he was a German. This is corroborated by the statement of Mr Yang, the chief representative of the Chahar Government in Kalgan, who expressed to Lieutenant Millar the view that Müller was released because he was a German, "and the relations of the Germans and the Japanese are friendly". This evidence lends colour to Mr Sylvester's allegation regarding a German-Japanese understanding. At the beginning of his report, Müller states that two Japanese were attached to the band which held Jones, and that these Japanese had proposed to despatch him, but the Chinese leader of the band had refused. Later he quotes the bandits as having declared that they had entered the Japanese service and had been commissioned by a Japanese authority in Jehol to cross the Chahar border and create as much trouble there as they could.

Chapter 18 – Lloyd George Contacts The Foreign Office

This despatch was written before Sir A. Cadogan had received copies of Mr Sylvester's letters but presumably the latter will not materially affect the conclusion quoted in the first paragraph of this minute, which represents the considered view of the Embassy after consideration of the very facts (i.e. Müller's evidence) on which Mr Sylvester's allegations and *The Week's* report are apparently based. But I am afraid that if we were to send Mr Sylvester the enclosures to this despatch it would be difficult to get either him or Mr Lloyd George to agree with Peking's conclusion, and Mr Lloyd George would probably be provided with some useful ammunition for awkward questions in the next Parliament.

I suggest that for the present we should take no action on this despatch, but await Sir A. Cadogan's considered views on the letters from Mr Sylvester which have been forwarded to him, before making any communication to Mr Sylvester on the matter.

The despatch also clears up one or two of the points raised in Mr Sylvester's original letter. For instance it informs us for the first time of the presence on the trip of Baron von Plessen. It also throws light on the question of Müller's release and his subsequent failure to return. Müller says that the bandits at first asked him to return after his negotiations for the release; later, however, they waived their demand that he should go back to them. He says that both Lieutenant Millar and Captain Scott agreed with him that his liberation must necessarily be final (i.e. that he need not return).

The following are hand written comments from the Foreign Office appraising this document:

I have now read this report and annexes, and agree that it is premature to disclose any of it to Mr Lloyd George. The Embassy in Peking has been asked for their opinion on the allegation of Japanese complicity and on the suspicions regarding Dr Müller. Until they reply we must do nothing and if Mr Sylvester asks we can tell him we are awaiting a complete report from Peking, with particular points raised by him.

In the meantime it will be noted that the allegations of Japanese complicity are mainly from a Chinese source (the report in Kalgan of the Chahar Government); without confirmation these may well be open to doubt. Yet there is sufficient evidence of the Japanese being mixed up in the case (bandits once being in Japanese service, Japanese directions as to the route) to cause Mr Howe to qualify to a certain extent his denial of direct Japanese connivance.

I am afraid that the wording of this despatch would be hell to justify Mr Sylvester's worst (and no doubt, largely unwarrantable) suspicions. We must therefore wait for a direct answer to our direct questions to Peking.
(SGD) A.W.G. Randall. Dated 8/11/1935

I agree with above appreciations and that we should wait for what is still to come from Peking. We must be very careful meanwhile what we say to Mr Sylvester and avoid if possible that there are 'complete reports' which we might then be asked to publish. Publication would serve no useful purpose and would only make trouble. These are facts which justify suspicions but we should never be able to get further than that.

Müller's frankness as to the route having been recommended by the Japanese rather tends against the theory that he was in league with them.
(SGD) C.W. Orde. Dated 11/11/35

In the Foreign Affairs debates of 1935 and 1936 in which Lloyd George spoke, there was no reference to Gareth's capture or murder. Questions were asked in Parliament in 1935 concerning the plight of British Nationals held for ransom in China during the previous four years and the reply was that Gareth was the only known victim of banditry despite a number of persons being made captive. A year later there was further reference to Gareth in Parliament and it was reported in Hansard that:

Chapter 18 – Lloyd George Contacts The Foreign Office

On Monday, July 13th, 1936, Mr H. Day, M.P., asked the Under Secretary of State for Foreign Affairs the names of British Subjects kidnapped in the past year and held for ransom; of which have now been released by their captors; what ransom was demanded; and what amount was paid.

Viscount Cranborne replied for the Government that:

During the period from July 1st, 1935, to the present time, there only occurred one case in which a British subject was involved. Mr Gareth Jones was captured by disbanded bandit soldiers in Eastern Chahar on July 27th, 1935. His captors originally demanded $100,000 and a supply of arms. Negotiations for his release were rendered impossible by the subsequent rapid movements of the bandits, who eventually killed their captive on August 16th.

The Foreign Office acted in line with the policy which later became known as 'appeasement'. If, in so doing, their aim was to thwart Lloyd George from discovering the truth about a possible German-Japanese alliance, then they were clearly successful. However in so doing they also prevented Sylvester and the Jones family from finding out the truth about Gareth Jones' murder.

ENDNOTE

Memorandum by the U.S. Minister to Austria (George Messersmith) regarding a conversation with the U.S. Ambassador in Germany (Dodd), Berlin, March 22, 1935.

I mentioned a despatch about the Chinese Minister in Vienna having said that I had told him that there was a Japanese-German understanding, if not alliance. I told him that I had not made such a statement but that I had told the Chinese Minister that in May and June, 1933 I had heard talk in Berlin that the Nazis and Japanese were trying to get together. I told the Ambassador that I had good reason to believe at the time that this was so, but I did not know how far it had gone. He said that he thought this had continued and that he felt that it had gone pretty far and he was not at all sure that there was not a very thorough understanding and perhaps even a very far-reaching one.

Chapter 19
Baron von Plessen

Prince Otto von Bismarck's cousin.[1]

Baron von Plessen.

Wolf von Dewall, a good friend of Gareth, who was the London correspondent for *Die Frankfurter Zeitung,* wrote to Gareth's parents on 26th September 1935 and told them that he had met Prince Otto von Bismarck, Counsellor at the German Embassy in London. The Prince had told him that:

> Baron von Plessen, his cousin was actually with Gareth and Müller in Mongolia, but had to leave them eight days before, as the end of his vacation demanded it. Since coming back I have read the awful story in *The Week*. I cannot say I believe every word of it.

---

[1] A descendant of the first Chancellor of Germany, Prince Otto von Bismarck.

Wolf von Dewall, his wife and a friend [from a Newport newspaper cutting date uncertain].

The Foreign Office, in reply to Mr Sylvester's request on the 3rd September, was told only that Baron von Plessen was a counsellor at the German Embassy in Peking and that they thought he had not accompanied the pair on their travels.

Sylvester, determined to get to the bottom of the mystery of his colleague's death wrote on 6th September from the Office of Mr David Lloyd George to Mr Timperley, the China correspondent for the *Manchester Guardian*. As the letter later caused so much anguish to Baron von Plessen the letter is quoted in full:

> I am writing to ask your kind assistance to see whether you can throw any light on the tragic death of my friend and late colleague Gareth Jones.
>
> His parents, whom I know very well, came to see me the other day and on behalf of Mr Lloyd George. I am in touch with the Foreign Office with regard to the whole affair. I have asked them to look into the matter of his property, his

books, his diaries, his camera, etc., etc., to see that all these things are returned to his parents. If however, you can be of any assistance in these matters, I know that his parents will be grateful, as I shall be myself.

There are things, however, which appear to his parents to be most unsatisfactory and upon which there is very little information.

For instance, the Foreign Office have informed us that Gareth Jones went on this trip to Inner Mongolia against the advice of the British authorities in Peking. On the other hand, I have an extract from a letter from Gareth Jones written to his mother, which reads as follows:

Then suddenly as I am drinking tea near the swimming pool of the club, where I am a temporary member, Baron von Plessen comes up and says: 'Would you like to join Dr Müller and me in an excursion into Inner Mongolia to visit Prince Teh Wang; at the meeting of the Princes? There will be a car at our disposal' - so I jumped at the offer. I shall be away about a week. ABSOLUTELY SAFE COUNTRY, NO BANDITS.

Surely if he went as a member of this private mission at the invitation of a German diplomat, one would suppose they had some responsibility for his safety. It is not clear whether Baron von Plessen went on the mission, but we do know that Dr Müller went. The question that is everywhere being asked is "Who is Dr Müller?" Newspaper reports have it that he was let out on parole for ten days in order to get the ransom, but one never heard of his ever returning either with the ransom or to try to help his friend who was left behind and who could not speak the Chinese language, which Dr Müller knew fluently. From all we know it seems that Dr Müller only returned to identify the body, which was found some 200 miles away from the place where it was supposed to have been.

It has been suggested to me that an effort had been

Chapter 19 - Baron von Plessen

made between the Germans and the Japanese to affect some sort of military arrangement. This was said to be very secret and they were most anxious that it should not leak out. Was Gareth Jones one of the few people who, with his enquiring mind, had found this out? And did Dr Müller realise this?

The suggestion has been made to me that Dr Müller may have been something more than a journalist and might have been a secret agent who was perturbed at what Gareth Jones had learned and the rest - I leave that to your imagination. Suffice it to say that Dr Müller, who now appears to be in Berlin, has not communicated one word to the parents - not even an ordinary letter of condolence. These suspicions may be totally unfounded - at any rate it is right that we should know the truth.

My purpose in writing to you is that Gareth informed his parents that it was through you and Mr Macdonald that he became a member of the Peking Club.

I have, therefore, sent a similar letter to Mr Macdonald and if you can throw any light on this tragic affair or help in any way, anything that you say, if necessary, will be regarded as strictly confidential, and will be greatly appreciated not only by his parents but all those who were the friends of Gareth Jones.

Two years after Mr Lloyd George had died, in 1946, Baron von Plessen wrote to Mr A.J. Sylvester with the request that the letter be forwarded to Gareth's parents. The text of the letter was printed in Graham Jones' article in the *National Library of Wales Journal* of December 1991. In the letter and account titled "Ill-fated Journey" Baron von Plessen wrote:

… But none other than Mr Lloyd George himself has blamed me for the death of the Englishman. His former secretary - not publicly, but in a letter which he wrote to a friend of mine in Peking. I saw the letter myself, Mr Lloyd George was wrong – I was not to blame for the death of Gareth Jones. I feel I have a score to settle with Mr Lloyd George.

Why did Mr Lloyd George have to write about my 'mission' to Mongolia implying, of course, that it was a secret mission? It was no more a mission than if he went to Brighton with his daughter Megan for the weekend. And what about Sir Charles Bell and the various members of the British Embassy in Peking who, like me, attended the celebrations of Prince Teh Wang's residence? Were they on a mission too? What was the meaning of that Japanese aeroplane which landed close by at luncheon time? And why were the two occupants closeted along with Prince Teh Wang in his tent for so long? We heard that they had asked for the names of all the Europeans present, without expressing a wish to see any of them. Possibly it was just a routine matter – the Japanese like to know what is going on in these parts – and yet!

The Baron must have read the letter that was written to either Timperley or Macdonald and he assumed that Lloyd George had implicated him in Gareth's death.

Certainly Gareth's parents would have liked to have known that Baron von Plessen wished to communicate with them. They had always wondered why they had never had a letter of sympathy from either Müller or von Plessen. Sylvester decided not to send it to Gareth's parents despite a number of letters from the Baron requesting him to do so. The reason Sylvester gave was that he did not want to stir up old memories of this ill-fated expedition. In his letter Plessen appears to be more concerned about his honour than family grief.

Was it Lloyd George who had blamed the Baron for Gareth's death? Mr Sylvester wrote the letters on notepaper from Lloyd George's office and dealt with Gareth's parents in their grief. Mr Sylvester was known to act on the elder statesman's behalf and, as the latter advanced in years, the loyal secretary undertook a great deal of responsibility for his employer's interests. None of the letters that Sylvester wrote in September 1935 either to the Foreign Office or the newspaper correspondents in China refer directly to Lloyd George ever having blamed the Germans, Baron von Plessen or Dr Müller for

Von Plessen's letter to Mr Fitzmaurice at the British Embassy.[2]

---

[2] Above is a letter, which the author discovered in Gareth's copy of 'Krieg in China' [War in China]. It is dated August 26th, 1935 and is from Baron von Plessen, written from the German Legation to Mr Fitzmaurice at the British Embassy in Peking. It reads: "I am herewith sending you a book which belonged to poor Gareth Jones and which he had lent to Countess Lichnovsky who returned it to me yesterday on her return to Peking from Japan".

the death of Gareth. At that time the former Prime Minister was known to wish to show the hand of friendship to Germany and he believed Hitler when the Dictator said that he did not want to attack France and the West. Lloyd George, as a consequence of the decisions made in the light of post war angst by those who signed the Treaty of Versailles in 1919, was aware of the burdensome legacy that had been imposed upon Germany resulting in the rise of National Socialism. Sylvester was in direct contact with the Foreign Office who gave him as little information as possible in their replies, little appreciating that his interest was that of a friend and colleague and that the questions might not be of a political nature.

In 1987, Sylvester at 99 years old still felt that Von Plessen was to blame. He was convinced in a letter that Baron von Plessen and Müller at the instigation of the Japanese were both implicated in Gareth's death:

> Again, I say from the very start in 1935 I have felt instinctively that Von Plessen, the supposed friend of Gareth, had a responsibility for his death. I feel strongly that Gareth's murder was deliberately planned. He had discovered too much. He died for his country.

Chapter 19 - Baron von Plessen

```
                                    Sept 18th 35
                                      London .
The Rt. Hon. D. Lloyd George M.P.


    Re the matter of Gareth Jones , if this
matter be properly gone into, if it is possible
properly to go into it, it will be found that
the poor man was treacherously betrayed by
his colleague the German.
They were both in possession of valuable
       information which was too vital for more
than one to have, one had to be got rid of ,
a very ingenious method was to do as the
German gentleman did , he saved his skin and
became sole possessor of the information.

The other was left to his fate,"Dead men tell no
tales", it will therefore be difficult if not
impossible to establish any sort of proof .
The bandits were more or less well paid to
take the action they did.

It was all part of the bargain .

The German made very little attempt to save
the "English Pig"as he was referred to.

One day this German will be known as a hero
in his country.

         I must remain
                      , Anonymous .
```

This strange letter was forwarded to Gareth's parents by Sylvester, which suggests that he took its contents seriously. It supports Sylvester's view that the Germans were in some way implicated in Gareth's murder.

Chapter 20
The German Doctor

Friend or Foe?

Who was Dr Herbert Müller? Very little is known about this elusive character.

Gareth's German journalist friend, Von Dewall,[1] who kept close contact with Major Edgar Jones during the ordeal, knew Dr Müller and said he would be a useful companion. Müller had been correspondent for the *Frankfurter Zeitung* in China for some years, but now was mostly a curio dealer. Those who knew Müller in Berlin gave a high opinion of him as a man and as a journalist and though none regarded him as a particularly likeable individual, they did not think him guilty of foul play. The Foreign Office had very little to say about him and certainly did not comment on his character to Sylvester.

A Miss Adelaide Hooker,[2] an American, who had been sent by Mr Kuhn of the *New York Times*, called at the office of Mr Lloyd

---

[1] Von Dewall, at one time in the employ of the China Customs and Postal Service under Sir Robert Hart, told Gareth before he left Britain that the bandits in China were merely interested in money and were not a blood-thirsty lot.

[2] Adelaide's father, Elon Huntington Hooker of Greenwich, Connecticut, was a former Senior Aide to Theodore Roosevelt and afterwards became the multi-millionaire founder of the Hooker Chemical Company. Adelaide had two sisters; Blanchette married John Rockefeller III in 1932 and Helen married Ernie O'Malley, an IRA intellectual in London in September 1935 (coinciding with her visit to Sylvester). Adelaide married the Pulitzer prize winner, John P. Marquand in 1936. Marquand toured the Orient in 1934 to gather background material for his stories. While in Japan, Marquand briefly aroused the suspicions of a Japanese detective who was rather short and exceedingly polite. The man tailed Marquand until he was satisfied Marquand was just an author on tour. This anonymous man intrigued Marquand, and he later developed the character of Mr Moto based on this individual. Mr Moto was first published in 1935 (and later played in Hollywood [1937-39] by Peter Lorre who also appeared in *Casablanca*) was one of Japan's top secret agents whose assignments and activities were always shrouded in mystery.

Chapter 20 – The German Doctor

George on the 26th of September 1935 and Mr Sylvester took an account of her statement in a memorandum. Mr Kiezler, Chairman of the Trans-Siberian Railway had told her of Gareth's death. On two occasions, while in New York, Gareth had stayed at her home. She had been in the Far East with a delegation of women who had been visiting Japan and on hearing of Gareth's capture by bandits she went to Kalgan to investigate the situation. She told Sylvester that she had met Dr Müller in Kalgan immediately after his release from the bandits and at that time the doctor was quite sure that Gareth would be released soon. Asked what kind of man Dr Müller was, Miss Hooker said:

> He was a very peculiar man who had "practically gone native" in China. He had been married to a German woman, but was now, so to speak, married to a Chinese woman by whom he had several children. He was not a particularly attractive man and people in Kalgan and Peking thought it dreadful that he had gone off and left Gareth who spoke no Chinese. He spoke the language fluently. "He is a kind of silent intelligence man keeping track of what goes on for the German Government."

Miss Hooker had seen the automobile in which Gareth and Müller had travelled. The truck belonged to the "Wostwag Company", supposedly a German Company, but which was really a Russian Company trading with Mongolia. It was a special kind of truck specifically designed for travelling in Mongolia. This 'peculiar' transport company was intending to move out of Kalgan. She saw four to five bullet holes in different parts of the vehicle body. Müller had shown her the special place for hiding silver money and said that the bandits went immediately to this hiding place.

Miss Hooker told Sylvester that the Japanese were intending to go into Kalgan in a few weeks time and take over a large portion of territory in Northern China. The Japanese attitude was that the Chinese civilisation was dead. They made no bones about taking over China. It was common knowledge amongst the Japanese that England, Germany and America had exploited China for years and now they felt that they had the same rights. Where there were White Russians, Chinese and Japanese, the only people who could organise them were the Japanese; the Japanese ran everything in Peking. An un-named official whom Miss Hooker styled as the equivalent of a mayor had been actually detained by the Japanese for three days.

When she met Müller in the office of the 'Wostwag', he did not seem to care what he said and many remarks had been anti-Japanese. This suggested he was not an agent for them. Miss Hooker had read the article in *The Week* and this tallied with what Müller had told her in Kalgan, but not with the article that she had read in the *Berliner Tageblatt*. Müller had told her that they had been definitely instructed to take the road they did by Japanese soldiers, not the soldiers from Manchukuo. Asked what motive Müller might have in writing press reports that differed so widely from the information he had given to Miss Hooker, she said her understanding was that he was afraid of what the Japanese might do.

A copy of the *Berliner Tageblatt*, which Miss Hooker cited above, has not been located, but supporting evidence of the Japanese, taking exception to Müller's allegation about the route was found in the *News of the World*, 25th September 1935:

> The Japanese Army is angry with Dr Müller, the German who was with Mr Jones when he was kidnapped. Major Takahashi, speaking in Peking on behalf of the Japanese Army, said they resented Dr Müller's statement if he intended to imply that the Japanese military authorities at Dolonor had purposely exposed Mr Jones and him to danger by dictating their route and by putting them on the wrong route. "I think that Dr Müller wished to escape his own responsibility for the incident", added Major Takahashi.

Shortly before this newspaper report was published, according to the *Peking Chronicle* (21st August), Müller called on Major Takahashi, the Japanese Military Attaché and expressed regret that his statement had been interpreted as a reflection upon the Japanese military authorities. After this apology, Müller then presumably retracted his story regarding the Japanese being responsible for the chosen return route in the *Berliner Tageblatt*.

Dr Herbert Müller in the centre with Ba-Wang-Yeh, the Prince of the Abaga Mongols on his left and the second living Buddha Diluwa Hutukin from Outer Mongolia on his right. Prince Teh Wang's son is in the front.

As to why Müller never returned with the ransom, the Foreign Office said that they only had his story of explanation: that he was told by the Kalgan local authorities that they would arrange for Gareth's release either by an offer of money to the bandits or by enrolling them in the Chinese army.

Müller explained his own release saying it was because he was a German National, suggesting there was an understanding between the Germans and the Japanese.[3] As Müller spoke Chinese fluently he probably was very persuasive which enabled him to engineer his own freedom.

---

[3] That Germany and Japan were liasing is born out by the following quotation: "The Japanese Military Attaché in Berlin, General Oshima's discussions with the Nazi leaders frequently centred on the possibility of a pact between the two countries. By August 1935 the [British] codebreakers reports of traffic passing on diplomatic circuits between Berlin and Tokyo had convinced the author of a military intelligence report that an alliance was inevitable." © Michael Smith 2000. Extracted from *The Emperor's Codes* by Michael Smith, published by Bantam Press, a division of Transworld Publishers. All rights reserved.

As it was, the bandits considered that Gareth was a far more valuable captive than Müller. There may have been intelligence surveillance on Gareth from the time he left Japan and unfortunately his connection with Mr Lloyd George was of no advantage to him on this occasion.

What was the relationship between Baron von Plessen and Müller? The latter was certainly an interpreter during the journey to Inner Mongolia as he spoke German and Chinese. In his diaries Gareth makes no note of the fact that there might be a secret mutual understanding between the Japanese and the Germans, but the German pair would have been wise enough to keep information of this nature away from the inquisitive young journalist. Chang Kai-shek was attempting to persuade the Germans to mediate in the dispute between the Chinese and the Japanese over the demilitarised zone in Chahar and Germany was still 'hedging her bets' at this time between the two nations - China and Japan - as to which of the two to make her ally.

There is no indication why Müller went to the town of Dolonor and why he was persuaded to take Gareth with him. In the quote from the letter 'The Ill-fated Journey', Baron von Plessen states that Gareth had thanked him for the invitation to attend the congress of the Mongol Princes though Müller wished to claim the credit for it himself. In letters Gareth had written, he certainly felt that the Baron had issued the invitation and was delighted to have been invited by him. Müller stated in his story that he preferred to travel alone, but on this occasion he had been persuaded by a third party to take Gareth with him on the trip to Inner Mongolia. It is not recorded who that third party was. The very fact that he gives no indication as to whom this was, is suspicious and makes one wonder whether he was by any chance bribed or coerced into taking Gareth to the town in order to affect his capture.

No more seems to have been heard about Müller in China after his apology to the Japanese and his subsequent retracted report.[4] The bandits had told the captured pair that they were in the pay of the

---

[4] Rumour has it that he sometime later visited Britain, but that he never contacted Gareth's parents.

Japanese, 'that they hated them, but they were compelled to obey Japanese orders for fear of retaliatory measures being taken against their families in Manchukuo.' Dr Müller had a Chinese family and it is for the same reason that he may well have feared for their safety.[5]

Anatoli, the Russian driver.

As to Anatoli Petrewschtchew, the Russian driver, he had reported to the Chief of Police and had given the ransom note written and addressed to him from Müller. He had been lent to the party by the "Wostwag Company" and was a White Russian. After the attack he had escaped along with Müller's Chinese servant, Liang, for although the bandits had poured water into the fuel tank to make the car useless they had overlooked the reserve tank. After the kidnapping, Liang, the manservant was never again mentioned. Lieutenant Millar interviewed neither him nor Anatoli and so their version of events is missing.

---

[5] Amelleto Vespa, an Italian, according to his book *The Japanese Secret Agent*. was forced to undertake intelligence work in Manchukuo. According to him, his family was kept as hostage in order that he should perform duties for the Japanese.

Chapter 21
The Japanese Involvement

Major Takahashi Tan, the Japanese Military Attaché.

"Make sound in the East and attack in the West". General Sunzi in *The Law of Warfare (4th century B.C.).*

"The Japanese intelligence has followed you in Japan, China, Manchuria and Russia". Amletto Vespa from his book, *The Japanese Secret Agent. 1939.*

In the complex, but incomplete story of Gareth's death there are three characters that figure in the incident: Prince Teh Wang, Doihara and Takahashi. The first is Prince Teh Wang, because though there is no evidence of him being culpable, he appears somewhere on the scene. He summoned Gareth to an interview. Shortly before this a plane landed with Japanese officials and, according to Baron von Plessen, they stayed quite some time with the Prince. They requested the names of the guests; Gareth's name would have been included in the list and perhaps the Japanese demanded this interview. The inquisitive journalist asked many questions referring to the articles he had read in the June editions of *The Times,* whilst in Peking, particularly as these referred to Doihara having visited the Prince. Doihara had then discussed with Teh Wang the building of an aerodrome at his headquarters and the establishment of telephone communications. Gareth referred to these delicate issues in the course of his interview. Teh Wang was skilful in his replies and cunningly fielded Gareth's questions.

Unbeknown to Gareth, in the previous year Major General Doihara had endeavoured to persuade the Mongolians to recognise the Japanese authority and in September 1934 Teh Wang's Chief of Staff was kidnapped and shot by the Chinese because they claimed he was a Japanese spy. Following this, Teh Wang had openly negotiated with the Japanese because he had one ambition, which was to unite the Mongols in China, Russia and Manchukuo. Gareth had asked Teh Wang some very searching questions, particularly with reference to Wang's approach to the Japanese in endeavouring to unite the

Mongols, but the Prince's answers were guarded and gave no indication that he had been liaising with them. It is curious that Gareth appears to have been the only guest who was singled out for a presence with the Mongol Prince; not even Sir Charles Bell, the High Commissioner for Tibet, was invited nor was the British Military Attaché. It is reported in the Foreign Office records that the Prince advised Gareth not to visit the eastern borders of Chahar.

The second character was the sinister, shadowy figure of Major General Doihara Kenji[1], the arch secret agent, whom Gareth never met. When Gareth asked in Tokyo the nature of the General's visit to China, General Hayashi, the Japanese Minister of War, and at one time Commander-in-Chief of the Kwantung army, gave him the terse reply that he was a friend of the Chinese and was there in a private capacity.

In the summer of 1935 on a number of occasions Doihara is mentioned in documents as being engaged in political activities in North China and may have been in the area when Gareth was captured. On 27th June he signed the Chin-Doihara[2] agreement in Peking nine days before Gareth arrived in the city. During the summer months of 1935, Japan was aiming to organise an Independence Movement in North China involving the five Provinces of Hopei, Chahar, Suiyuan, Shansi and Shantung. Major General Doihara was endeavouring to persuade General Sung Che-yuan to become its Chairman. The Chinese General, after the Changpei

---

[1] Major-General Doihara was one of Emperor Hirohito's 'eleven reliables' and had been appointed by him as the Chief of Special Service Organ and Director of the Military Intelligence Bureau in Mukden, the army's political espionage agency there. It is very likely that he had direct connections with the Kempeitai, the Japanese Secret Police in Manchukuo. He spoke Chinese fluently and had served in China since 1913. He had a wide acquaintance with petty warlords and malcontent mandarins. He was known as the 'Lawrence of Manchuria' and described as the 'stormy petrel of the Japanese army'.
[2] General Chin Te-chun replaced General Sung. The terms of the Chin-Doihara agreement included the dissolution of anti-Japanese organs in Chahar, an end to Chinese immigration into the province and the withdrawal of Sung's army from the area.

incident[3] in early June, had been dismissed by Nanking from the position of Governor of Chahar Province, but by September 9th (as stated by *The Times*) he had become acceptable to the Japanese authorities. According to Edgar Snow in his book *The Scorched Earth*, the Japanese General wished to bribe Sung to achieve his objective with 100 million dollars, to finance his government, and to re-arm and train his troops and to reinforce this offer Snow writes:

> Doihara discovered some "bandits" (actually they were in Japanese pay) in East Hopei (Hebei). Doihara brought some troops in to "restore order". He let it be known to Sung that he was holding a number of divisions at Shanhaikuan, the 'seagate' of China in readiness if his offer was declined.

There is a startling similarity between Doihara's intrigue in this, the Hopei (Hebei) incident involving Sung Che-yuan and in the capture of Gareth by Sung's disbanded soldiers, forced to become bandits, in the demilitarised zone of Chahar. In Sung's incident troops were kept in readiness at Shanhaikuan to "restore order" whilst in Gareth's case Japanese troops were held in Dolonor with a view to rescuing the young journalist and to use this as an excuse to invade the Province of Chahar.

On 9th December 1935 there was a mass demonstration against Japan's drive for an independent North China by Chinese students in Peking. Following this the Japanese Government forbade further action in Chahar and the movement for autonomy that Doihara was endeavouring to achieve ended in ignominious failure.

The third character in this picture is Major Takahashi, the suave Japanese Military Attaché who had been instrumental in June in arranging a demilitarised zone in Chahar into which Gareth and Müller had ventured. This was the Japanese officer who apparently was so zealous in endeavouring to obtain Gareth's release from the bandits. Was he really sincere in his endeavours? Gareth had asked many relevant questions in Peking pertaining to the situation of the

---

[3] Four Japanese Special Service Agency members were detained overnight for questioning on June 5th 1935 at Changpei. The Japanese were incensed at this action and Chiang Kai-shek, complying to their demands, dismissed General Sung Che-yuan from the position of Governor of Chahar Province.

Japanese in Inner Mongolia, their views on autonomy for the Mongolians and their fears concerning the Communist menace so uppermost in the Japanese strategic planning for the area. Gareth wrote in his diary at the end of the interview with Takahashi, the words: "he grinned and showed his gold teeth" appreciating his cunning nature.

Takahashi stated that he had heard of Gareth and Müller's capture through the press. Immediately he received the news, it was reported that he ordered the Kwantung Army to be of assistance and on 2nd August he flew to Dolonor.[4] The Major knew that they had captured a very important prisoner, a 'rare treasure' as one Chinese described him. It is curious that the following day it was reported that Gareth had been handed over to another band of bandits, more than a hundred in number, that there were at least two Japanese advisors with them and that Pao, the original bandit leader, had been put in detention. Was it a coincidence that a locally motivated incident had changed into an international one with a strong political overtones? Why were the bandits constantly on the move and 'curiously obdurate' in their wish to accept the ransom and release their prisoner? For four days after Gareth was last seen there was no news of the bandits until his death.

On 15th August, in a report to Sir Samuel Hoare from the British Embassy,[5] it was stated that Major Takahashi and Colonel Matsui had flown from Taiyuanfu to Kalgan on 13th August to meet Chang Chu-chang, Commander of the Chahar Peace Corps, at Kalgan. They advised him in the strongest terms to find Gareth by putting up the ransom. Chang declared: "We have already made an exhaustive search". Major Takahashi replied: "Now look in the right place."

Did Takahashi know that Gareth had died on the previous day? He seemed well informed about the bandit activities. Suffice it to say that this was the first known case of banditry in the area for some considerable time. Nor was it the usual custom of Chinese

---

[4] "It would appear that the Japanese authorities wished to make certain that any kudos that might be gained from the release of Mr Jones should accrue to the Japanese." Sir Alexander Cadogan's report to Sir Samuel Hoare at the Foreign Office on 3rd September.
[5] Also quoted in *The Western Mail & South Wales News* on 14th August.

brigands to kill their captives; in most cases they held them prisoner for many months and then released them without harm. The Japanese authorities gave an official denial to the European press that they were responsible for the capture and they appeared to have had some grounds for wishing to cover their tracks. On the same day as his visit to Kalgan, Takahashi requested that the Chinese Chief of Police at Kalgan furnish him with a written statement, which Takahashi then in turn showed to Colonel Lovat-Fraser, the British Military Attaché who was present in the town. The approximate translation of the Chinese statement is as follows:

> After the release of Müller, the Chahar authorities despatched a special police force to Kuyuan and Pao Ch'ang to warn the bandits that no harm was to be done to Jones. In addition they despatched special representatives in order to open up secret negotiations with the bandits and therefore proceeded to clear up other bandit bands in that area. This had the effect of frightening the bandits who are now holding Jones and they have split up into small parties of three to five and are hiding in the mountains. They have discarded their uniforms and are now wearing civilian clothes.

Why did Takahashi demand this statement from the Chinese authorities and insist that it was shown to the British Military Attaché? He was extremely zealous in his desire to affect Gareth's release and this arouses suspicion as to whether he was implicated in the kidnap. To add to this, why did Takahashi vehemently deny that the Japanese army had directed the pair along the wrong road and put pressure upon Dr Müller to retract his original allegations against the Japanese army in Dolonor? These suggestions all help to substantiate the theory that the act of banditry and capture of Gareth was politically motivated.

"The Japanese intelligence has followed you in China, Manchuria, in Mongolia and in Russia". A Japanese colleague told Amelleto Vespa this and he quoted it in his book *The Japanese Secret Agent* (published in 1939). It could so easily have applied to Gareth. Gareth said in Tokyo that he was going to visit Manchukuo, but he would not have appreciated that this colonial territory was a breeding ground for the Kempeitai, the Japanese secret police. Amau Eliji, the Japanese Foreign Office spokesman had reported to *The Times*

Chapter 21 – The Japanese Involvement

correspondent in Tokyo at the time of Gareth's death that: "the Japanese authorities had given Mr Jones all the facilities in their power including introduction to Japanese officials in Manchukuo and China". This confirms that it was known that he would be visiting this area and by the time of his capture by bandits, he would have visited all these countries, as mentioned by Vespa. In articles in the *Manchester Guardian* and other newspapers, Gareth exposed the famine of the Russian peasants which had resulted from Stalin's Five Year Plan of collectivisation and industrialisation. Following these articles the Russians refused to give Gareth a visa to return. The Japanese without doubt would have felt equally uneasy about his inquisitiveness as to their activities and as a result probably feared that Gareth might expose them to the world in the same way as he had disclosed Russia's fallibility. To the Japanese, a foreign journalist was not a popular breed of person. Gareth was a well-known journalist and in Tokyo he asked very influential Japanese politicians extremely searching and pointed questions. He was also seen by the Japanese to be Lloyd George's 'Private Secretary' and in their eyes, this would have carried sufficient weight to open doors and create opportunities. In Baron von Plessen's letter entitled 'Ill-fated Journey', he remarked how outspoken Gareth was in Inner Mongolia and that he had wished Gareth had kept the fact to himself that he was going to write about Japan's policies.

Gareth visited Japanese Consuls in every port of call and interviewed each of them in the course of his travels. It is the author's opinion that he was followed by the secret police from the time he left Tokyo and no doubt they had a dossier on him. In the Philippines, the Japanese Consul, Kimura, was very frank about Japan's intentions in the country and said that he would not be averse to coming to the island. The Philippines had abundant raw materials for commercial and military needs. Kimura gave Gareth the feeling that Japan had the upper hand in Pacific domination. The Japanese Consul-General in Bali was most hospitable and took him in his elegant limousine to the botanical gardens and saw him to his ship before it sailed. He said that Japan had a policy of peace in the Far East. In Siam Gareth saw the Japanese Minister with whom he had a brief interview and in Canton he spoke to the Japanese Consul-General who said he had just come back from a 10 day trip to Manchuria. If Vespa is to be believed, then it is likely that these diplomats reported back to their mother country, particularly if Gareth quite innocently told the Consuls about his intentions of writing an investigative book on Japanese policies in the Far East. All of this is informed speculation and not fact, but it is certain that the Japanese had every opportunity to follow his movements.

Gareth's friendship with the daughters of General Tsai and General Chen may have been purely coincidental, but were the Chinese or Japanese intelligence services aware of the friendship? These two Generals were strong adversaries of the policies of Chiang Kai-shek and leaders of the Southwest Faction. They too had every reason to hate the Japanese. The Mayor of Canton was highly critical of the Generalissimo and very derogatory of Major General Doihara. Doihara aimed to organise autonomous regions in the southwest of China as well as in the north. In Hankow, Gareth conveyed the views of the Canton faction to Marshall Chang Hsueh-liang, Chang Kai-shek's deputy Commander-in-Chief, the Commander of the disbanded Northeast Army in the Province of Hopei; a man who had every reason vehemently to hate the Japanese. Gareth appeared to trust the Japanese and it would not have been difficult for their intelligence service to follow his progress. The bandits who had captured Gareth had been soldiers in General Sung Che-yuan's disbanded army and were wearing uniforms of the Pao An-tui, the Peace Corps. Pao was their leader and it was known that these men were in the service of the Japanese. The bandits had few sympathisers in the area, were strangers there and pressed-ganged local Chinese to act as their guides. The Rengo representative at Peking informed the Reuters' correspondent on about 15th August, before Gareth's death had been reported to the British Embassy, that Takahashi had told him that some bandits had been employed by the Japanese the previous January in another incident and thereafter had been paid off.

Müller stated in his account that just prior to their capture the bandits had been unsuccessful in capturing a Mongol prince as instructed by the Japanese. According to Amelleto Vespa, banditry was conspired by the Japanese and ransom money was paid into the army coffers. It was an organised activity by the Japanese army in Manchukuo.

Chapter 21 – The Japanese Involvement

Documents have been found in the Naval Archives in Tokyo in Japan, which referred to the "Jones' Murder" case. It described the circumstances of his death:

> The party [Gareth Jones and Dr Müller] arrived in Tarin [Japanese name for Dolonor] and visited the social services organisation. It afforded the party various conveniences on the 25th such as the purchase of horses! On the way back against the instruction from the Japanese, the party did not take the official road to Kalgan, but the road to Hosho and were kidnapped by bandits (reportedly the Chinese army which had deserted and turned into bandits). The incident occurred in the Province of Chahar in which area the Japanese denied responsibility. The Kwantung Army made every effort in the rescue operation. Müller was released and returned to Peking on August 1st. On August 17th the Provincial Government informed the Japanese Consulate at Zhangjiakou (Kalgan) that: "Jones had been shot and found dead".

The document further reported on the public comments relating to the incident and Müller's statement:

> In Europe and U.S.A. there were slanderous and exaggerated reports. Lloyd George made a statement that Gareth had documents of which a certain country wished to know the contents. British political circles rumoured that Gareth might have been the victim of Japanese Intelligence Services and that because Müller was immediately released, it was considered that Gareth was the only target.

Though the contents of these documents referring to Gareth that were found in the Tokyo Archives on Jones' murder appear insignificant, they do reveal the great interest that the Japanese had in the incident. Some details of the pair's visit to Dolonor did not appear in any British newspaper and were probably issued directly from the town of Dolonor. The Japanese intelligence service followed the press reports worldwide. The Japanese authorities denied any responsibility for Gareth's capture and death and sent an official denial to this effect to the European press. The Japanese were particularly sensitive to the comments from Mr Lloyd George and

Chapter 21 – The Japanese Involvement

from British political circles. This supports the political reasons for the Foreign Office's reluctance to give more than the barest information to the distinguished parliamentarian for fear of offending the Japanese.

The mystery of Gareth's death is made more confusing by evidence provided by Gareth's friend in Hong Kong, Mr R.T. Barrett of *The Critic*. He called attention to the contrast between Japanese duplicity and the Chinese anxiety not to 'lose face'. The Chinese authorities were to all intents and purposes doing all they could to release Gareth; they promised to pay the ransom. Mr Barrett pointed out that the Chairman of the Chahar Government was supposed actually to have sent an emissary to the bandits with an instalment of $10,000, but Dr Müller reported that they never had received it. Despite having warned Gareth that they could not be responsible for his safety, the Chahar Government had offered to pay the ransom. Yet, at this very time, the Chahar Government was informing Nanking that the treasury was empty and that no dues could be sent to the Central Government. Mr Barrett suggested that the murder was a deliberately bungled affair by a Chinese District Magistrate with Gareth becoming the victim of oriental intrigue. This District Magistrate had not informed his neighbouring colleague into whose area Gareth had been taken, that negotiations with the bandits were already in hand. He thereby deliberately allowed his uninformed colleague to send troops out to reprehend the bandits who in turn doubted the sincerity of the previous negotiations and therefore took the straightforward course of murdering Gareth, as 'dead men tell no tales'.

The Chinese accused the Japanese of obstructing their negotiations and wished to show them that the demilitarised zone was a haven for banditry without the security that the Chinese army offered previously. Mr Barrett continued:

> It may all have been genuine, that is the efforts of the Chahar Government and the good offices of the Japanese, but intrigue is so much part and parcel of the East, that no one believes that it was suddenly suspended and replaced by clear wells of sincerity.

Chapter 22
A Manchukuo Incident

Gareth Jones: a man who knew too much?

"The Japanese have always treated me with respect, but I too was deceiving myself." **Marshall Chang Tso-lin.**

"The innkeeper says they intend to occupy Kalgan about August 15th, about 40,000 troops have assembled not far away." **Extract of the narrative, taken from Gareth's final diary entry.**

When I commenced my investigation into the mystery of Gareth's death, I never considered it would be solved to my satisfaction. But I have no doubt that it was politically motivated. The secrets that he knew died with him. The countries involved have much to answer for and none can be given any credit for trying to save him. He was merely a pawn in an international game of chess. Each had its own selfish motive not to save him and laid blame upon each other. Why was the British Government so secretive and why did they make no attempt to raise the ransom to aid the impoverished Chahar Government? Was it from fear of the rise of National Socialism, Hitler and German rearmament that it did not wish to offend the Japanese for fear of a confrontation in the East? What bearing did Japan's insidious territorial expansion in China have on his death? Did the Japanese think that Gareth had access to secret information? Would the Chinese have been able to pay his ransom, which was quite a considerable sum at that time? The Germans themselves would not have been interested in Gareth's release for he was not one of their nationals. The Japanese must have been aware of his considerable knowledge of Nazi Germany and Communist Russia, particularly as they were hostile to the Soviets on the northern borders of Manchukuo.

Gareth's death should be seen in the light of the political situation of the time, each country rearming with the escalating fear of an impending global conflict. David Lloyd George's speeches in Parliament in 1935 and 1936 portrayed a fear of this rearming and requested the means to save "civilisation from a great catastrophe".

As for the powerful United States of America, this country's policy of isolation merely left a void in the Far East.

The capture of the two men by bandits would appear to originally have been an engineered act on the part of the local Japanese Army in Dolonor. The army may have suggested their route in order to divert the party from the main road to Kalgan along which military transport was proceeding. Gareth and Müller had ventured into this area, into Dolonor, a town that was assembling troops and armaments in preparation for the invasion of East Chahar. Major Takahashi became aware from the press reports that it was Gareth Jones who had been captured. Gareth was an embarrassment to the Japanese. He was an inquisitive journalist who wanted to know what the Japanese were up to and made it widely known that he intended to write a book to expose the nation's intentions in the Far East; a man whom the Japanese secret police had possibly followed since his departure from Tokyo. Takahashi had previously been prominent in the crisis of Northern China and delivered an ultimatum to the Chinese precipitating the crisis which resulted in the signing of the He-Umetsu Agreement. The Military Attaché then turned the whole Gareth affair into a politically motivated incident of worldwide interest intended to compromise the Chinese not only in the Province of Chahar but also throughout the whole of China.

To Japan, a proud and aggrieved country imbued with a desire for colonial expansion, it was a thinly veiled 'incident' like so many more that had been contrived by them in order to implicate the Chinese in a zone which they wished to acquire by stealth. Through the auspices of Major General Doihara, Japan was pressing to make North China independent of Nanking and the local governments to become autonomous. Doihara was known to have engineered other incidents in China and was present in the area at about the time Gareth and Müller were captured. Is there a possibility that he also was implicated? Though Japanese troops were massing in Dolonor and on the road to Kalgan, there was no reported invasion in August 1935 by the Kwantung army in the area. The innkeeper in the town of Dolonor had informed Gareth that the Japanese intended to occupy Kalgan by about 15th August. The unanswered question is whether Gareth's incident, which had worldwide press coverage, curtailed a planned offensive in the next Japanese 'drive for Asia'. Historically though, it

Chapter 22 – A Manchukuo Incident

is a fact that by 6th December 1935, the Japanese had merely occupied the border areas of Eastern Chahar.

Though he was a keen observer and asked many pertinent and delicate questions, Gareth was not a secret agent. Although the Japanese thought he was, as intimated in newspaper reports from Dairen in the Japanese territory of Manchukuo, there is no evidence in any document, letter or even in his diaries to give even the slightest indication of such a possibility. Duncan Stewart, the British Special Operations Executive archivist wrote to the author in 1998 stating that he had looked up Gareth's name:

> in some archival indexes which would have been quite likely to contain some reference to Gareth had he been involved in intelligence-gathering on behalf of the British Government. No such reference was located ... It would, however, have been natural for the Foreign Office, War Office or even Lloyd George himself to ask Gareth to: 'keep his eyes and his ears open and let us know what you think when you come back'.

There was an exuberant nature to Gareth's character; he talked freely and openly and to everyone.[1] Therefore any interested party would have been able to gain useful information given in trust by Gareth though probably little would have been volunteered in return.

Lloyd George's Private Secretary Mr Sylvester may have been very near the truth in questioning whether there was a close understanding between the Germans and the Japanese. In Peking, according to the British Embassy, the Germans were in touch with the Japanese. Rumours from the Far East probably emanated from Japan. Secret negotiations were tentatively commenced in the late spring of that year between Joachim von Ribbentrop and General Oshima Hiroshi, the Japanese Military Attaché in Berlin. The Reichswehr (German War Ministry) and the Wilhelmstrasse (Foreign Office) were

---

[1] In Tokyo, for instance Gareth socialised with his journalist colleague Günther Stein (later alleged to have been a Soviet spy) in *The Case of Richard Sorge* by Deakin, F.W. and Storry, G.R. (1966). See endnote in Chapter 2 - Japan.

all unaware of the secret negotiations. General Werner von Blomberg, the German War Minister was informed of the plans on 23rd September 1935 and was very much against an agreement. The German Foreign Office was not aware of them until October or November. The German Ambassador, Oskar Trautmann, wished to keep a balanced policy in Germany's approach to China and Japan and he may not have known of the plans. It would appear that he directed his sympathy more to Chang Kai-shek than towards Japan though he tried to remain unbiased. Baron von Plessen's views are not known, but he was still living in Peking in 1938 when Sir Harold Acton met him there. Then, according to Acton's book *More Memoirs of an Aesthete*, the staff in the German Legation were Nazi sympathisers and pro-Japanese. The German Ambassador to Japan, Herbert von Dirksen, a known Nazi sympathiser, supported these negotiations, but even he did not know of them until November. In Hitler's view, it was to be an ideological agreement only in name.

Tass, the Russian News Agency, released a report from London (in late December 1935) to the effect that Ribbentrop and the Japanese Military Attaché in Berlin had initialled a military convention and that an agreement of co-operation against the Communists was signed at the same time. On 20th January of the following year, a pact between the Germans and the Japanese was denied. On October 23^{rd,} the Anti-Comintern Pact was initialled and on 25th November 1936 was signed by von Ribbentrop and the Japanese Ambassador Mushakoji. There is no evidence to be found in the German Foreign Ministry archives of proceeding negotiations nor any reference to any such negotiations in Gareth's diaries.

Baron von Plessen of the German Legation in Peking was surely blameless in respect of being involved in Gareth's death even though Mr Sylvester was suspicious of him and implied that the Baron was probably aware of a secret liaison between the Germans and the Japanese. According to his relative Prince Bismarck, the Baron returned to his duties on the 15th July at least eight days before the pair left for Dolonor, long before the fatal episode. The reason why Sylvester implicated Baron von Plessen in Gareth's murder must be that full disclosure was kept from Lloyd George. The Foreign Office clearly suppressed the circumstances surrounding Gareth's death at the hands of bandits for fear that the former Premier would make

Chapter 22 – A Manchukuo Incident

political capital in Parliament by embarrassing His Majesty's Government (whose foreign policy at the time was one of appeasement). It is questionable that even if Lloyd George had been made aware of the true nature of events whether he would have made any political capital from the tragedy, as he felt true affection towards Gareth, (always having referred to him as 'My Dear Boy') - he was merely trying to discover the truth for personal reasons.

Gareth's life seemed less important than the British Government's anxiety of offending either Hitler or the Japanese Emperor or both. In July Sir Samuel Hoare, the Foreign Secretary, spoke in Parliament of the importance attached to Britain having friendly relations with Japan.

Caricature of David Lloyd George taken from a postcard.

Why was Dr Müller released after two days? Was it because of the friendly understanding between two war-minded countries? He always insisted that it was because he was a German National. Was this because the Japanese in Manchukuo desired formal recognition of their state by the Germans? From another source it was reported that Dr Müller had been set at liberty at the instance of Chang Chung-Chi, a former bandit and now Commander of the local militia - the Peace Preservation Corps. Chang was a friend of the bandit leader Pao, who captured the two men and because of their displeasure at Müller's release the Japanese detained Pao, and Gareth was then put in the charge of another group of bandits.

Whatever reason there was for Müller's early release there remains a suspicion that he was implicated in Gareth's death. It is the author's belief that he was not directly involved and he appears to have told the truth about the pair's capture when he first returned to Peking, though clearly much of this was suppressed in British newspaper reports. After Müller's interview with Takahashi, when he went to apologise for saying that the Japanese put himself and Gareth on the wrong route, he remained silent. The Japanese had many means of coercion. Was Müller's silence in order to save his own life or for fear that the Japanese might harm his Chinese family? Perhaps Pao released Müller to recount his findings in Dolonor to the Chinese authorities or even to get his own back on the Japanese. Pao and his men were loyal Chinese despite the fact they were bandits. The Japanese detained Pao, and this throws further suspicion as to the involvement of the Japanese army into whose service they had been coerced. We shall never know the answer. Gareth gave no reason in his letters or diaries as to why he had wished to go to Dolonor with Dr Müller except that he had told a friend before leaving Peking that he wanted to see "what the 'Japs' were up to". Gareth would have read in *The Times* of June 1935 that Dolonor was a centre of Japanese military activity.

The Japanese Army in Manchukuo was noted for intrigue and was not past compromising the Chinese by implying that the latter were incapable of controlling banditry in their own territory. They considered that conditions in China were anarchic. By fabricating an incident in Chahar the Japanese may have wished to imply that the Chinese were incapable of keeping law and order, particularly as Sir Frederick Leith Ross, the Chief Economic Adviser to the British Government, intended to visit China in the late summer to advise on financial matters.[2] This would have been a glorious opportunity for a Japanese propaganda coup to help influence the eventual outcome of the planned visit to the detriment of the Chinese Government.

"The Japanese have always treated me with respect, but I too was deceiving myself." These were the words of the Manchurian warlord, Marshall Chang Tso-lin,[3] who was believed to have been murdered by the Japanese as he returned by train to his capital of Mukden. These may also have been Gareth's sentiments as he rode alone on horse back, hands bound and saddle sore; a hostage of bandits in the service of the Japanese; a man who trusted them. On a number of occasions Gareth wrote regretfully that he considered it was to be a very quiet summer in the Far East. The sight of amassing troops and armoured vehicles in Dolonor would have been the 'scoop of his life', but it turned out to be so in a very different sense from anything which he could have ever anticipated.

Gareth was a young man who asked too many embarrassing questions, knew too much and would not have been afraid to expose to the world Japan's ambition to dominate China by writing leading articles in the national newspapers of Europe and America. It is the author's opinion that Gareth's capture was an act of banditry orchestrated by the Kwantung Army and intended to be a political incident with the excuse of invading the Province of Chahar - the Province which the Japanese had recently forced the Chinese Government to demilitarise. Though Manchukuo was Japanese territory, the army and its officers were a law unto themselves. Gareth's death may not have been part of their plan, but as he was too weak to remount his horse and because the Pao An-tui was in hot pursuit of the bandits, his captors shot him. The local militia may well have been intent on seeking revenge for the loss of one of their own men at the hands of Gareth's captors. Alternatively, though less convincing, according to Mr Barrett of *The Critic* there was a breakdown of communication between two neighbouring District Magistrates, which led to the bandits fleeing for their lives.

---

[2] The United States had brought China to the verge of bankruptcy by its Silver Purchase Act of 1934.
[3] He was the father of Marshall Chang Hsueh-liang, whom Gareth interviewed in Hankow. See List of Characters for more information.

However with Gareth's murder on 12th August, any 'devious' scheme in which the Japanese might have planned for *A Manchukuo Incident*, went tragically wrong. As a direct result, any immediate designs for further Japanese territorial expansion of Northern China were temporarily postponed. With Gareth's death, the Japanese were clearly embarrassed by all the adverse publicity from the attention of the international media.

The question remains as to what would have been the outcome had Gareth lived? Would the Japanese troops who were already assembling in Dolonor, have been sent into the Province of Chahar to "restore order", using Gareth's rescue from the hundred strong "curiously obdurate" bandits as an excuse to effect their plans? The Japanese would then have been able to achieve by stealth a political objective of occupying Kalgan by about 15th August – and without any need for direct military action against the Chinese. Gareth's untimely death ultimately meant that the Kwantung army in Manchukuo no longer had any pretext in pursuing a covert plan of expansion into Chahar Province.

The Japanese's ultimate aim was the independence of the Northern Provinces of China from Nanking and had hoped to achieve this without resorting to the use of force. Had their plot of rescuing Gareth been successful, then Major General Doihara might not have needed to present his later ultimatum to General Sung Che-yuan to declare autonomy on November 18th 1935.[4]

In consequence, the course of history in the Far East might have been profoundly changed. Had Japan succeeded in her aims by peaceable means, then the ensuing 1937 Sino-Japanese War might have been averted.

On July 30th 1935, *The Western Mail* printed an article by Gareth entitled "Anglo-American Relations from the Japanese Point of View" which highlighted the conflicting opinions of Western politicians concerning Japanese intentions in the Far East. He wrote:

---

[4] Major-General Doihara threatened that Japanese forces would take action, but "The Japanese government was afraid of arousing international complications and forbade the use of force." Quotation from *China and the Origins of the Pacific War* by Youli Sun.

"Which is the right point of view? I shall not be able to make up my mind until I have been through the Far East, visited China and Manchukuo and returned for a second visit to Japan." Had Gareth survived his kidnapping ordeal he would have undoubtedly written a sensational book revealing Japan's desire to build an Empire. This startling exposé would also have emphasised Japan's plans of infiltrating North China for defensive reasons because of the fear of an invasion by Communist troops massing in the north, on the Soviet Union's border with Manchukuo. The worldwide publicity given to Gareth's controversial articles on his return from Russia in 1933 would have perturbed the well-informed Japanese Intelligence Service.[5] In the summer of 1934 Gareth correctly predicted the conflict in Europe against Germany. In Java he anticipated that while Britain was occupied by this war, Japan would exploit the situation and strike to expand her Empire. This prediction was confirmed when on December 7th 1941, the American fleet was bombed in Pearl Harbour, Hawaii and simultaneously Japan invaded and occupied in rapid succession many of those countries that were "coloured as colonies of Nippon" on Ishihara Koichero's map; the map that Gareth was shown in the Dutch East Indies. For a short time during the Second World War Japan's ambition of imperial power became a reality.

Had Gareth lived he certainly would have achieved a distinguished career. In his death, Wales lost a remarkable son, but the world sadly lost a journalist with an exceptional knowledge of global affairs - "It is bitter to think that brilliance and vigour and promise should be wiped out by the bullet of a miscreant".

He did however leave us with a legacy of articles which encompassed an entire spectrum of these events. After his 'Fact Finding Tour of the World' Gareth would have been able to fully comprehend the worldwide repercussions that followed the misjudged and acrimonious decisions taken by the politicians at the Treaty of Versailles. In many respects, the resentments resulting from these decisions, precipitated the Second World War and they may have had

---

[5] These internationally published articles in addition to his lecture tours of Britain and America brought worldwide attention to the tragic famine and terror resulting from Stalin's Five Year Plan of industrialisation and collectivisation.

some bearing on Gareth's death. In 1931, Lloyd George, one of the signatories of this Treaty, wrote a testimonial to Gareth in which he said: "I noticed a spark of venturesomeness in him combined with solid study and the gift of getting on with people. I feel confident in predicting a brilliant future for this young man."

Gareth's grave in Merthyr Dyfan cemetery in the Colcot, Barry, inscribed:

YMA
Y GORWEDD LLWCH
GARETH JONES
MAB ANNWYL EDGAR A GWEN JONES
IEITHYDD TEITHIWR CARWR HEDDWCH
A LADDWYD YM MONGOLIA AWST 12 1935
YN 30 MLWYDD OED
HE SOUGHT PEACE AND PURSUED IT.[6]

---

[6] [Here lie the ashes of Gareth Jones, the dear son of Edgar and Gwen Jones, linguist, traveller, lover of peace, killed in Mongolia August 12 1935, aged 30 years. He sought peace and pursued it.]

APPENDICES

Appendix I
Historical Background

Gareth's travels in the Far East and in particular his visit to Japan must be seen in the context of the social mores and the political history of the 1930s. The intrigues of the Japanese and their Emperor Hirohito are difficult to comprehend at the beginning of the 21st century. Our culture at that time was so different. The East has its fascination and it is not surprising that Gareth was captivated by it. It stimulated his enquiring mind to ask so many questions and I feel that his tremendous zeal and enthusiasm carried him away. He came from a Welsh Non-Conformist family and from his father came to believe that all men were good. To quote the letter of condolence to Major Edgar Jones from Mr R. Barrett of the *The Critic* in Hong Kong:

> There is no doubt that Gareth was in deep waters, for the swirl of Far Eastern politics is more ruthless and treacherous than anything conceivable in the West, more a mixture of petty interests of money and 'face' with the enormous clash of national interests. They knew what he had discovered in Russia and they knew what he had found out in the East.

According to the eminent historian, Edward Bergamini, behind the Emperor Hirohito's pretence of virtue and innocence was a devious man. From the early 1920s when he was Crown Prince, he wished not only to rid Asia of the Western influence: "Asia for the Asiatics", but was also contriving to build a Japanese Empire. Gareth was not to know, or suspect at the time, of the intrigues, the ruthless suppression, even assassination, of those who deviated from the path or opposed the plan of expansion. Nor could he have suspected Japan's devious orchestration of incidents in China with a view to eventual domination and colonisation of that country. Still less that he would be at the centre of such international intrigue. The Japanese history of the period runs red with cruelty. Gareth was thoroughly informed about the news of the time, but most probably unaware of the merciless side of the Japanese Government. Though he asked penetrating questions, he must have been unaware of their sensitive nature when directed towards a government that had something to hide. Those ministers, or ex-ministers, he interviewed do not seem to be as culpable as some were, but they were responsible to their Emperor.

Japan in the late twenties was going through a period of depression and was planning a campaign of expansion as the country was overcrowded and lacked natural resources for home and for war. At this time China was in a state of political unrest, ruled by local warlords. Chiang Kai-shek was trying to unite his country and endeavouring to rule South China. At the time he had a greater fear of the Communists than he had of the Japanese. In 1928 his Northern Expedition drove Marshall Chang Tso-lin, a bandit turned warlord, north to the Eastern Provinces known as Manchuria of which he was the Governor. He was returning to his capital, Mukden, from Peiping (Beijing or Peking) when explosives blew up his train. Following his murder, the Kwantung Army planned to seize the city of Mukden and much of Southern Manchuria, but this failed because dissent among the senior officers prevented decisive action. Marshall Chang Hsueh-liang, known as the Young Marshall, succeeded his father and was to become a very key figure in China during the early 1930s. Chang Hsueh-liang was to find out that his father's murder had been perpetrated by the Japanese, and for this reason he hated the Japanese vehemently.

Three years later Chang, who was Commander-in-Chief of the North Eastern Frontier Army, was to lose his Eastern Provinces and Mukden to the Japanese. On September 18th 1931, the Japanese planned and then executed an explosion on the South Manchurian Railway destroying a small section of it. This provocative deed, known as the Mukden Incident or to the Japanese as the Manchurian Incident, was merely an excuse to attack the Mukden garrison and the Young Marshall's small air force base. Coolly planned and orchestrated by Ishiwara Kanji to implicate the Chinese, the faked derailment of a Japanese train was created purely as an excuse to invade Manchuria. Thus the Young Marshall had further reason to hate the Japanese.

Having briefly toyed with the option of direct negotiations with Japan, as was the wish of Shidehara, Chiang Kai-shek concluded that he had no alternative, but to appeal to the League of Nations because he was in no position to fight the Japanese. Further to this, in

January 1932, the Japanese engineered another incident, known as the Shanghai Incident. Carefully orchestrated demonstrations hostile to those Japanese living there were organised. To protect her nationals, Admiral Shiozawa sent in his marines. Unexpectedly fierce resistance was encountered. The 19th Route Army Commander, General Tsai Ting-kai, and his troops fought very bravely and announced that the 19th Route Army would: "fight the Japanese to the last man if it has to dye the Whampoa river red with its blood". Chiang Kai-shek did not wish to escalate the war against the Japanese and gave orders to Tsai that the: "19th Route Army should take advantage of its victorious position, avoid decisive fighting with the Japanese and end the war now". Another interesting source gave a fascinating reason for the cessation of hostilities, in that the infamous female Japanese spy, Eastern Jewel, a distant relative of Pu Yi, had betrayed Tsai. In 1933 General Tsai led an unsuccessful coup d'état against Marshall Chiang Kai-shek known as the Fukien Rebellion. He proclaimed martial law in the name of the people and announced that the lack of financial provision for the 19th Route Army had compelled him to take over Fukien revenue. This coup, though not successful, suggests that it was Chiang who had influenced the outcome of the end of the fighting in Shanghai and it seems the more feasible historical fact.

The Japanese Year Book of 1934 states that:

On March 1st, 1932 a manifesto was promulgated announcing that Manchukuo was founded in response to the unanimous aspirations of the 30,000,000 people living in Manchuria and Mongolia and on March 7th Mr Pu Yi who once ruled over the entire territory of China as the 12th Emperor of the Ching Dynasty, consented to become the Chief Executive of Manchukuo.

The League of Nations set up a commission headed by Lord Lytton, which denounced Japan for its conduct in annexing Manchuria. The League Assembly convened a special meeting and an almost unanimous majority of the members accepted the report. Siam was the only nation to abstain. Due to this unfavourable result the Japanese delegation, headed by Mr Matsuoka Yosuke, left the assembly. In March 1933 Imperial Sanction was given for Japan to withdraw from the League.

In *The Last Emperor,* Edward Behr describes how Major General Doihara, a Japanese secret agent, persuaded Pu Yi to leave Tientsin. The Japanese officer convinced him that the Young Marshall wished to destroy the deposed Chinese Emperor and that there was a contract out on his life. The Japanese provoked riots, which were blamed on Chang Hsueh-liang and eventually Pu Yi was smuggled out of China. He was then formally enthroned as Emperor of Manchukuo on March 1st, 1934.

In his *China and the Origins of the Pacific War,* Youli Sun states that the Tanggu Truce of May 31st, 1933 legitimised Japan's control of China, north of the Great Wall. According to the Japanese version of events this practically put to an end the long protracted state of affairs known as the 'Manchurian Incident'. They declared that they had no other intention than to maintain peace in the Province of Jehol and pacify the provincial people from local banditry and the invading troops from across the Great Wall.

On April 17th 1934, the Japanese Foreign Ministry spokesman, Amau Eliji, stated that Japan had a special mission to maintain peace and order in East Asia and opposed any financial assistance to China by foreign countries and in particular any Western military or political aid. This statement in fact confirmed the status quo and was proof of Western inaction. The British and the United States responses to what became known as the Amau (Amŏ) Doctrine were extremely indifferent and both were unwilling to offend Japan by giving support to China. In May 1935 the Japanese Army presented a series of demands to the Chinese authorities in Peking, including the withdrawal from North China of Marshall Chiang Kai-shek's Central Army and the termination of all anti-Japanese activities.

According to Youli Sun, the Marshall conceded to every demand except withdrawal of the Central Army. Premier Wang Chin-wei and War Minister He Ying-qin were eager to avoid conflict at any price and they verbally agreed to all the demands requested by Major Takahashi Tan, the Military Attaché. Nothing was provided in writing and the crisis mounted. The British Ambassador to Japan, Sir Robert Clive, made representations to Japan, but wished to remain friendly with this country, because the British Government had to contend with the troublesome issue of Germany. America was following a policy of isolation and had just granted independence to the Philippines. With the world powers indifferent to China's fate on July 9th 1935, Wang wrote to General Umetsu (Umezu), the Japanese Commander in Tientsin, to concede the demands. This became known as the He-Umetsu Agreement.

Japan obtained similar concessions in Chahar Province as in the Hebei Province and Chiang Kai-shek realised that China would have to stand firm against further demands from the Japanese. Much of his time had been spent combating the Communists in the south. Mao Tse-tung and his Communist followers were in the southwest and 1935 was the year of the Long March. During these last negotiations Gareth was travelling north of the Great Wall of China with his German companions Baron von Plessen and Dr Herbert Müller to Prince Teh Wang's court. Prince Teh Wang, leader of the Mongol Princes was keen to establish his own independent government of Inner Mongolia. Wang's arrangements with Nanking failed and then he turned to the direction of the notorious Japanese secret agent Major General Doihara. He had the task of sponsoring Chinese leaders to establish their own autonomous regimes in 1933. From then on Prince Teh Wang was secretly in league with the Japanese at the shrine of a Hundred Spirits. Little by little, Teh's Mongol Government gained allegiance of Inner Mongolia's seventy-seven tribes or 'Banners', but realising that they would be entirely dependent on Japan, many of the Silingol banner and others eventually stopped supporting him.

Early attempts at southwards expansion had failed because the Japanese (Kwantung) Army believed the northern warlords could be bribed into declaring independence from Nanking. In November 1936 Prince Teh Wang, his Mongol roughriders and the Kwantung Army, underwrote a Mongol expedition force to establish an independent Inner Mongolia. The Chinese National Forces at Pai Ling-miao in Suiyan Province soundly beat Teh's troops. Though he had once been a strong supporter the Young Marshall, Chang Hsueh-liang, lost faith in Chiang Kai-shek following the He-Umetsu Agreement, as the 51st Army in Hebei (Hopei) was his army. Chang established contact with the Communists in 1936 and also with Zhou En-lai. He captured Chiang Kai-shek in Xian on December 12th 1936 and persuaded him that the Communists (CPP) and the Kuomintang (KMT) should present a united front against the Japanese. He kept Chiang Kai-shek captive for two weeks until he agreed to abandon his anti-Communist campaigns and resist the Japanese in their aggressive plans. Chang persuaded Chiang Kai-shek to become the leader of a united China. It was this unity of the Chinese nation that the Japanese feared. Following a further fabricated incident, the 'China Incident', the Chinese and Japanese armies clashed near the Marco Polo Bridge outside Peking. On July 29th 1937 the Japanese troops entered Peking and China was formally at war with Japan. On the 10th December the city of Nanking was entered by the Japanese and there followed for the next three months atrocities of an inconceivable nature. This reign of terror by the Japanese Army became known as the 'Rape of Nanking'. In September Prince Teh Wang joined the Japanese in the war against China and occupied the Province of Suiyan. He was designated a traitor of the National Government.

The history of China at this time was so closely linked with Japan that one must now turn one's attention back to that nation. During the thirties Japan experienced a period of unchecked aggression abroad and murderous conspiracy at home. The Japanese-inspired murder of Chang Tso-lin, by blowing up his train, led to the resignation of the Japanese government following which in 1928, Hamaguchi Yuko became Prime Minister. Two years later he was shot and wounded by a right-wing 'patriot' at a Tokyo station and later died of his wounds. For a short time Shidehara Kijuro, the Foreign Minister became Acting-Prime Minister after the attempted assassination of the Prime Minister though at the time of the 'Mukden Incident' he had resumed the office of Foreign Minister.

The next year, 1931, the 'Young Officers' plotted a 'coup d'état' to assassinate the entire Cabinet and recommended that Araki Sadao be made Prime Minister. He had urged the high command [following the murder of Chang Tso-lin] to send an army to overrun Manchuria. He headed the 40,000 strong Kodokai: an organisation based on the philosophy of Koda 'the Imperial Way', which recommended reform at home and expansion abroad. "There is a shining sun ahead for Japan in this age of Showa", prophesied Araki. Showa or 'Enlightened Peace' was the title given to the period of Hirohito's reign. The coup was suppressed and Araki was appointed Minister of War in December 1931 with the Seiyukai party. [Seiyukai means Association of Political Friends.] This party favoured economic, rather than military, expansion. He also favoured the Strike-North rather than Strike-South movement, which was the vehement intention of Hirohito and with whom he eventually fell out of favour. The Strike-North faction favoured expansion into Communist Russia rather than southwards into China and other Asiatic countries where there were raw materials in which Japan was lacking. He believed there would be war with Russia by 1936. Araki put short-term military preparations in hand. He was the most powerful man in the cabinet. He and his friend, General Mazaki, were regarded as leaders of the Kodo-ha or the 'Imperial Way School' (Strike-North Faction). The Kodo-ha began to lose ground in 1934 and General Araki resigned, supposedly from ill health. In January 1934 he accepted elevation to the ranks of the Supreme War Councillors.

Emperor Hirohito and Empress Nagako.

256   *Appendix I – Historical Background*

Hirohito in Imperial robes.

EMPEROR CHI-YUN OF MANCHUKUO.
Formerly the "Boy Emperor" of China, and after his deposition known as Mr. Pu-Yi, he is now the titular head of Japan's new foster State of Manchukuo, a country twice as large as the British Isles and inhabited by some 30,000,000 people, mainly Chinese. In the larger picture he is seen receiving congratulations after his coronation last March. The right hand picture shows him in Western dress.

The Emperor Pu Yi of Manchukuo.

The rival faction was the Tosei-Ha or 'Control School'. General Hayashi, who had once been Commander-in-Chief of the Kwantung Army, took over office as Minister of War from Araki and came under the influence of Major General Nagata. In 1935 he was active in opposing the Strike-North Faction and ridding those in the army that supported it. After much intrigue, he effected the resignation of Mazaki. In the spring and summer of that year there were plots and counter-plots culminating in the assassination of Nagata on the same day that Gareth was killed. On August 12th 1935, outraged by the virtual dismissal of Mazaki, an obscure lieutenant colonel cut Nagata down with a sword. Hayashi then had to resign to save the government. In August 1935 Matsuoka was appointed to the Presidency of the South Manchurian Railway. He identified the Railway Company as the economic spearhead of Japan's expansion into China and predicted that:

> Because of the activities of the Soviet Union and the situations prevailing in China, Japan is going to start operations in North China. Most of the people of Japan do not yet quite understand the great importance of the future operations and their lack of understanding, I believe will beyond doubt bring about a really serious crisis in the nation. Regardless how serious the crisis may become, Japan cannot halt her Chinese operations. The arrow has already left the bow. The progress of these operations will decide the destiny of the Yamato race.

The history of the Far East following the First World War should not be seen in isolation, but should be viewed from a global context. Japan had entered The Great War on the side of the Allies in August 1914. She soon captured the German fortress of Tsing-tao and became firmly established in Shantung as well as Manchuria. The ruthless German submarine campaign in the North Atlantic forced President Woodrow Wilson to join the Allied cause in April 1917. Prior to the entry of the United States, Britain and France had secretly negotiated with Japan that she should acquire Germany's Chinese Concession of Shantung. President Wilson was very much against this secret agreement, though he had to concede to it despite American affiliation with China and growing anti-Japanese sentiments. This acquisition incited Chinese students to demonstrate against the Imperialists on May 5th 1919. (It was relinquished in 1922 following the Washington Conference.) It was partly on account of this settlement that the Congress of the United States failed to ratify the Treaty of Versailles or join the League of Nations, which had been suggested by the President. On her part Japan was aggrieved at the outcome of the Treaty because she felt she deserved more recognition for the support that she had given the Allies. Japan was merely given the mandate for the Pacific Islands that she had taken from the Germans in the First World War, despite the fact that she wanted permanent sovereignty. Japan failed to have a clause inserted into conditions of the League of Nations declaring the principle of racial equality. Further indignities were piled on this sensitive nation. In 1922 at the Washington Disarmament Conference she was only given the smaller quota of a 3-5-5 proportion of capital ships and the United States persuaded Great Britain to end the Anglo-Japanese Alliance. In the following years America became very anti-Japanese and denied the immigration to the U.S.A. of Japanese workers because in their opinion the Japanese émigrés did not assimilate into the American way of life. In 1930, while Gareth was working for David Lloyd George, the London Naval Disarmament Conference was held. He mentioned having seen some of the delegates in one of his diaries and records his and Lloyd George's unfavourable comments. The ratification of the Treaty by Prime Minister Hamaguchi and his cabinet had far reaching repercussions, because it was considered by the Japanese that he had conceded to the Americans to accepting a below the minimum number of warships. They agreed to a lower ratio for auxiliary warships than the 10-10-7, which had been laid down as the accepted minimum. This issue caused a bitter protest and, with the Nationalists demanding action in Manchuria, culminated in the attempted assassination of Hamaguchi.

Following the 'Mukden Incident' in September 1931, Japan felt that the Imperialist nations supported China and were excluding Japanese merchandise through tariff barriers and the restriction of free trade. An article in Gareth's possession by Ishihara Koichiro expressed the opinion that the world was dominated by the white nations and that Japan had long put up with insults by them. "Japan's present solitary position, international, economic and racial, in the nature of things stimulates Japan to greater activity and advance. Up to the present the white powers have been oppressing the coloured races, and through exploitation of the latter have enjoyed luxury and prosperity." Ishihara considered that German-Japanese co-operation was the only step to save Germany from total collapse and was also an effective way for Japan to challenge the advance of the United States, Britain, France and Italy into the Asiatic continent.

Contemporary national sentiments have a way of influencing the politics of a country. Gareth was well versed in the reasons for American isolationism. The depression of the early thirties caused great hardship with much unemployment and financial loss in the country. The Americans blamed this on the failure of the repayment of the war debts and war reparations. They failed to understand that insisting on the payments of war debts was causing them far greater loss than the millions owed to them. It was not understood that the method of repayment and tariff barriers prevented free trade and was causing poverty in the countries that they felt owed them money. When Gareth visited the Philippines he was to see the problem of this isolationism and political lobbying. Just prior to the 1932 election Gareth wrote in *The Western Mail* an article entitled: 'How America sees the Debts Question', portraying her ignorance and mistrust of Europe. The previous year an American Congressman had even declared the President of the United States was a 'German Agent', because he had declared the Hoover Moratorium. Circumstances of the financial crisis had forced President Hoover to pronounce this moratorium. Franklin Roosevelt bowed to the strong lobby of farmers and America voted him into power as President of their country.

In the summer of 1934, Gareth interviewed Randolph Hearst, the newspaper magnate at his Welsh home, St Donat's Castle, initiating the conversation with the remark: "Was not the Americans' contribution to the War millions of dollars, whilst that of Britain and France millions of men?" He replied that: "It was not their War, but the Allies". Gareth went on to say that in Wales they were amused by Hearst's remark: 'Welshing on a debt'. Hearst's response was that it would be more accurate and more definitely descriptive to say: "that a man who had repudiated on an obligation had 'Englished' on his debt. It was a phrase devised by Englishmen to gratify the vanities and prejudices of Englishmen".

Gareth standing directly behind President Hoover at the White House, Washington together with the Children of the Revolution, April 23rd 1931.

Gareth was aware of the interdependence of the great nations of the world. As David Lloyd George's Foreign Affairs Adviser, he would have fully understood the repercussions of the Treaty of Versailles, which were reverberating more than a decade later. The British Prime Minister was one of its signatories in 1919, after the Great War. The Treaty was sacred to the French and she was against its revision. In Germany it had fermented great bitterness. In an article he published in *The Western Mail* entitled: "The World in Banking Crisis in 1931" he wrote graphically of how the collapse of the major bank, Credit-Anstalt in Austria, had been sufficient to cause a knock-on effect resulting in a financial crisis of global proportions - a spark as small as that which set Europe afire in 1914. He poignantly wrote: "the rumblings of disaster have grown more ominous. Japan has taken advantage of the trouble in Europe to send troops into Manchuria. The forces of Hitler, the fascist, have mounted in Germany". Appearing in *The Western Mail* on July 30th 1935, two days after bandits captured him, was an article by Gareth entitled: "Anglo-American Relations from the Japanese point of view". Lloyd George, General Smuts and other statesmen were in favour of an Anglo-American alliance and such an understanding was supported by one of his colleagues in Japan. The latter considered that Japan was aiming to dominate North China. Another view from Tokyo was that speeches by Western politicians who had never visited the East, advocating such an alliance, only antagonised a sensitive nation like Japan and increased her feeling of isolation. A 1934 trade mission had improved relations with Britain. The British Ambassador believed that Japan was becoming friendlier towards the Soviet Union. A third colleague considered an alliance with America was nonsense and that the Americans could not be relied upon, that they had a passion for isolation and that they had no great interests in the Far East. They were abandoning the Philippines and would not help Britain defend Hong Kong or Shanghai. The only alternative would be a close understanding with Japan. Gareth closed his article with these words: "Which is the right point of view? I shall not make up my mind until I have been through the Far East, visited China and Manchukuo and returned for a second visit to Japan".

As a consequence of the war loans of the First World War, Britain was indebted to the United States. Despite these debts, in the period prior to the Second World War, the British Empire was considered a great and a dominant power in the Far East. On the other hand, Germany had become an impoverished country. Following her defeat in the Great War and as a result of the conditions of the Treaty of Versailles, which financially crippled the nation, she lost her Empire. The German economic and financial paralysis of 1930-32 made repayment of the war reparations prohibitive and after the temporary moratorium these were permanently repealed. Gareth was to see for himself the poverty of the people and the demoralised youth who were unemployed and who had no hope of finding work. Rebelling against the bondage of war reparations and the failure of democracy, a disillusioned Germany allowed Hitler and the National Socialists to come to power in early 1933. She began to re-arm and turned to China, away from the "Jewish-Bolshevik" state of Russia to import raw materials including wolfram (for tungsten) and antimony required for armaments. In return, with the knowledge of the War

<u>PERSONAL</u>.

BRON-Y-DE,
CHURT,
SURREY.

May 3rd.1933

My dear Gareth,

    Thank you so much for your interesting article. Whether you are right or wrong about my speaking, it is a first-class piece of writing.

    The notes from the Unemployed Camps are valuable.

    The papers here do not fully report Hitler's speech. What is it he definitely proposes to do and how? I am particularly anxious to know what his intentions are about Land Settlement.

                Best wishes,

                    Ever sincerely,

Gareth Jones Esq.,M.A.,
c/o "WESTERN MAIL"
<u>CARDIFF</u>.

Personal letter to Gareth from David Lloyd George.

Ministry, the Reichswehr, she gave advice and military equipment to Marshall Chang Kai-shek for the purpose of suppressing the Communists and the eventual war that might take place against the Japanese.

    The retired General, Hans von Seeckt, one-time Commander-in-Chief of the Reichswehr, went as a German military adviser to the

Marshall and introduced an industrialist, Klein, to him. With General von Seeckt's knowledge, Klein was also involved with the development of an armaments factory and an arsenal in Canton for Marshall Chen Chi-tang's Army. On Gareth's first visit to Hong Kong he saw Von Seeckt with a Chinese General in mufti. The German Foreign Office (the Wilhelmstrasse) wished to keep a balanced foreign policy between China and Japan. Unbeknown to this department in the late spring of 1935 the Nazi, Joachim von Ribbentrop, began secret negotiations with the Japanese Military Attaché, General Oshima Hiroshi, in Berlin against the Soviet Union. The significance of these negotiations, in the light of the suspicions of Mr David Lloyd George's Secretary, Mr A.J. Sylvester as to Gareth's inexplicable death, should become apparent to the reader on completing this book, *Gareth Jones: A Manchukuo Incident.*

Appendix II
Tributes to Gareth Jones

"Cut off in his prime as by frost in the midst of high summer."
Tribute to Gareth by the Chahar Commissioner for Foreign Affairs at Gareth's Chinese memorial service in Kalgan.

Though his stay was very short in Peking, Gareth had made many friends there. A brief, but impressive memorial service was held in the British Embassy Chapel. There were many tokens of respect and sympathy in the form of wreaths, especially from Chinese organisations and the congregation was very representative. At home, there were many moving tributes to him

In *The Times* on August 19th 1935, Dr H.F. Stewart, a Fellow of Trinity College, Cambridge wrote:

> I desire to add a pebble to the cairn of my friend and pupil, Gareth Jones. He was an extraordinary linguist; he had literary ability of no mean order; he had, to my knowledge the makings of a good teacher. An academic or official career lay open to him; yet he preferred a life of independent activity, with its attached perils. Nevertheless, through all his adventures, he kept in touch with those who live less dangerously and I had a cheerful postcard from him at Nanking a few days before his capture. His wit, his irrepressible sense of humour, his story and shrewd and penetrating comments on men and things in America, Germany and Russia were to his friends an unfailing source of delight. "Les premiers jours de printemps ont moins de grâce que la vertu naissante d'un jeune homme". [The first days of spring are of less favour than budding virtue of a young man.] It is bitter to think of all that brilliance, vigour, and promise brutally wiped out by the bullet of a miscreant.

Sir Robert Webber paid tribute in *The Daily Telegraph:*

> The news of the tragic death of Gareth Jones has brought a feeling of deep personal loss to all his colleagues on *The*

Western Mail and the *South Wales Echo and Evening Express*. It is like the death of a brother. He had the rare quality, which on the instant endeared him to all that met him. When we read last week that the bandits were charmed by his personality and his singing of Welsh airs, we said how like Gareth Jones. He was Gareth to everyone, young and old and nobody thought of addressing him formally. He was a delightful, loveable boy. His youthful, jubilant spirits made us forget that he was grown up and that we were talking to a most brilliant scholar. In Wales his loss will be felt in every home.

It was not just in his mother country of Wales, but throughout the whole world that the news of his death reverberated. Countless tributes were received from people of all walks of life, both young and old. All these affirmed that although he was disarming in his modesty, this belied the fact that he was a gifted student who would have had a brilliant future ahead of him had his life not been so tragically cut short. All knew that he was a Welsh patriot and a great lover of the land and its people.

A letter to the editor of *The Western Mail and South Wales News* from Geoffrey Crawshay and Elfan Rees at the end of August 1935 suggested a University of Wales Travelling Scholarship and that a memorial fund be established in the name of Gareth Jones. *The Western Mail and South Wales News* quickly took up the idea with Sir Robert Webber consenting to act as its Honorary Treasurer.

Many people donated to the fund including Mr Harold Bucquet of Metro-Goldwyn Mayer Corporation, as did Mr Barnett Janner, M.P., Randolph Hearst, the American newspaper magnate, gave a donation saying Gareth was a fine man and a great journalist:

We had a delightful conversation at St. Donat's and I was greatly impressed by his ability, knowledge, fearlessness and fairness. These qualities are important in any man, but particularly important in a journalist. I was greatly shocked to hear of Mr Jones' death. A memorial is all we can do to show our respect and admiration for him.

Gareth walking with Mr William Randolph Hearst – the American newspaper magnate in the grounds of St. Donat's Castle, Llantwit Major, South Wales.

These sentiments of understanding between foreign nations have stood the test of time and ring as true today as they did in 1935. The travelling scholarship is still awarded to one young person every year, and students of outstanding ability are benefiting to this present day.

Appendix III
Gareth's Eulogy

[Barry & District News – Friday 30th August 1935.]

Apostle of International Understanding

Reverend Gwilym Davies's Tribute to Mr Gareth Jones

Mr Gareth Jones, the brilliant 30 years' old journalist, who was murdered by Chinese bandits was described as an apostle missionary of international understanding by the Rev. Gwilym Davies, M.A., at a beautiful but simple memorial service at the Barry Memorial Hall on Sunday evening.

Mr Jones' parents, Major Edgar Jones, M.A., O.B.E., a Welsh adviser to the B.B.C. and headmaster for many years of the Barry County School, and Mrs Jones, Eryl, Porth y Castell, Barry, were present, with members of the family. The packed Hall, used for the first time for a memorial service for a civilian, was representative of every phase of Welsh national life, of Parliament, County and municipal councils and education authorities, old Barrians, and other prominent South Wales public bodies.

Councillor John Ireland, J.P., chairman of the Barry Council presided.

The ministers taking part were the Revs. W. Austin Davies, B.A. (rural dean), Idris Evans, M.A., W.R. Jones, D.D., and J. Mydyr Evans while Professor Joseph Jones, Brecon, pronounced the benediction. The singing was led by the choir of Tabernacle, Barry Docks, conducted by Councillor Dan Evans.

Mr Ireland said they were there to pay their tribute of respect and affection to the memory of a Barry boy. He felt sure he had interpreted the wish and desire of the whole of Barry in arranging this service in the Memorial Hall so that, as a town, they could have an opportunity of showing their pride in one whose career was so distinguished and whose life was such a remarkable example of character and ability.

The Rev. Gwilym Davies addressed Gareth's mourners in Barry Memorial Hall on Sunday, August 25th, 1935:

In the Book of Psalms - and the Bible is a wonderful book at a time like this - in the 39th Psalm there are words which set out exactly the feeling that possessed us all when we heard the news of Gareth Jones. 'I was dumb with silence,' said the Psalmist. 'I held my peace.' And even tonight that silence is hard to break. But we owe it to the town of Barry that the silence should be broken, we owe it to the country to which he belonged and whose name was written upon his heart. And we owe it to ourselves for there are truths to be pondered and there are messages of comfort and of inspiration to be gained from the sorrow which has darkened not only the home of "Eryl" but all our homes.

He was a Barry boy. How much of a Barry boy he was I realised one evening about two years ago outside this Memorial Hall. It was at the close of an Armistice service at which he was present and where I had to speak. After the service we were outside, waiting for his father and mother. We had been looking at the names of the men of Barry who fell in the War. He was only nine when the war broke out, so that he could have taken no part or lot in it. But there he was - I can see him now - taking off his hat and standing bare-headed in the cold of a November night - beside the Memorial to the men from his town who never came back. There was a pride about it, a pride in Barry. One could see that. And there was something else - so true of him - there was a reverence in the presence of a mystery he could not understand. Indeed, if I were asked to name, straight off, one of the deep things in him, I should say it was reverence - the reverence whose flower was that humility which made of him the friend of everybody he met.

We here, tonight, have no need to be told anything about his career. We know the steps from school to college with the prizes and the honours then to the various posts which brought him into living contact with famous men of three continents, Europe, Asia and America; and we know of that additional endowment of a gift of tongues which was almost a miracle in itself. But you and I rarely thought of all this when he was with us. To us, as it was put in a delightful tribute – 'he was Gareth - Gareth to everyone young and old' - the Gareth to whom life was a joyful adventure, filled with laughter and good humour and friendliness.

And with all this boyishness and love of fun, the spirit of youth personified, there was seriousness on the grave, moral issues of life that made him every inch a man. I suppose if we were to ask his colleagues in the great and exacting profession to which he belonged, they would all say of him that he was 'steel true and blade straight'. Like every born journalist - like every man with ink in his blood - he loved best to work at high pressure. I remember him one day coming round to my room at the office. He wanted to write a two or three columned article for the paper next day - it had to be next day, May 18th, on the reception all over the world of the 'Welsh Children's Message'. Here was a task which made a compelling appeal to him if only for his love of children. It was 12.30 p.m. when he came. He told me he was leaving Cardiff by train before three o'clock. He had before him on the table scores of replies in various languages; he quickly picked out those he needed. 'But, surely, Gareth,' I said, 'you cannot do the article now - it's one o'clock'. 'Certainly,' he replied, 'you go to lunch. I will get it done'. And done it was there and then, and a first rate article appeared next morning. He worked like that - sixty seconds to the minute. He lived like that - intensely in the present. But if he lived in the minute, he did not live for it.

He could forget the things that were behind, no one better, but he did strive for the things that are before, no one harder. There was a 'something' about him that it would be presumption on the part of any of us to say that we fully understood. There was an atmosphere about him which I can best describe to myself as the consciousness of a 'call'. That he would devote himself to public service went without saying. He owed that to the tradition of public duty of his home - a tradition which is a household word not only in Barry but all over Wales. He would not be the son of his father and mother if public spirit did not find in him a ready and an unselfish response.

But it was more than that. It was more than that because he brought to it his own, his original contribution - a conviction best expressed, perhaps, in the words of Browning's 'Paracelsus' – 'I can devote myself, I have a life to live'. I am convinced, knowing him as I did, that years ago he had heard distinctly the call - 'Whom shall I send?' He answered very firmly - 'Here I am, send me'. And what was it - this call - this task - to which he became 'a dedicated spirit'?

Well, this world is a rapidly changing world - continents are being dwarfed into countries, and countries into counties. And one of our greatest needs presently will be men, and women - not with a command of languages, that is a small part of the equipment - but with powers of intellectual and spiritual interpretation - the interpretation of nation after nation, of people after people in this strange new world in which we are living.

He had this gift of international understanding; he had this genius of becoming the interpreter of nations to one another. To him was given, for example, the power, the rare power of an instinctive reaction to an international dispute not as a quarrel, which it seldom or never is, between 'a right and a wrong' but between 'two rights'.

I am not exaggerating when I say that there are very few men in the whole world equipped with the knowledge and endowed with the sympathy for this new vocation of international interpretation on a world scale. I asked a high authority last year how many men living had it -'Twenty?' 'Twenty,' he replied, 'there are not ten, there are not five.' 'I can only think,' he went on, 'of three living men who have got it'. And he named them - one was an American, the second was an Englishman, and the third a Spaniard. But there was a fourth - a fourth at about half their age - nearly ready for it. That, my friends, is the measure of the world's loss.

And with all this passion for internationalism he was no internationalist in the narrow sense of the term - the internationalist who is like a cut flower in a vase; the internationalist with no roots, who belongs to all countries and to none. Not at all - his internationalism was rooted in the rich soil of a healthy and a vigorous nationalism. He was British and a democrat, a lover of political freedom in every fibre of his being and Welsh to the very core - 'Cymro i'r carn'.

In article after article - those sketches, often unfinished, which he tossed off rapidly like an artist getting ready to paint on a big canvas - in whatever foreign land the article was written - you can see Wales peeping out - Wales constantly breaking through.

If he was writing of hospitality offered him in Java - he was thinking of the hospitality in a Welsh farmhouse.

If he was writing in the Philippines and of the Philippines - his mind instantly went back to Barry and to Mr Ifor Powell of the County School, an authority on the subject.

Or if he was in the Saar Valley on the eve of Plebiscite - to him it became the valley of the Taff, with the industrial importance of East Glamorgan.

I cannot trust myself to speak about something which is in all our minds - something which will become a legend all over the East - the singing of the songs of Wales - in the Babylon of his captivity.

But there is a problem about his death that we ought to face bravely and honestly: it is this - this murmuring in our hearts - and we have all done it - we have said: 'why should a life like this - pure and precious and fearless - why should it have been poured out like water?' Could it not have been preserved? Could it not have been stored up for other and greater things?

So it is here. A sacrifice like this is of the very savour of life, enriching it, ennobling it. It is deeds of daring, with no hope of material gain, that keeps our civilization from becoming stagnant and selfish. What would this world be without the pioneers, in age after age, who make a magnificent venture of themselves, in scaling heights that life may become richer for us who dwell in the valleys?

In our hearts we know that the world owes most to those who said, as Gareth Jones said in deeds not words - 'not for me any calling that is easy, uneventful, safe - that I may be free to quest the horizon - and to push further back the boundaries of knowledge.'

I shall never forget Dr Clifford, broken with grief, speaking of his irreparable loss in a fine illuminating phrase after the death of a young and brilliant minister: 'He is more to us today,' he said of his young friend, 'than he has ever been - Death has brought to light his wholeness. We knew him before only in fragments. Life hid him; death has revealed him'.

That is true of us tonight. We knew Gareth Jones only in fragments. Life hid him and now death has revealed him - it has revealed him; even to the family at 'Eryl' in the hundreds of letters and messages they have received bearing witness to what Gareth Jones was and did—the most touching of them perhaps from humble people to whom he was a friend. Death has revealed him to us to whom God gave the privilege of his comradeship. And it will go on revealing him to the world and especially to the Youth of Wales as a missionary apostle of the great gospel of international understanding.

We have been dwelling upon the horror of the end—those who come after us will not do that; they will speak not of the horror but of the heroism of it - the heroism which will make them say triumphantly what we ought to be able to say just as triumphantly, 'O Death, where is thy sting, O Grave, where is thy victory'. "Nid i ni, O, Arglwydd, nid i ni, ond I'th enw dy hun dod, Ogoniant Yn Oes Oesoedd."

Lord Davies, who was represented by Mr Dudley Howe, J.P., telegraphed his regret at being unable to attend, stating how deeply he felt his loss in the New Commonwealth to whose aims Gareth rendered such loyal and devoted service. His enthusiasm and courage would always remain an inspiration and example to all those who worked for peace and mutual understanding among nations.

Appendix IV

Lieutenant Millar's Identification of Gareth Jones' body.

The body examined by me at Pao Ch'ang on the 18th August 1935, was that of a foreigner (i.e. not Oriental), male, probable age about 30.

Physical characteristics as far as it was possible to determine, were identical with those of Mr Gareth Jones as described to me by Mr Baker-Carr and Dr Müller.

Owing to the condition of the body and the fact that no disinfectants were available, a detailed examination was impossible.

The following were the physical characteristics of the corpse height five foot six/seven inches, Hair dark - chest very hairy - neither teeth nor eyes could be examined.

A bullet had apparently entered the back of the head and passed out near the mouth, two other bullets appeared to have been fired into the back and come out through the chest.

A monogram was woven on the breast pocket of the vest or shirt in which the corpse was clad. I could not distinguish the letters. Before leaving Kalgan, I ascertained that only two other foreigners were known to be anywhere near this area - they were both Russian Fur Traders. I saw the photos of these two men, the body I examined was not that of either of these men.

Everything possible had been done by the Chinese Authorities in Pao Ch'ang to preserve the corpse, but none of the necessary materials were available. Decomposition had not actually commenced, as far as was visible to the eye, but the face was extremely swollen and blackened.

The body had been placed in the best coffin available, and wild flowers had been placed in and around the coffin which rested in a small temple. Incense was burned night and day.

Chang Yun Chui of the Pao An-tui, who saw Jones and Müller with the bandits on the 29th July, and returned with the latter to Pao Ch'ang, identified the body in my presence on the 19th August at 10.15 a.m.. He stated that the body was that of the foreigner whom he had seen in the bandits' camp with Müller on the above date. He had no difficulty, he said, in recognising the corpse.

Appendix V
Bibliography

'Author, The'. (1932). *Experiences in Russia – 1931. A Diary.* The Alton Press Inc. [Written anonymously by Jack Heinz II, with a preface by Gareth R.V. Jones.]
Acton, Harold. (1948). *More Memoirs of an Aesthete.* Methuen Press.
Behr, Edward. (1987). *The Last Emperor*: MacDonald and Co..
Bergamini, David. (1971). *Japan's Imperial Conspiracy.* William Morrow. New York.
Colley, Philip. (1987). *Short Account of the Life and Murder of Gareth Jones. A Dissertation.* Newcastle University.
Crozier, Andrew. (1997). *The Causes of the Second World War.* Blackwell.
Deakin, F.W. and Storry, G.R. (1966). *The Case of Richard Sorge.* Chatto and Windus.
Fleming, Peter. (1936). *One's Company.* Jonathan Cape, London.
Fox, John. (1982). *Germany and the Far Eastern Crisis 1931-1938.* Clarendon Press.
Kirby, William. (1984). *Germany and Republican China.* Stanford University Press.
Harris, Meirin and Susie. (1991). *Soldiers of the Sun.* Heineman.
Han Suyin. (1966). *A Mortal Flower.* Jonathan Cape.
Jones, Gareth. (1936). *In Search of News.* The Western Mail, Cardiff.
Lamont- Brown, Raymond. (1998). *Kempeitai. The Dreaded Japanese Secret Police.* Sutton Publishers.
Muggeridge, Malcolm. (1995). *'Winter in Moscow'.* Extract from *The Biography of Malcolm Muggeridge.* Gregory Wolfe.
Nuechterlein, Donald. (1965). *Thailand and the Struggle for South East Asia.* Cornell University Press.
Power, Brian. (1986). *The Puppet Emperor.* Corgi Books.
Secrest, Meryl. (1998). *Frank Lloyd Wright. A Biography.* The University of Chicago Press.
Smith, Michael. (2000). *The Emperor's Codes.* Bantam Press – subsiduary of Transworld Publishers.
Snow, Edgar. (1937). *Red Star Over China.* Gollancz Press.
Snow, Edgar. (1941). *Scorched Earth.* Gollancz Press.

Storry, Richard. (1960). *A History of Modern Japan*. Pelican Books.
Sylvester, A.J. (1947). *The Real Lloyd George*. Cassell.
Trott, Adam von. (1989). *A Good German*. MacDonogh. Quarter Books.
Vespa, Ameletto. (1938). *Secret Agent of Japan*. Little Brown and Co. New York.
Youli Sun. (1993). *China and the Origins of the Pacific War 1931-1941*. Macmillan Press.
Zephir Thierry. (1997). *Khmer - Lost Empire of Cambodia*. New Horizons Series. Thames and Hudson.

Other sources

Gareth's letters and diaries.
Hansard. 1935-1936. Speeches by Lloyd George.
German Foreign Office letters.
Journals of Institute of World Affairs 1934 and 1937.
Public Record Office documents. 1935. No 7699. Ref FO371/19768
The Japan Year Book. 1934.
Various newspaper publications and documents including *The Western Mail, The Times, Daily Telegraph, Manchester Guardian* and others. 1935.
U.S., Department of State, Publication 1983, *Peace and War: United States Foreign Policy, 1931-1941* (Washington, D.C.: U.S., Government Printing Office, 1943, pp. 255-256).

Appendix VI
List of Characters

British

Alley, Rewi: (New Zealander); Inspector of Factories in Shanghai who endeavoured to improve the working conditions of the contract labourers in Shanghai.

Barrett, Mr R.T.: Journalist for *The Critic* of Hong Kong.

Buchan, John: 1st Baron Tweedsmuir (1875-1940). War correspondent in World War One. Governor General of Canada. Author of many books including *The Thirty-nine Steps*.

Cadogan, Sir Alexander: The British Ambassador to China in 1935.

Clive, Sir Robert: The British Ambassador to Japan in 1935.

Cox, Melville James 'Jimmy': The Reuters' correspondent in Tokyo who was arrested on 27th July 1940 by the Kempeitai and died mysteriously a few days later.

Davies, Elwyn: An American missionary teacher. Family came from Pennorth, Breconshire.

Davies, Lord David, of Llandinam: Prominent in the formation of the League of Nations Union. Wartime (First World War) Parliamentary Private Secretary to the Prime Minister, Mr Lloyd George.

Fleming, Peter: Author of *One's Company*, brother of spy novelist Ian.

Garvin, John: Famous journalist and newspaper editor.

Howe, Dudley: J.P., Chairman of the Barry Urban District Council.

Hoare, Sir Samuel: Foreign Secretary in June, 1935.

Jones, Annie Gwen: (1868-1965) J.P., Gareth's mother. Known to the author as Nain and in the convention of the day as Mrs Edgar Jones.

Jones, Major Edgar: (1868-1953) O.B.E., T.D., and M.A., LL.D., Gareth's father. Headmaster of Barry County School for Boys. B.B.C. Wales, Welsh Religious Adviser in 1932.

Jones, Miss Gwyneth Vaughan: (1895-1996). Gareth's sister. Headmistress of Barry County School for Girls for 20 years from 1938.

Jones, Miss Winifred: (1880-1952). Always known as Auntie Winnie or to the children as Ninnie.

Leith-Ross, Sir Frederick: The chief economic adviser to the British Government who led the failed Treasury mission to the Far East in 1935-36.

Lewis, Mrs Eirian Vaughan: Sister of Gareth and mother of Siriol Colley and John Lewis.

Lloyd George, Right Hon. David: Later Earl Lloyd George of Dwyfor. Chancellor of the Exchequer, 1908-1915. Minister of Munitions, 1915-1916. Prime Minister of Great Britain from 1916 to 1922.

Lytton, Lord: Headed the League of Nations commission following the Mukden Incident and the establishment of the state of Manchukuo.

Millar, Lieutenant: Language Officer at the British Embassy.

Muggeridge, Malcolm: Author and journalist.

Shaw, George Bernard: (1856-1950) Irish dramatist and playwright. Member of the Fabian Society.

Simon, Sir John: Foreign Secretary from 1931 to 1935.

Stewart, Dr H.F.: Fellow of Trinity College, Cambridge.

Sylvester, Mr A.J.: David Lloyd George's Private Secretary until Lloyd George's death.

Timperley, Mr H.J.: Peking correspondent for the *Manchester Guardian.*

Webber, Sir Robert: Managing Director of *The Western Mail.*

Yorke, Gerald: Freelance journalist and part-time Reuters' correspondent; Companion of Peter Fleming in *One's Company* and adviser to Gareth on his trip to Changsha.

Chinese

Chang Chung-Chi: Commander of the local militia, the Chahar Peace Corps.

Chang Hsueh-liang: Governor of Mukden until the Mukden Incident and Chang Kai-shek's deputy Commander-in-Chief. Known as the Young Marshall. Son of Chang Tso-lin.

Chang Tso-lin: (1875-1928): Manchurian warlord. Murdered by Japanese as he returned to his capital of Mukden.

Chen Chi(Ji)-tang: General and Warlord of Canton. Leader of the Southwest movement. An adversary of Chiang Kai-shek and opponent of the Japanese.

Chiang Kai-shek, Marshall: (1887-1975): Leading nationalist leader of the Kuomintang (KMT), dictator of China until he had to flee to Taiwan in 1949.

Ch'ien Lung: (Qing Long) Emperor of China (1736 to 1795). Founder of the Qing dynasty.

Diluwa Hutukin: The second living Buddha from Outer Mongolia.

Appendix VI – List of Characters

He Ying-qin: War Minister in Chiang Kai-shek's Government and endorser of the He-Umetsu Agreement.

Hsu Mo, Dr: Vice-Minister of Foreign Affairs.

Mao Tse-tung; Communist leader. Lead the 'Long March' in 1935. Assumed control of the People's Republic of China in 1949.

Pao Fang Wu: The bandit chief, a former Chinese Military Officer and a resident in Japanese concession at Tientsin.

Pu Yi: (1906-1967): The last Emperor of China. Enthroned as Emperor of Manchukuo on March 1st, 1934. Imprisoned by the Communist Chinese after the Second World War, but released in 1959.

Sung, General Che(h)-yuan: Commander of the 29th Army based in Peking and Governor of Chahar until he was forced to resign prior to the demilitarisation of the Province following the He-Umetsu Agreement.

"Sylvia": General Chen Chi-tang's daughter.

Teh Wang: Leader of the Mongolian Princes. He fought on the side of the Japanese in 1937 and was considered an enemy of the people. He was released from custody in 1963.

Tsai Ting-kai, General: the 19th Route Army Commander who held the Japanese at bay during the Shanghai Incident of January 28th, 1932. Lead an unsuccessful revolution in Fukien in 1933 against the Kuomintang.

Wang Ching-wei: Premier in Chiang Kai-shek's Government. He established the puppet regime in Japanese occupied China.

Yang, Mr: Chief Representative of the Chahar Government in Kalgan.

Zhou En-lai: Premier and Foreign Minister under Mao Tse-tung from 1949. Died in 1976.

Germany

Baum, Vicki: Austrian author of *Grand Hotel*.

Dewall, Wolf von: The London correspondent for the newspaper, The *Frankfurter Zeitung*. A close friend of Gareth. One time in the employ of the China Customs and Postal Service under Sir Robert Hart.

Dirksen, Herbert von: A Nazi sympathiser. The German Ambassador to Japan.

Hitler, Adolf: Leader of the National German Socialist Workers Party in 1921. Author of *Mein Kampf*. Chancellor of Germany in 1933. Nazi Dictator.

Müller, Dr Herbert: Gareth's companion into Inner Mongolia. Freelance journalist and representative of Deutsches Nachtichenburo, the German news agency.

Plessen, Baron Johan von: German diplomat in Peking and Gareth's companion into Inner Mongolia.

Ribbentrop, Joachim von: German Nazi Leader, Secret Agent in U.S.A. during World War One. Ambassador to Britain 1936-1938. Foreign Minister in Germany until 1943. Negotiated the Anti-Comintern Pact with Japan. Executed as a war criminal in 1946.

Seeckt, General Hans von: Commander-in-Chief of the Reichswehr. In retirement, he went as a German military adviser to Marshall Chang Kai-shek.

Stein, Günther: A known socialist and a committed Communist. Spent time as a correspondent for the *Berliner Tageblatt* in Moscow prior to 1933. In Tokyo, he became associated with double secret agent, Richard Sorge.
.
Trautmann, Oskar: German Ambassador to China until 1937.

Indian

Nair: With the Japanese at Dolonor. Secretary of the Pan-Asiatic League.

Japan

Amau, Eliji (Amŏ): Japanese Foreign Office Spokesman. Proposed the Amau (Amŏ) Doctrine on April 17th 1934, which opposed Western aid to China and considered that Japan had a special mission to maintain peace and order in East Asia.

Araki Sadao: General: Appointed Minister of War in December 1931 with the Constitutionalists. He supported the Strike-North faction, which favoured expansion into Communist Russia.

Doihara, Kenji, Major General: One of Hirohito's 'reliables'. A secret agent, experienced in subversive techniques. Endeavoured to convert the China Provinces north of the great wall to autonomous government. Executed following the International Military Tribunal for war crimes.

Hamaguchi Yuko: Prime Minister after the death of Chang Tso-lin. His assassination was attempted in November 1930 and he died one year later.

Hayashi Senjuro, General: Assumed the position of Minister of War after General Araki. He supported the rival faction of the Tosei-Ha or control school, which favoured striking south into China.

Hirohito: Emperor of Japan.

Hiroshi, General Oshima: The Japanese Military Attaché in Berlin who discussed with Ribbentrop secret negotiations against Bolshevik Russia in 1935.

Hirota, Koki: Foreign Minister and then Prime Minister in 1936. Executed following the International Military Tribunal for war crimes.

Matsui, Colonel: Chief of the Japanese military mission in Kalgan.

Matsuoka Yosuke: Headed the Japanese delegation, which denounced Japan for its conduct in annexing Manchuria. He left the meeting and in March 1933 Imperial sanction was given for Japan to withdraw from the League of Nations.

Nogi, General Maresuke: The victor in the battle for Port Arthur against the Russians in 1905. He imposed a high standard of discipline upon his troops.

Osumi Mineo, Admiral: The Naval Minister when Gareth was in Japan.

Shidehara Kijuro: The Foreign Minister in 1930. Became Acting-Prime Minister after the attempted assassination of the Prime Minister, Hamaguchi. He assumed the position of Prime Minister when General MacArthur was Supreme Commander in Japan following the cessation of hostilities in 1945.

Shiozawa, Admiral: Fought General Tsai during the Shanghai Incident.

Takahashi Tan, Major: The Military Attaché so influential in the negotiations during the crisis involving the demilitarisation of Chahar.

Russian

Iswolski, Aleksander Petrovich: Russian Minister to Japan from 1900 prior to the Russo-Japanese War 1904-1905.

Nadezhda Krupskaya: Lenin's widow, Minister in the Commissariat of Education in Moscow.

Petrewschchew, Anatoli: Russian driver of the Wostwag truck in Inner Mongolia.

Sorge, Richard: Tried by the Japanese, found guilty of spying for the Russians and executed by them. He informed Stalin of the intended invasion of Russia by Germany on June 21st 1941. Stalin disregarded this information.

Stalin, Joseph (1879-1953): He was active in the plot to overthrow Kerensky in 1917. On Lenin's death he assumed his place and became Dictator of the United States of Soviet Russia.

Siam

Ananta Mahidon: The young King of Siam.

Pridi Panomyong: Law graduate who became leader of a group of idealists who were dissatisfied with the arrogance of the Royal Princes. He was given the title Luang Pradit. In 1932 Pradit was involved in a coup d'état to overthrow the Princes.

United States of America

Durranty, Walter: United States correspondent who disputed Gareth's exposure of the folly of Stalin's five year plan in the American press.

Hearst, Randolph: The famous newspaper magnate.

Heinz, Jack II: Grandson of the founder of the Heinz Organisation. In 1931 Gareth travelled with Jack throughout the Soviet Union as detailed in Jack Heinz II's privately published and 'anonymously written' book entitled: *'Experiences in Russia - 1931'*. (The foreword was written by Gareth).

Hooker, Adelaide Ferry: Socialite friend of Gareth's from New York, who met Müller in Kalgan after his release and was later interviewed by Lloyd George's Private Secretary in London regarding her suspicions of a German- Japanese conspiracy. For family history - see footnote in Chapter 20 – The German Doctor.

Hoover, President Herbert: Defeated by Roosevelt in 1932. Proposed the Hoover Moratorium of 1931.

Lee, Dr Ivy: Said to be America's greatest public relations expert. [From his obituary in an unknown newspaper.]

Lloyd Wright, Frank: Architect of worldwide renown.

Roosevelt, President Franklin (1882-1945): American President from 1932 until he died in 1945.

Snow, Edgar: Author of *The Scorched Earth* and *Red Star over China*.

Wilson, President Woodrow (1856-1924): Committed United States to join the Allied cause in April 1917. Took active part in the Peace negotiations after the Great War and he suggested the League of Nations, but U.S. Senate rejected this and the Treaty of Versailles.

Index

(Bold pages references refer to entry in List of Characters.)

Aberystwyth. i, 94.
Acton, Sir Harold. 240.
Alley, Rewi. 145, 146.
Amau Doctrine. 51, 252, **282**.
Amau, Eliji. 50, 59, 62-3, 252.
Ananta Mahidon, King. 101, 103, **284**.
Angkor Wat. 55, 105-9.
Anglo-Japanese Alliance. 64, 258.
Anti-Comintern Pact. 240.
Araki Sadao, General. 55-58, 65-67, 254-257, **282**.
Baker, Mr, American. 98.
Barrett, R.T.. ii, 73-74, 120, 236, 247, 249, **277**.
Batavia. (Jakarta) x, xiii, 78, 81-89.
Baum, Vicki. 89, **280**.
Bell, Sir Charles. ix, 11, 31, 162, 185, 188, 218, 229.
Behr, Edward. 251.
Beidzemiao. 22-28, 186.
Berliner Tageblatt. xx, 43, 61, 142, 241.
Bismarck, Prince Otto von. 214.
Blomberg, General Werner von. 208, 239.
Bolsheviks. 4, 26, 261, 263.
Borobudur. 81-87.
Buriats. 25-31.
Cadogan, Sir Alexander. 202, 208, 211, 231, **277**.
Cambodia. 55, 107-110.
Cambridge University. i, xiii, 92, 97, 101, 155, 264.
Canton (Guangzhou). x, xiii, 59.
Chahar. xiii, 3, 35, 143, 153-155, 164, 165, 170-174, 180-189, 192, 194, 200-201, 205, 207,
210-213, 226, 229-232, 235-238, 242-244, 253, 264.
Chang Chu-chang. 231.
Chang Chung-chi. 164, 242, **279**.
Chang Hsueh-liang. 119, 142-144, 234, 243, 250, 252-253, **279**.
Chang Pei Incident. 143, 230.
Changsha. ix, x, viii, 118-119, 120, 129, 132, 139, 140, 142, 144.
Chang Tso-lin, Marshall. 237, 243, 254, **279**.
Chen 'Sylvia'. 125-128, **280**.
Chen Chi-tang, General. 124, 130, 132, 234, 263, **279**.
Cheng, Pax. 48, 71, 146.
Chiang Kai-shek, Marshall. 66, 71-73, 124, 119, 129, 137-138, 142, 147, 154, 226, 230, 234, 250-253, 262, **279**.
Chiang Yung Kui. 196-198.
China Incident 1937. 254.
Clive, Sir Robert. 54-55, 64, 252, **277**.
Communism. xix, xiv, xxi, 10, 26, 52, 61, 63, 66, 71-72, 74, 102, 120, 138, 142-143, 147-148, 154-155, 189, 204, 231, 250, 253, 255, 262.
Cox, Melville James. 52-53, 61, **277**.
Cranborne, Viscount. 213.
Crawshay, Geoffrey. 265.
Critic, The (Hong Kong.) ii, 73, 117, 236, 249.
Dairien (Dalien) 62, 239.
Davies, Elwyn. 97-98, 100, **277**.
Davies, Rev. Gwilym. 267-268, **277**.

Day, Mr H., M.P.. 213.
Deutsches Nachrichtenbüro. 163.
De Valera, President. xx, 61.
Dewall, Wolf von. 43, 151, 152, 214, 215, 222, **281**.
Diluwa, (The living Buddha). 25-26, 31, 225, **279**.
Dirksen, Ambassador von Herbert. 250, **281**.
Doihara, Major General Kenji. 59, 129, 143, 154, 228-230, 234, 238, 244, 251, 253, **282**.
Dolonor. ix, 23, 31-35, 162, 163, 165, 179-180, 182, 185-187, 191-192, 202, 205-206, 210, 224, 226, 230-232, 235, 238, 242-244.
Donetz. (Hughesovska/Stalino). xii.
Durranty, Walter. xxiv, **284**.
Dutch East Indies. (Indonesia). x 55, 75, 77-81, 84-85, 89, 139, 245.
Erskine, Dr. 18.
Evening Standard. 172, 177.
Fianna Fail Party. xx.
Fleming, Peter. vi, 47, 118, 129, 135, 155, **277**.
Fletcher, Mr. 82-83.
Frankfurter Zeitung, Die. 43, 214, 222.
French Indo-China. viii, x, 55, 86, 107, 111, 113, 116,
Fukien rebellion. 251.
Garvin, John. xxx, **277**.
Genghis Khan. 28-29.
Great War, The. v, xxvi, 57, 63, 257-261.
Hammond, Mr. 68-72.
Hamaguchi Yuko. 54, 254, 258, **282**.
Hankow. ix, x, 119, 132, 138-139, 142-143, 234.

Hashimoto. 174.
Hayashi Senjuro, General. 55-56, 58, 67, 229, 257, **282**.
He Ying-qin, War Minister. 252, **279**.
Hearst, Randolph. vii, 45, 46, 259, 265-266.
Heinz II, Jack. xix, xx, **284**.
He-Umetsu Agreement. 154, 238, 253.
Hirohito, Emperor. 57, 65, 66, 229, 249, 254, 256, **282**.
Hiroshi, General Oshima. 239, 263, **283**.
Hirota Koki. 64, **282**.
Hitler, Adolf. xxi, xxvii, xxviii, 17, 56, 65, 76, 85, 147, 208, 220, 237, 242, 260-261, **281**.
Hoare, Sir Samuel. 231, 242, **278**.
Hong Kong. ii, viii, x, 47, 55, 61, 67, 72, 73, 116-118, 120-127, 130, 136, 236, 249, 261, 263.
Hooker, Miss Adelaide. 203, 222-224, **284**.
Hoover, President Herbert. xxvi, 259-260, **284**.
Hoover Moratorium. 261.
Hsu Mo, Dr. 147, 208.
Hughes, John. xvii, 68.
Imperial Hotel, Tokyo. 49-50, 53.
In Search of News. xxx.
International News Service. xx, 52, 90.
I.R.A.. xx.
Ishihara Koichiro. 84, 244, 258-259.
Ishiwara Kanji. 250.
Isvolsky, (Iswolski) Aleksander. 64, **283**.
Iwanaga, Mr. 52, 56, 59.
Janner, Sir Barnett. M.P.. 265.

Index

'Japanese Asia Monroe Doctrine.' 51-52.
Japan Chronicle, The. 67, 69.
Jehol. 64, 118, 165, 170, 174, 184-185, 189-190, 192, 194, 197, 206, 210, 252.
Jones, Major Edgar. vii, xvi, xviii, 43, 162, 173, 202, 222, 249, 267, **277**.
Jones, Miss Gwyneth Vaughan. v, vii, **278**.
Jones, Miss Winifred, (Auntie Winnie). xvii, 33, **278**.
Jones, Mrs Edgar, (Mrs Annie Gwen). xi, 168, 173, 202, **277**.
Jones, Graham. 217.
Kangpao. 35.
Kanin, Prince. 64.
Kempeitai. 61, 229, 232.
Kiangsi. 71, 142, 145.
Kimura, Consul. 77, 78, 233.
Kitson, Mr. 207-209.
Klein, Herr. 263.
Kobe. viii, x, 67-69, 81, 88.
Krupskaya, Nadezhda. xxi, xxv, **283**.
Kublai Khan. 1, 33.
Kuomintang. 143, 253.
Kuyuan. 35, 174, 184, 189, 191, 194, 196-197, 232.
Kwangtung Army. 26, 147, 148, 180, 182, 192, 229, 231, 235, 238, 243-244, 250, 253, 257.
Kweichow. 143-144.
Larsen, Mr. ix, 4, 6, 31, 153, 185, 186.
League of Nations. 29, 48, 56-57, 63, 205, 250-251, 253, 258.
Lee, Dr Ivy. xix, xx, xxii, **284**.
Leith Ross, Sir Frederick. 243, **278**.
Lewis, Mrs Eirian Vaughan, nee Jones. xix, **278**.
Li. 118.
Liang. 21, 33, 179.
Lichnovsky, Baroness. 152-153, 219.
Lloyd George, David. i, ii, vi, vii, xix, xx, xxiii, xxvi, 29, 55, 61, 66, 102, 117, 162, 177, 202-207, 209, 211-213, 215, 217-218, 220, 226, 233, 235, 237, 239, 241, 245, 258, 260-262, **278**.
Lloyd George, Megan. 218.
Lloyd Wright, Frank. vii, 43, 44, 49.
London Naval Disarmament Conference.1930. 258, 265.
Lytton, Lord. 251, **278**.
Lytton Report. 56, 251.
Manchester Guardian, The. xx, xxiv, 45, 67, 139, 151, 174, 215, 233.
Manchurian Incident. (See Mukden Incident).
Mao Tse-tung. 75, 142, 185, 198-200, 253, **280**.
Matsui, Colonel. 154, 184, 190, 231, **282**.
Matsuoka, Yusoke. 56-57, 61, 65, 67, 144, 251, 257, **282**.
Mazaki, General. 255, 257.
Meiji, Emperor. 576.
Merthyr Tydfil. xvii.
Millar, Lieutenant. 165, 173-174, 184, 188-189, 190, 193-194, 200, 210-211, 227, 273, **278**.
Müller, Dr Herbert. 1-38, 151-156, 161-170, 179-187, 189-193, 198, 204-222, 234-238, 242, **281**.
Muggeridge, Malcolm. xxiv, **278**.
Mukden Incident. 62, 102, 186, 243, 250.
Munhok. 89.
Mushakoji, Ambassador. 240.
Mussolini, Benito. xx, 65, 147.

Index 289

Nagata, Major General. 257.
Nair, Mr. 190, 205, **281**.
Nanking. 26, 71, 139, 143-147, 149, 154, 184, 186, 188-189, 208, 236, 238, 253-254.
Nazi. xxii, xxvii, xxviii, 84, 89, 225, 237, 250, 263.
Newton, Mr. 208.
Nine Power Treaty. 51.
Nogi, General. 30, 57, **283**.
Open Door Policy. 51, 63.
Orde, Mr. 203, 205, 207, 212.
Osumi Mineo, Admiral. 56, 57, 66, 67, **283**.
Otcheroff, Prince. 26, 31.
Pai Ling-miao. 6, 8, 21, 23, 153, 187, 200, 253.
Pan-Asianism. 65, 98, 190, 205, 206.
Panchen Lama. 2, 7, 10, 28.
Pao An-tui. 181-182, 184, 195, 199, 200, 234, 243, 274,
Pao Ch'ang. 35, 163-169, 172-174, 181-184, 188, 194-199, 202, 232, 273-274.
Pao Wang Wu. 191, **280**.
Pearl harbour. 244.
Pekema, Mr. 83, 86.
Petrewschtschew, Anatoli. 22, 24, 34, 35, 179, 227, **283**.
Philippine Bulletin, The. 76.
Philippines, Independence of. 75-76.
Phnom Penh. iii, 110 114-115.
Pingshek. 132-136.
Plessen, Baron von. 1-3, 6, 9, 11, 21-22, 151-156, 179, 211, 214-220, 226, 228, 233, 253, **281**.
Powell, Ifor. 75, 271.
Pra Riam. 98-99.
Prachadhipok, King. 101, 103.
Pridi Panomyong, Luang Pradit. 96, 98, 101-102, **284**.
Pronk, Prime Minister. 83.

Pu Yi, Emperor. 27-28, 50, 52, 251-252, 256, **280**.
Purpis, Mr. 2, 6, 179.
Rape of Nanking. 254.
Rebecca Riots. 43.
Rees, Elfan. 265.
Rengo. 52, 98, 234.
Reuters. 67, 71-73, 118, 124-125, 164, 167, 170, 173, 234.
Ribbentrop, von Joachim. 239, **281**.
Robb, Mr. 75, 78.
Rockefeller. xix, xxii, 222.
Roosevelt, President. Franklin. 43, 75, 132, 259, **285**.
Royal Institute of International Affairs. xi, xii.
Russian 5 year plan. xxi, xxiv.
Russo-Japanese War. 30, 59.
Saigon. viii, 107, 110-113, 116.
Sakhalin. 64.
Seekt, General Hans von. 130, **281**.
Semarang. viii, 80-82.
Shanghai Incident. 130, 250.
Shantung Province. 69-70, 155, 229, 257.
Shaw, George Bernard. xxi, 65, **278**.
Shidehara Kijuro, Baron. 54, 61, 67, 250, 254, **283**.
Shiozawa, Admiral. 251, **283**.
Siam. The 1933 Revolution. 96, 102.
Siemreap. 107, 110.
Silingol Banner. 25, 253.
Silver Purchase Act. xx, 48, 132.
Simon, Sir John. 56, **278**.
Singapore Naval Base. 89-94.
Snow, Edgar. 22, 75, 230, **285**.
Smuts, General Jan. 261.
Sorge, Richard. 53, 61, 239, **283**.
South Manchurian Railway. 257.

South Wales Echo and Evening Express. 161-162, 164, 265.
Soviet (Union). xix, xxii, xxiv, xxix, 1, 18, 21-22, 24, 25-26, 28, 59, 62-66, 239, 257.
Stalin, Joseph. xxi, xxiv, xxv, xxviii, 65, 147, 233, **284**.
Stein, Günther. 53, 61, 239, **281**.
Stewart, Dr H.F.. 264, **278**.
Stewart, Duncan. 239.
Suiyan. 153, 186-187, 253-254.
Sun Yat-sen. 62, 126-127, 148.
Sung, General Che-yuan. 143, 154, 162, 182, 229, 230, 234, 244, **280**.
Sunnit Tribe. 1, 7, 12, 31, 179, 186.
Sylvester. A.J.. vi, vii, 202-213, 215-220, 222, 239, **279**.
Szechuan. 52, 72, 138, 143-144, 148, 189.
Taganrog. xvii.
Takahashi Tan, Major. 154-155, 165, 171, 185, 189, 224, 228, 230-232, 234, 238, 242, 252, **283**.
Takahashi, Baron Korekiyo. 55.
Tanggu Truce. 252.
Tanaka, Baron Tokichi. 59.
Tibet. 2, 7, 11, 71, 162, 229.
Teh Wang, Prince. 1, 6, 7, 12-13, 18-19, 20-21, 29, 142, 151-152, 154-156, 179, 216, 218, 228, 253-254, **280**.
Timperley, Mr. 151, 215, 218, **279**.
Times, The. xx, 52, 134, 151, 153-154, 156, 228, 230, 232, 242, 264, 276.
Trautmann, Ambassador Oskar. 239, **281**.
Tsai Ting-kai, General. 124, 129-131, 234, 251, **280**.
Tsing Tao. 69, 155, 257.

Tientsin. 31, 191, 192, 252-253.
Ueyama, Major. 182.
Ujmutchin. ix, 25-27, 186.
Ukraine. xxi, xxv.
Umetsu, General. 154, 238, 253.
United States of America. xxii, xix, xxx, 43, 56, 66, 68, 74, 76-77, 237, 243, 252, 257-259, 261.
Urga. 2-4, 21, 35.
Vallette, Mr. 84.
Versailles, Treaty of. xxiii, 220, 245, 258, 260-261.
Vespa, Amelleto. 43, 227, 228, 232-234.
Wakatsuki, Counsellor. 155.
Wang Chin-wei, Premier. 147, 252.
Wang, Mr. 184.
Washington Conference. 1922. 62, 258.
Webber, Sir Robert. xx, 264-265, 279.
Week, The. 187, 205, 211, 214, 224.
Weigle, Dick. 38-39, 129, 137.
Western Mail, The. i, xx, xxi, xxx, 45, 73-74, 165, 169, 203, 259-260, 265, 275-276, 279.
Wilson, President Woodrow. 257, **285**.
Windlaw, Commodore Mark. 91-93.
Wostwag Company. 2, 4-5, 179, 184, 223-224, 227.
World War Two. xvi, xxvii, 48, 54, 245, 261.
Yang, Mr. 191-193, 200, 210, **280**.
Yorke, Gerald. 72-74, **279**.
Yunnan. 143.
Zaragoza, Mr. 77.
Zentgraff, Mr. 83-84, 87.
Zhou En-lai. 253, **280**.